Light on the Web

Essentials to Make the 'Net Work for You

Wendy. G. Lehnert

University of Massachusetts, Amherst

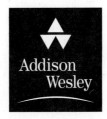

Boston San Francisco
London Toronto Sydney Tokyo
Mexico City Munich Paris Cape Town

D1377205

SENIOR ACQUISITIONS EDITOR:	Susan Hartman Sullivan
ASSISTANT EDITOR:	Elinor Actipis
SENIOR PERMISSIONS EDITOR:	Mary Boucher
EXECUTIVE MARKETING MANAGER:	Michael Hirsch
COPYEDITORS:	Laura Michaels and Roberta Lewis
PROOFREADER:	Holly McLean-Aldis
COMPOSITION AND ART:	Gillian Hall, The Aardvark Group
DESIGN MANAGER:	Gina Hagen
TEXT DESIGN:	Leslie Haimes and Gillian Hall
COVER DESIGN:	Gina Hagen
COVER ILLUSTRATION:	Susan Cyr
PREPRESS AND MANUFACTURING:	Caroline Fell
MEDIA PRODUCER:	Jennifer Pelland

Access the latest information about Addison-Wesley computer science titles from our World Wide Web site: http://www.awl.com/cs

The programs and applications presented in this book have been included for their instructional value. They have been tested with care, but are not guaranteed for any particular purpose. The publisher does not offer any warranties or representations, nor does it accept any liabilities with respect to the programs or applications.

Library of Congress Cataloging-in-Publication Data

Lehnert, Wendy G.
    Light on the Web: essentials to making the 'Net work for you / by Wendy G. Lehnert.
        p. cm.
            ISBN 0-201-73734-5
            1. World Wide Web. 2. Internet. I. Title.

    TK5105.875.I57 L3933 2002
    004.67'8—dc21

                                              00-054844

12345678910-CRK-0403020100

For Mark, Michael, Kate, and Annelise

Preface

The year 2000 marked a turning point for the Internet. For the first time, over 50% of all American homes and more than 90% of all American college students had Internet access. As a group, college students are relatively savvy about the Internet, quick to exploit online resources and eager to embrace technological innovations. Out of necessity, most students have learned what they know about the Internet on their own. They've learned by word-of-mouth, by browsing the Web, and by asking friends for help. This hit-or-miss process works to some extent, but it does have its limitations. For one thing, it takes a long time to cover the basics when your lesson plan relies on serendipity. In addition, some things are likely to be learned the hard way, and the school of hard knocks can be downright painful when it comes to computers.

This book is for anyone who wants to learn more about the Internet. These pages cover all the basics for those who are just starting out. At all times, our emphasis is more practical than technical, although we aim for a level of understanding that is more general than the operation of specific software applications.

FROM NEWBIES TO NETIZENS

In these chapters you will find a solid foundation of basic concepts and practical know-how for everyone from the novice to the self-taught expert. You don't have to have any experience with the Internet to get started with this book—we explain it all from scratch. On the other hand, if you've been online for a few years and think you know everything, you might be surprised to find out how much you still have to learn. This book was written for a range of readers, from Internet newcomers (the "newbies") to seasoned regulars (the "Netizens").

In order to address a wide range of readers, we have structured our topics in a way that makes it easy to pick and choose. Each chapter is written in two parts: The first part contains core topics that cover the basics. A newbie could cover just these core topics and learn enough to make the Net a valuable asset. The second part is easily identified by sections titled "Above and Beyond" the core topics. This material is for those who already know the basics and want to dig a little deeper.

WHAT'S IN THE BOOK

Chapter 1 starts by explaining some basic computer and computer networking concepts as a foundation for all that follows. We develop a working vocabulary in Chapter 1 before moving on to an in-depth tour of the Internet. Chapter 2 surveys important pitfalls and precautions before the real hands-on learning begins—we don't want anyone to get into trouble, and there is danger out there. Starting with Chapter 3 on e-mail management, we encourage readers to dive right in and use the Net. E-mail is a good place to start because many people have an e-mail account and are already familiar with at least one e-mail program.

No book about the Internet would be complete without an introduction to Web-page construction. We cover the basics of HTML in Chapter 4 for beginners.

Although the Internet is clearly about computers, computer networks, and computer software, the Internet is also about information. We cover online search strategies (Chapter 6). To be knowledgeable about the Internet also means being educated about a wide range of contemporary issues, including intellectual property law, software piracy, and personal privacy in a digital age. These topics are all introduced and discussed, with advice and guidelines for all Internet users.

WHAT'S ON THE WEB

As one of the reviewers for this book commented, timely Internet topics have the "half-life of a May fly." As soon as you put something about the Internet into print, it's out of date. This is true of the technology that drives the Net, the software we use to tap the Net, and all the information that lives on the Net. Any book about the Internet is not just a shot at a fast-moving target; it's also a shot at a shape-shifting target as well.

With so much in flux, it makes sense to turn to the Net itself for updates. Each chapter of this book contains pointers to resources on the Net. The most important pointers are grouped inside special sections titled "Where Can I Learn More?" Others are scattered throughout the text but printed in blue to help you spot them. You can visit our Web site and find links to all of the online resources referenced throughout these pages:

```
http://www.awl.com/lehnertlightweb
```

Many of the Web sites mentioned throughout this book are accompanied by URLs, but not all. Web page addresses are notoriously short-lived and require frequent updates. We cannot update a URL that appears in these pages, but we can update the links at our Web site. We will update any URLs at the Web site as needed in order to keep these resources readily available. You will also find a software index with links to software sites, documentation, and tutorials (if available) for all of the software mentioned in this book.

SOFTWARE THAT STUDENTS CAN USE

It is impossible to discuss software without showing examples of specific software packages in action. This is tricky in an educational text because we are not trying to endorse specific products, we just want some concrete examples for good pedagogy. We are also aware that it can be discouraging for students to see software that they cannot afford, and many popular software titles (e.g., Web-page construction kits) may be out of reach for a large number of students. In an effort to avoid commercial endorsements and pricey software, this book emphasizes the use of freeware (with two or three exceptions where no good freeware was available).

This policy may perplex some instructors and experienced Netizens, who may find themselves wondering why the book showcases an obscure piece of freeware instead of a popular shareware alternative. In all cases, I have tested each of these freeware options myself and have found them to be largely comparable to their better-known $20–$30 counterparts. When it comes to software, high prices and high quality do not always go hand in hand. Some students need to cut corners, and software is one place where students can exploit the Internet to great advantage.

For those who prefer to see a perfect match between the software in front of them and blow-by-blow instructions in a textbook, I would suggest putting more emphasis on the underlying functionality of comparable software packages and less emphasis on software-specific details. There is nothing terribly unique about most Internet software applications. The underlying functionality of a Web browser, an FTP client, or a download manager does not vary a great deal from program to program. It's a rare piece of software that distinguishes itself with truly original operations and features. This is good news for users: If you master one application, you can master any other application of the same type without much trouble. The menus and check boxes won't be identical, but the basic commands and preferences will all be there.

Software is constantly being upgraded and replaced, just like everything else on the Net. If we publish detailed instructions for a particular software exercise, there is an excellent chance those instructions will be obsolete within a year. Once again, it makes sense to focus on the basic functionality of an Internet application rather than on specific command lists and instructions. We do illustrate selected preference settings with screenshots for the sake of having some concrete examples, but no attempt has been made to provide comprehensive coverage at this level of detail.

HANDS-ON LEARNING

We may steer clear of in-depth software tutorials, but we emphatically stress that there is no substitute for hands-on software experience. No one can learn about the Internet without getting online and working with Internet software applications. To facilitate software mastery, many chapters have software checklists that enumerate the most important things you should be able to do with a given piece of software. We do not tell you how to do them, just that you should be able to do them. For readers who have trouble with a software checklist, solutions for all of the most popular software applications are available at `http://www.awl.com/lehnertlightweb`. In this way, readers using different software can still tackle a software checklist and get the help they need—not from the book, but from the book's Web site. When the software changes, we will update our checklist solutions with solutions for new software releases or entirely new software packages as needed. Additional opportunities for first-hand software experience will be found in exercises that have been marked **[Hands on]**.

PEDAGOGICAL FEATURES

Each chapter is divided into two sections: a section containing core topics, followed by a separate section containing optional topics. At the end of each core section you will find:

Things to Remember—Facts, tips, and reminders

Important Concepts—Key terminology and definitions

Where Can I Learn More?—URLs for relevant Web sites

Problems and Exercises, Including three special types of questions:

- **[Find It Online]**—Find the answer on the Web
- **[Hands On]**—Gain experience with software
- **[Take a Stand]**—Present and defend an opinion

Throughout the text, we also distinguish notable material using a system of five reference boxes:

Tips and Tricks—Useful information of practical value

Definitions—Definitions for important terms or phrases

Checklists—Do-it-yourself software checklists

For Your Information—Related facts or background material

Quotations—Relevant quotations by Internet experts

Glossary Terms

Important words and phrases appear boldfaced throughout the text.

Web Sites to Visit

References to Web sites are printed in blue. Links for all of these Web sites can be found at `http://www.awl.com/lehnertlightweb`

Index

A comprehensive index makes it easy to track down all references to specific terms or concepts.

TOPICS AND CHAPTER SELECTION

First Things First - Chapter 1

To get off the ground, we introduce the Internet in Chapter 1. Most importantly, we use this chapter to introduce a core vocabulary which will be used throughout the book. We cover important Internet concepts and practical tips for working with Web browsers. Most of this material should be familiar to a seasoned Netizen, but the newbies will find Chapter 1 an important prerequisite for everything that follows.

Personal Safety Online - Chapter 2

There are some very real dangers online. Many will be discussed in great detail throughout the book. But we have devoted Chapter 2 to the topic of personal safety so you'll have everything you need to know in one place. If you master Chapter 2, you'll steer clear of the most serious mistakes that people make online.

E-Mail Management - Chapter 3

Everyone uses e-mail these days, but not everyone has it under control. Chapter 3 begins with the basic operations of any good e-mail program and covers the rules of e-mail netiquette that everyone should know. We look at different e-mail services (POP, IMAP, HTTP) and discuss the pros and cons of each service. Then we move on to filtering, routing, and some general mail-management tips.

Basic Web Page Construction - Chapter 4

Web pages are easy to create and can be a lot of fun. Chapter 4 introduces HTML, the language of all Web pages. We explain and illustrate the elements of beginning HTML, concluding with a presentation of tables and frames. With this level of knowledge, students can construct a recreational Web page, spruce up a seller's listing at eBay, or add some pizazz to an e-mail newsletter. For those who want to learn more, this is a good foundation for intermediate tutorials and more advanced topics in Web page construction.

Find What You Want—Fast! - Chapter 5

You might be wasting a lot of time if you keep going back to the same old search engine every time you need to hunt down information on the Net. Chapter 6 presents a systematic approach to online searching. We describe three different types of search tools, and explain which tools are best for what types of questions. We show how to use successive query refinement to get the best possible results, and we finish up with a discussion of quality assessment.

A NOTE TO THE STUDENT

As the Internet evolves, we all have to struggle to keep up, and the first step is a solid foundation. Seemingly mundane activities such as a trip to an e-store can turn into a regrettable undertaking if you don't know how to spot a secure Web server, how to protect personal information from data resellers, or to expect the unexpected. Other problems creep in over time. For example, e-mail is a breeze until you start getting 100 messages a day. Then you need to get organized and take advantage of specialized tools for e-mail management.

Ignorance of computer security is another pitfall for newcomers to the Internet. Each time you connect to the Internet, you open the door to possible hacker attacks. If you visit a poorly designed e-store, your credit-card number could be stolen. Spend some time at another site, and highly personal or sensitive information can wind up in countless databases. You can break the law by downloading the wrong file, or you could find yourself visited by the FBI, or on the receiving end of a lawsuit for speaking candidly about the wrong subject in an online forum.

Whether you expect to use the Net personally or professionally, this book will give you the skills you need to make the Net a real asset. No one can say what the Internet will be like five or ten years from now, but the people who are using the Internet today will help shape the Internet of tomorrow. In a very real way, this technology belongs to you and is yours to mold. Every week, some Congressional hearing in Washington touches on the Internet in one way or another. Children need to be protected. Consumers need to be protected. Musicians and artists need to be protected. A burgeoning e-commerce needs to be nurtured, and a digital divide between the rich and the poor needs to be crossed. Learn about the Internet today, and you will get the Internet you want tomorrow.

A NOTE TO THE INSTRUCTOR

If you've taught an Internet course before, you know the Internet is not your only moving target. Your students are changing at least as fast as the Net itself, and it may be necessary to take their collective pulse two or three times a year. We know that college students tend to be very interested in music: Many students already know how to find and download music files from the Net. Some students have mastered the know-how needed to find and download software from the Net because they've investigated their MP3 player options (the software needed to play music files found on the Net). These same students have probably been using e-mail for at least a year or two, they may have dabbled in Web-page construction, and they have probably purchased at least one item online. We know that online chat is also quite popular among students, and a growing number of students are learning to use the Internet to make long-distance phone calls at reduced rates. We hope that students are also using the Internet to enhance their education and find valuable information. Evidence suggests this is true: We know that 80% of all students graduating in 1999 used the Internet to search for a job or research a prospective employer.

The Digital Divide

If you conduct a survey of your students, you will find that many are knowledgeable about e-mail and Web browsers, others are very experienced with a wide range of

Internet resources and applications, and a few have managed to miss out on everything and are desperate to catch up. This wide range of expertise is a major challenge facing all instructors of the Internet. You need to hold the interest of the more experienced students while getting the less experienced students off the ground. If the digital divide is dramatically apparent in your classroom, your syllabus must be flexible and your assignments must somehow accommodate everyone.

In the Instructor's Manual (IM) that accompanies this text, I address the very real problem of the digital divide. Students who do not have their own computers will not be able to do some of the hands-on chapter exercises, even if computing facilities are available to your students in computer labs. Security concerns usually prohibit students from downloading and installing software from the Internet in educational computer labs, and this will be a problem for some of the exercises in Chapters 8 and 9. I have some suggestions in the IM for handling this, as well as other problems related to the digital divide.

Wizards in the Classroom

Courses about the Internet are usually fun for both students and teachers, but neither should underestimate the amount of work involved. Everyone is struggling to keep abreast of the most valuable Internet tools and resources. You should expect to find at least one or two students who are more experienced than you are with some aspects of the Internet (the "wizards"). I tell you how to identify these individuals early on and give you some suggestions on how to turn their expertise into a classroom asset.

With each new class, an instructor should always revisit the question of where to start, how fast to move, and how much material to cover. In the case of the Internet, initial class assessments are even more important. In the IM, I show you how to assess your class with a few casual questions during your first class meeting. Not only can you benchmark your class in general, but you can smoke out the wizards right from the start.

The Instructors Manual

The IM also contains all the usual things you hope to find in an IM:

- Solutions to all the problems and exercises in the book
- A large archive of test questions, indexed by chapter and section
- Chapter notes and teaching tips
- Suggested classroom demonstrations
- Suggested class projects
- A checklist of things to do at the start of the semester
- A sample class syllabus (with variations)

All recipients of the IM are also welcome to join my Internet 101 Mailing List for Internet instructors (see `http://www.awl.com/lehnertweb101/` for instructions on how to subscribe). Members are welcome to post questions, ask for advice, report on classroom experiments, and look for inspiration in our collective classroom experience.

I've had a lot of fun teaching undergraduates about the Internet, and I have written the IM for both the inexperienced first timer as well as for the experienced teacher who is looking for ways to improve an existing course offering. Students bring considerable enthusiasm to the subject of the Internet; all you have to do is sustain it. The Internet itself is always a plentiful source of timely Internet-related news items. Plus, students who have been online for a year or more have probably had their own first-hand learning experiences. If you draw from the news as it happens, and encourage selected students to participate in your class presentations, you can sustain a high level of interest and involvement (your own included) for an entire semester.

WHY THE IGUANA?

For those who are curious about the cover of this book, I suppose I should say a few words about the iguana. The green iguana is a fitting symbol for everything that is unique and wonderful about the Internet. Iguanas are surprisingly popular in the United States as pets, especially among college students and the 20- or 30-something crowd. Unfortunately, much published misinformation is available to a prospective iguana owner about what constitutes a healthy diet or how an iguana should be housed. Luckily for the iguana, many iguana enthusiasts are active on the Internet and talking to each other. Questions from beginners are being answered in great detail by herpetologists and experienced iguana owners. Thanks to the Internet, this native inhabitant of tropical rain forests now thrives in Arizona, Alaska, and all kinds of intemperate regions. The iguana community is not a place you will find on any map, but it is alive and well on the Internet!

ACKNOWLEDGMENTS

Many people helped make this book possible. First and foremost, I am indebted to my colleagues in the Computer Science Department at the University of Massachusetts who encouraged me to develop an undergraduate course on the Internet. I am also deeply indebted to the many undergraduate students who have taken my course and given me valuable feedback on my choice of topics, exercises, and examples. The enthusiasm and achievements of my students have kept me interested in the challenge of teaching the Internet to non-Computer Science majors in spite of all the work that necessarily accompanies a moving-target curriculum.

My best defense against inaccuracies and outright errors were my many reviewers, who were remarkably generous in providing me with detailed feedback, corrections, and suggestions. My reviewers assisted me greatly in my humble attempt to produce a manuscript that is free of errors and omissions. Heartfelt thanks to Jeffrey R. Brown (Montana State University—Great Falls), Janet Brunelle (Old Dominion University), Jack Brzezinski (DePaul University), Peter G. Clote (Boston College), Paul De Palma (Gonzaga University), Michael Gildersleeve (University of New Hampshire), Martin Granier (Western Washington University), Stephanie Ludi (Arizona State University), Jayne Valenti Miller (Purdue University), Lori L. Scarlatos (Brooklyn College—CUNY), and Scott Tilley (University of California—Riverside). This book benefited greatly from their expertise. With all of this excellent assistance, any errors that may have found their way onto these pages are mine and mine alone.

Many thanks also to everyone at Addison Wesley who supported me in this endeavor. This book would never have been written without the support and encouragement of Acquisitions Editor Susan Hartman Sullivan, whose enthusiasm and confidence kept the project on target in spite of an accelerated production schedule. Assistant Editor Elinor Actipis marshalled reviewer feedback, kept an eye on all the copyright permissions, answered all my questions, and helped me keep my priorities straight when too many deadlines began to get the better of me. Production Editors Helen Reebenacker and Patty Mahtani tackled the unenviable job of putting it all together and remaining cool in the face of upstream delays (mea culpa). Mary Boucher, Senior Permissions Editor, gave us invaluable support by handling the copyright permission requests for over 400 screen shots. My copy editor, Laura Michaels, moved through a remarkable amount of text in short order, sorting out the mess produced by imperfect typing and speech-recognition software. Webmaster Jennifer Pelland takes full credit for the design of the Web site that accompanies this text. I am grateful to Regina Hagen, who designed the book cover, and especially to Susan Cyr, our cover artist, whose fertile imagination produced a thoroughly believable iguana with a taste for MP3's.

Special thanks go to my husband, Mark Snyder, who contributed to these chapters by poring over my text and suggesting countless improvements. Finally, I want to thank my whole family for putting up with the ambiguous shadow of a mother who was simultaneously there and not there for the six months it took me to write this book. Unexpected life forms flourished in the fridge, dust bunnies roamed the hallways with confidence, and the kids acquired important macaroni and cheese survival skills. As the mathematician in *Jurassic Park* remarked, "Life finds a way . . ."

Wendy Lehnert (February 2001)

Contents

CHAPTER 5   Find What You Want—Fast!   **141**

APPENDIX A   Internet Service Providers   191

APPENDIX B   When to Talk to Technical Staff   195

APPENDIX C   HTML Tags and Attributes   197

First Things First

CHAPTER**GOALS**

- Understand the purpose of your computer's CPU, RAM, and hard drive.
- Learn about bits, bytes, kilobytes, megabytes, and gigabytes.
- Find out how the Internet is structured and how computers become part of the Internet.
- Discover how IP and DNS addresses are used.
- Master the basic navigational features of your Web browser.

1.1 TAKING CHARGE

As a college student, you have probably spent quite a few hours on the *Internet*, also called the *Net*, even if you don't own a computer. In 1999, over 90% of U.S. college students had access to the Net, and 80% of graduating college students used it to search for a job or research a prospective employer. It's time to set aside all of the hype about how the Internet is changing everything—the ability of the Internet to transform our lives is a given. Now we need to get down to the serious business of really putting the Internet to work for us.

Each of us brings our own interests and needs to the Internet. By using Internet resources intelligently, we can be better informed, better connected to others who share our interests, and better able to pursue our goals. However, attaining this ideal won't happen automatically. We can easily spend too much time socializing in chat rooms or surfing for entertainment or exploring online games. In order to make time online productive and professional, we must begin by learning about the Internet and software applications for the Internet.

Most people do not fully appreciate how many choices color our experience of the Internet. Surveys show that most Internet users start with one Web browser (typically the one that came with their computer) and never experiment with alternative browsers. Chances are, these people have never bothered to think about their browser options and whether they're working with the browser that's best for them. However, the choice of a browser is simply one in a long list of software options that can make the difference between a productive Internet experience and an ineffective or frustrating one.

The Internet has evolved rapidly in recent years, and this pace will likely continue well into the future. Keeping up with it can divert us from other interests and goals that deserve attention. However, the Net can be tamed and put to good use if we are serious about using it wisely. The trick is to figure out when we are using the Net effectively and when we are floundering. Then, we can take charge, of our expectations and of our time, in order to maintain the right balance between our online activities and the rest of our lives.

Taking charge means cutting a swathe through the overwhelming number of choices and options that the Net offers. Our lives are shaped by choices that we make at each step along the way. We each choose our friends, our interests, and our beliefs. We also choose clothes, cars, hair styles, music, meals, pets, and insurance plans. The list is long, and at times, overwhelming. The Internet can help us make better choices by showing us available options, useful facts, and provocative opinions. The Internet also puts us in direct touch with a dizzying rate of technological change unparalleled in human history. We are clearly dealing with a transforming technology. The trick is to make sure that we stay in charge of the transformation.

Much of the challenge before us comes down to plain old time management and the realization that the Internet can be a time sink just as easily as it can be a time-saver. We can conserve and optimize time, in part, by making informed selections of Internet software, based on a practical understanding of the Internet and its resources. For example, if you dial into the Internet over a telephone line, a *Web accelerator* might cut in half the amount of time that you spend waiting for Web pages to download. If you are dealing with large amounts of e-mail, you can take steps to save time and manage those mountains of messages more efficiently (see Section 3.7). If you download a lot of files and a download needs to be resumed or scheduled during off-hours, a good download manager can free you to concentrate on other things. And if you spend a lot of time tracking down information using search engines, some powerful browser enhancements can speed you through those searches by cutting through all of the garbage (see Sections 5.7 and 5.8). Of course, when you're still learning it's hard to know what you need to know. That's why it pays to take some time to learn about the Internet software options available for Internet users today.

This book is a good place to start. It will introduce you to the most powerful Internet tools that every Internet user should know about. It will also prepare you to choose your Internet tools wisely regardless of how you intend to use the Internet: for work, for pleasure, or both.

Before we start, let's make sure that we're all speaking the same language. Computer jargon is a stumbling block for many Internet newcomers (often called *newbies*) because they've never bothered to learn the basics. This chapter will help you demystify the most commonly encountered jargon. Computers are typically characterized by the software that they run, how fast that they run, and the amount of memory that they contain. We will tell you what you need to know about computer software, computer speed, and computer memory in the next section.

1.2 ▚ COMPUTER BASICS

1.2.1 The Operating System

The heart of any computer is its operating system. An **operating system (OS)** is a large program that starts whenever you turn on your computer. The most important program running on your computer, the OS is necessary for other programs, called *application programs*, to run. It is like a computer's nervous system. It recognizes input from the keyboard and mouse, keeps track of files, updates the time display, tells you when you have a problem—it generally is there to respond to your input. Without an OS, your computer cannot perform any of the fundamental tasks that make it useful. If something is wrong with your OS, you have major problems.

The world of *personal computers* has long been divided into two camps based on the OS that they run: *Microsoft Windows*™ or *Apple's OS for the Macintosh*. The vast majority of personal computer users run Windows. However, other OSs are available. For example, **Linux** (a version of *UNIX*) is popular primarily with programmers and experienced computer users, but it is gaining a foothold in business environments as an increasingly popular alternative to Windows. Another alternative OS is *BeOS*. A computer that runs Windows is often called a **PC** (**personal computer**) to distinguish it from a Macintosh computer, called a Mac for short. For simplicity, this book uses the term *personal computer* to mean both PCs and Macs. When it comes to the Internet, PCs and Macs are largely indistinguishable, although software is generally written for one or the other: As a rule, software written for a PC will not run on a Mac and software written for a Mac will not run on a PC. We will explain why in the next section. Throughout this book, you will find many examples of Internet software in action. These examples are based on software for PCs, but if you have a Mac, don't worry. Whenever you hear about a piece of PC software, there is something analogous for Macs.

A newly purchased computer usually comes with an OS already installed. Upgrading to a new version of the OS is usually easy, although you'll want to set aside half a day for the process. Switching to an entirely new OS is a major project and is best managed with a second computer on hand so that you can revert to your old OS if needed.

1.2.2 The Central Processing Unit

The part of the personal computer that performs instructions is the **central processing unit** (**CPU**). The hardware unit that houses the CPU in a personal computer is called a **microprocessor** (the Pentium III and the G4 are two examples of microprocessors). Microprocessors normally contain additional hardware that supports the CPU, but the two terms are often used interchangeably in casual conversation. The CPU is the brain of the computer—it is where most of the computation takes place. In terms of computing power, it is the most important part of the computer—in general, the faster the CPU, the faster the computer. A CPU is distinguished by three characteristics:

- its speed (called the *clock speed*)
- its instruction set
- bandwidth (the amount of information it can manipulate at one time)

A CPU's **clock speed** determines how many instructions per second that it can execute. Clock speed is given in megahertz (MHz), a unit that refers to one million cycles per second, where a **cycle** is the smallest unit of time recognized by the computer's internal clock. A CPU running at 800 MHz goes through 800 million processing cycles in one second. You may also see descriptions of CPU speed in terms of MIPS (1 MIPS = 1 million instructions per second) although this measure is less meaningful because different instructions require a different number of cycles. CPU speeds in personal computers get faster and faster each year. If your computer is three years old, its CPU is probably running at less than a third or even a quarter of the CPU speed of personal computers sold today. You can do little to speed up an old CPU. As a result, used computers are not in great demand, unless they are relatively new.

Moore's Law

Computers double in speed at least every 18 months and do so without any increase in cost.

A CPU is also distinguished by its instruction set. An **instruction set** (also called **machine instructions**) describes the collection of operations that the CPU can execute. One instruction may be used to negate an integer, while a different instruction is used to add two integers. While instructions like these are standard fare, other instructions may be specific to a particular microprocessor. As a result, a Motorola CPU runs a different instruction set than does an Intel CPU. At the lowest level, all software operates by executing operations in a specific instruction set. For example, Macs use a Motorola CPU because the Mac OS relies on the Motorola instruction set. To run Windows, you need an Intel CPU (or another brand that supports the Intel instruction set) because Windows relies on the Intel instruction set. It is possible to simulate the Intel instruction set on a Motorola CPU and therefore run Windows on a Mac. However, OS simulations tend to run slowly because the target instruction set has to be simulated by the native instruction set. For this reason, OS simulations are never as satisfactory as an OS running on native hardware (the microprocessor that runs the required instruction set directly).

Computer engineers can achieve significant speed-ups by increasing the **bandwidth** (sometimes called the *data width*) of a microprocessor. More bandwidth means that a CPU can receive, manipulate, and return more data during each processing cycle. Instruction sets need to be modified so they can keep up with larger data transfers—it will do no good to hand a CPU a larger block of data if all of its instructions are still designed to handle smaller amounts of data. CPU speed, instruction sets, and bandwidth all work together to determine the overall computing power of your computer.

1.2.3 Memory

A computer's memory is its internal storage area and consists of several different types, including

- random access memory and
- long-term memory.

Random Access Memory The memory that the CPU uses when it executes its machine instructions is **random access memory** (**RAM**), also called **main memory**. RAM is often called **fast memory** because the CPU can write to and read from it very quickly, thereby enabling the CPU to perform its operations as quickly as possible. RAM is also *volatile* memory: when you turn off your computer, all data in RAM is lost.

RAM is sometimes described as a computer's version of human short-term memory. That is, the amount of space is limited and the information that it contains doesn't stay there for long. However, it is a crucial gateway to your computer; much of the information going in and out of your computer moves through its version of short-term memory.

Each program that you run on your computer requires some minimal amount of RAM. When running more than one program at a time, your computer allocates a fixed amount of the available RAM to each program. If there is enough RAM to go around, everything works as it should. But if those running programs collectively require more RAM than is available, then the OS resorts to various *memory management strategies*, which might or might not work very well. Your computer might respond very slowly when it is working with less RAM than it needs or might crash more often when you try to run too many programs at once. It is usually a good idea to buy as much RAM as you can afford (although all computers do have limits on the amount of RAM that can be installed). When you buy a new computer, never settle for the minimal RAM configuration. Research the software you want to run and then ask for at least twice as much RAM as the various software manufacturers say you should have. If you already have a computer that tends to crash when you open too many applications, check to see if your computer has room for more RAM. An ailing computer can often be made healthy with a RAM upgrade.

Long-Term Memory A different type of memory is used for long-term storage. Sometimes called **slow memory**, this is the memory on your hard drive. Whereas data in RAM disappears when the power goes off, data saved on the hard drive remains in long-term memory. The hard drive can be used to save, for example, computer programs, word processing files, and spreadsheet data, as well as that partially completed tax return. The larger your hard drive, the more files you can save and the more programs you can store on your computer. Whereas a lot of RAM can help your computer run faster, a large hard drive allows you to install many applications, such as word processors and games.

Personal computers may contain other types of memory and microprocessors. For example, some CPUs include their own built-in short-term memory that is faster than RAM (for example, the L1 cache in Power Macintosh computers). In addition, most computers contain a **floating-point unit** (**FPU**), a special microprocessor designed to handle floating-point arithmetic, which is crucial for speedy graphics displays. However, for the purposes of this book the most important hardware components are the CPU, RAM, and the hard drive as described here.

Computer Checklist: Get to Know Your Computer

Find out the hardware specs for your home computer:

1. How much RAM do you have?
2. How large is your hard drive?
3. How fast is your CPU?

If you don't know the answers, consult the Help feature for your OS and look for information about your *system resources.* Depending on your OS, you might need to find the answers in a few different places.

1.3　UNITS OF MEMORY

As people have become increasingly enamored with the Internet, many applications have surfaced to enhance the online experience. Many of these enable multimedia communication (audio and video) over the Internet. Software designers are always pushing the envelope regarding what can be done on available hardware. In turn, hardware manufacturers labor to produce faster CPUs and larger hard drives at affordable prices. Many leading-edge software applications tend to stress all but the most current and powerful computers, but software manufacturers know that hardware advances will make these products more accessible in a year or two—at least for those users who have access to the latest computers.

To understand how computing limitations can affect your experiences on the Net, you need to understand how files work. A **file** is a collection of data that has a name (the filename). Almost all the information stored in a computer is stored in a file. Thus the file is the building block of everything that we see and hear online. Files are constantly being moved across that Net, and different software applications work with different types of files. The size of a file often determines how long you must wait for an application to do something with the file, so it is important to know how big your files are. Files come in all sizes, from tiny to gigantic. In the next two sections we will explain how file sizes can be described with great precision.

1.3.1 The Bit

The smallest unit of measurement for computer data is called the bit. A **bit** is a memory unit that can hold one of two possible values: 0 or 1. All data inside of a computer is represented by *patterns* of bits. Small amounts of information can be represented by a small number of bits and larger amounts of information require more bits. The value of a bit stored in RAM or on your hard drive can be changed by software. When your CPU executes an instruction, it often stores a bit pattern in RAM, performs some manipulation on that pattern, and produces a new bit pattern as the result of the instruction. When you write over old files on your hard drive, you erase old patterns of bits and replace them with new patterns of bits. By contrast, read-only media such as a read-only CD-ROM or DVD disc consists of bits that cannot be changed.

What Is a 32-Bit System?

If you are a Windows user, you might have seen references to a *32-bit system* or *32-bit software*. The number of bits refers to the amount of memory that a CPU can reference by naming specific memory locations (also known as *addresses*). The range of addresses that a CPU can reference is called an *address space*. In a 32-bit system, both the OS and the CPU can work with 2^{32} memory locations (this is called a *32-bit address space*) by chunking 32 bits into a single unit that can be moved in and out of the CPU in a single cycle. Video game consoles have progressed from 8-bit CPUs (for example, the original Nintendo game) to 128-bit CPUs (for example, the Sega Dreamcast system).

Software described as 32-bit has been programmed to take full advantage of a 32-bit CPU. Windows 95/98/NT (Win95/98/NT) are 32-bit OSs; Windows 3.1 was a 16-bit OS. Applications for Win95/98 can be either 16-bit or 32-bit, but a 32-bit application will run faster because it can move twice as much information in and out of the CPU in a single cycle. The Macintosh G4 computer is a 128-bit system.

The actual speed of a computer depends on, as mentioned earlier, the CPU's clock speed, the intrinsic power of the CPU's instruction set, the number of bytes that can be transferred into and out of the CPU in a single instruction, as well as other features not described here.

1.3.2 The Byte and Beyond

The next level up from the bit is the byte. A **byte** is a pattern of 8 bits, for example 00101110. Patterns of bits are used to represent the letters of the English alphabet (among others). It takes only 5 bits to create 32 (= $2 \times 2 \times 2 \times 2 \times 2$) distinct patterns, more than enough to code the letters A through Z. Only 7 bits are required to code both lowercase and uppercase characters, numerical digits, and punctuation marks, with room to spare. Even the extra bit is put to good use for something called *error checking*, which makes it possible to detect transmission errors when bytes are moved from one computer to another. Therefore a byte is quite convenient when you want to represent all of the symbols that a keyboard can produce.

Interestingly, Japanese was initially a problem for software designers because Japanese characters could not be adequately represented using 8-bit bytes. To handle the Japanese language, computers had to be programmed to work with 16-bit patterns (sometimes called *16-bit words*).

The set of visible characters that you can type on a standard keyboard are referred to as **ASCII characters** because they are represented by a code for encoding 128 characters called the **ASCII character code** (see Figure 1.1). **ASCII text files** are files that contain only ASCII characters. **Binary files** contain additional characters not found on any keyboard (these files are usually generated by computer programs). The size of a file (either ASCII or binary) is measured by the number of bytes used to represent its contents. This number is more or less equivalent to the number of characters in the file. For example, a page of text that contains 60 lines of text, and 110 characters per line, contains 6,600 characters, which consumes 6,600 bytes of memory.

Figure 1.1:
The ASCII
Character Set

	0	1	2	3	4	5	6	7	8	9	A	B	C	D	E	F
0	NUL	SOH	STX	ETX	EOT	ENQ	ACK	BEL	BS	HT	LF	VT	FF	CR	SO	SI
1	DLE	DC1	DC2	DC3	DC4	NAK	SYN	ETB	CAN	EM	SUB	ESC	FS	GS	RS	US
2	SPC	!	"	#	$	%	&	'	(	)	*	+	,	–	.	/
3	0	1	2	3	4	5	6	7	8	9	:	;	<	=	>	?
4	@	A	B	C	D	E	F	G	H	I	J	K	L	M	N	O
5	P	Q	R	S	T	U	V	W	X	Y	Z	[	\	]	^	_
6	'	a	b	c	d	e	f	g	h	i	j	k	l	m	n	o
7	p	q	r	s	t	u	v	w	x	y	z	{	|	}	~	DEL

Kilobytes, Megabytes, and Gigabytes For easy reference, bytes are grouped into larger units. For example, a **kilobyte** (**KB**) consists of 1,024 bytes. (In casual writing, you might see the abbreviation K instead of KB.) Although the term *kilo* means 1,000, a kilobyte contains 1,024 bytes rather than 1,000 bytes as might be expected. This is because the arithmetic of computers works with binary (*base-2*) representations for numbers—recall that a bit can hold either of only two values: 0 or 1. This contrasts with a base-10 system, such as the decimal system that is used to represent numbers throughout the industrialized world. Just as the number $1,000_{(base\ 10)} = 10^3$ is a nice round number in the decimal system, The number 1,024 is a nice round number in base-2 because $1,024_{(base\ 10)} = 1,000,000,000_{(base\ 2)} = 2^{10}$. When you need only a rough estimate, you can think of a kilobyte as being 1,000 bytes. However, for precision, use 1,024 bytes. Thus one page of text that contains 6,600 bytes consumes approximately 6.6KB of memory, or, more precisely, 6.45KB (rounded to the nearest hundredth).

The Sinclair Computer

One of the first personal computers sold in the late 1970s, the Sinclair ZX81 came with 1KB of RAM and cost $100. If you could afford it, you could spend an additional $100 and add an extra 16KB of RAM. This was considered a tremendous amount of memory in those days.

If you need to deal only with text, you can go far with just kilobytes. For really large numbers of bytes, however, a more convenient unit to work with is the megabyte. A **megabyte** (**MB**) is 2^{20} = 1024KB—roughly 1,000KB, if you need only a quick estimate. Therefore 1,000 pages of text formatted like the previous example will require 6,445KB of memory or 6.4MB approximately and 6.3MB (rounded) precisely. Most of us do not need such large amounts of memory for our text files, but megabytes are a useful unit when referring to RAM. The new larger and more powerful computer programs can consume many megabytes of RAM, and RAM installations have been increasing to handle them (see Figure 1.2).

In addition, large amounts of RAM are needed to handle the many complicated graphics that are commonplace on the Net. Compared to text, graphical images require significantly larger amounts of memory. Whoever said that a picture is worth a thousand words was lowballing the amount. One thousand words that consist of approximately 5,600 characters require an estimated 5.5KB of memory. For graphics, this would be enough memory for only one black-and-white drawing of, say, Dilbert or perhaps a small, colored arrow on a Web page. Larger images can consume 60KB or more of memory, and a high-resolution photograph (see I-1 in the color insert) can eat up as

Figure 1.2:
Typical RAM
Configurations
for New
Computers

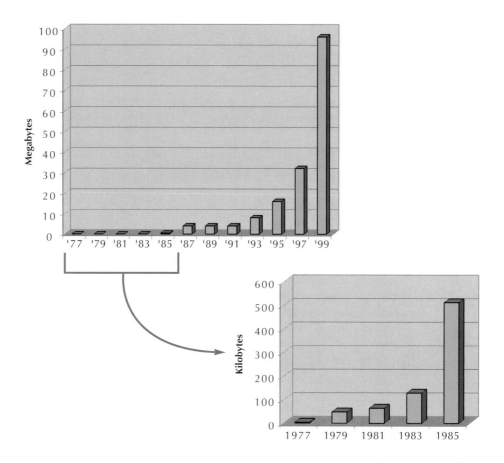

much as 600KB if nothing clever has been done to conserve memory. Three large photographs might be too big for a 1.44MB **floppy disk** (although that same floppy can hold 200 pages of plain ASCII text).

As people started working more with graphics on their personal computers, they began to need larger storage devices for handling many large files. In 1995, the storage capacity of hard drives for high-end personal computers crossed the line from megabytes to gigabytes. A **gigabyte** (**GB**) is 2^{30} bytes = 1,024MB. During the same period, floppy disks began giving way to **zip disks**, which can hold 100MB to 250MB per disk, and to **Jaz disks** (1GB to 2GB per disk), and to writeable **CD-ROMs** (640MB).

At the time of this writing, entry-level computers are typically configured with 13GB hard drives and high-end computers come with 40GB hard drives. Some people can easily fill up 10GB in only a few months; heavy users, in only a few weeks. Where does all of that long-term memory go? Figure 1.3 shows a few benchmarks. Win98 requires 100MB all by itself. A large collection of screen savers could eat up another 100MB. A family photograph album can easily consume 100MB. A Web accelerator for your Web browser requires a minimum of 200MB (you can opt to give it as much as 3GB if your appetite for the Web tends toward insatiable). With what else can you fill up a 13GB hard drive? A photographer or an artist would have no trouble using that amount of memory. Neither would the average college student.

A Music Revolution Massive amounts of long-term memory in countless dormitory rooms on hundreds of college campuses across the country are consumed by something that was a college preoccupation long before computers became a standard fixture: music. Music is a true memory hog. For example, a 3-minute music file can require from 3MB to 45MB, depending on how it's stored. To minimize a hefty music file without sac-

Figure 1.3:
Where Does All
the Memory Go?

One page of plain ascii text (54 single-spaced lines, 10pt)	5KB		One Iomega Zip Disk	100MB
One color cartoon on a Web page	50KB		Three minutes of video (compressed MP3 format)	400MB
One high-resolution photograph	500KB		One CD-ROM	640MB
One floppy disk (high density—double sided)	1.44MB		A hard drive for a new PC (in the year 2000)	13GB
Three minutes of music (compressed MP3 format)	3MB		One DVD disc	4.7–17GB
One medium sized Web site (text and graphics)	50MB			

rificing its content, you can use any of various *file compression techniques*. Without compression, for example, 10GB on a hard drive can store the equivalent of 15 audio CDs. With compression, that 10GB will store a respectable music library of approximately 200 audio CDs.

You can listen to this music on your computer, or you can invest $200 on an *MP3 player* (see the box, What Is File Compression?) designed to play digital audio files wherever you go (the programmable equivalent of a Walkman).

All of this indicates that a music revolution is underway, fueled by digital technology. And where do we get these audio files? The Internet, of course.

What Is File Compression?

Large files can be stored either in their original format or in a *compressed format* to save space. Different types of file compression are used for different types of files, such as text, graphics, and audio. You usually can reduce a large file by at least 50%, depending on the type of file and the type of compression.

In the case of audio files, for example, the **MP3** (**MPEG audio player 3**) format can be used to reduce audio files by as much as 90% to 93%. Bigger is never better when you're trying to move a large file across the Net.

Other ways to fill a 13GB hard drive include storing video files. These files require even more long-term memory than do audio files. Currently, few people collect video files from the Internet because they are so memory intensive. However, the introduction of Apple's iMac DVD SE, with its easy-to-use video editor designed for family use, is making personal computers and camcorders a powerful combination. Long-term memory requirements for video and audio files are driving consumer demand for larger hard drives on personal computers. As the cost of a hard drive continues to drop, users can be counted on to find new ways to use all of the long-term memory on their computers. In a culture in which you can never be too rich or too thin, you also can never have too much computer memory.

1.4   SPEED AND BOTTLENECKS

You will also encounter bits and bytes on the Internet. When you "go online," or connect your computer to the Internet, you create a communication channel between your computer and other computers. Data is exchanged between computers at the rate of *bits per second (bps)*. If you're connecting to the Internet from your home, you're likely dialing in over a telephone line or using a special service, such as ISDN, DSL, or cable. If you are connecting from your outside work office or a computer laboratory at school, you might have an Ethernet connection. The actual rate of data flow between any two computers on the Internet will vary, depending on competing traffic.

If you don't have broadband, then your Internet connection probably acts sluggishly sometimes. You might be feeling the effects of too much traffic on a specific server or of other traffic patterns on the Net. To find out why your connection is bogged down, you can visit the **PC Pitstop** and take the *ping test* (see Figure 1.4). Pinging is discussed in further detail in the Above & Beyond section. For now it's enough to know that a ping is a way to measure the speed of a data transmission between two computers. Ping values between 200 and 300 milliseconds (ms) are typical for computers connected via phone lines. The PC Pitstop displays test outcomes in this range with a yellow background. Unusually fast times and unusually slow times are shown with green and red backgrounds, respectively. If all of the ping test sites come back red, your ISP is probably having difficulties. If the tested sites are all green or yellow, these slowdowns are probably due to overworked servers. A mix of colors might indicate a routing problem on the Net or that some servers are overloaded. To find out what's normal for your type of connection and your ISP, take your computer's "pulse" by taking the ping test at different times of the day and on a few different days.

For most home users, the major bottleneck is the computer's modem and the telephone line. A 28.8K modem can transfer data at a maximal rate of 28,800 bits per second, or 28 kilobits per second (28.8 kbps). A 56K (56 kbps) modem is capable of 56,000 bits per second. However, achieving true 56K exchange is not possible because no telephone line can keep up with that rate. A poor-quality telephone line can slow you down to about 20 kbps no matter what your modem can do. The best transmission rate you can hope for with a 56K modem is probably in the 40 kbps to 45 kbps range.

Figure 1.4:
Testing Your Internet Connection at the PC Pitstop

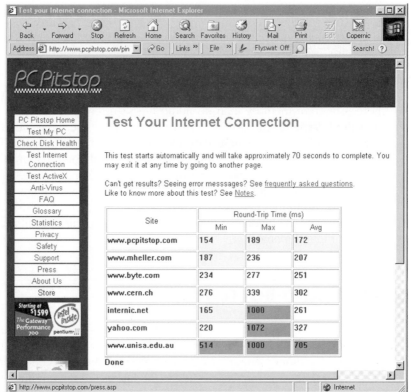

K (1,024) vs. k (1,000)

Why does 56K when referring to modems mean 56 × 1,000 bits per second (56 kbps), whereas 56KB (often written as 56K) of memory means 56 × 1,024 bytes? The ambiguity surrounding the letter "K" results because the same symbol is being used to represent both a base-10 (decimal system) kilo (1,000) and a base-2 kilo (1,024). In the context of data transmissions, K always means 1,000. In the context of computer memory, K always means 1,024. You need to know in which context the K is being used.

Some authors are careful to use a lowercase "k" for the decimal system version (as in kbps) in an effort to distinguish the two usages. However, you will see Kbps as well as kbps (with both meaning 1,000 bits per second). Further, modem speeds are often described in terms of K (as in a 56K modem), even though what is meant is kbps.

Most authors are careful at least to keep their bits (b) and their bytes (B) straight, although context is useful here, too. Usually, bits (b) describe data transmission rates, whereas bytes (B) describe quantities of computer memory. If this is too confusing, simply remember that most of the time, K means KB (1,024 bytes), unless you are talking about transmission speeds, in which case K means kbps (1,000 bits per second).

Figure 1.5:
LeechFTP Moving a File across the Internet at 2.33 kbps

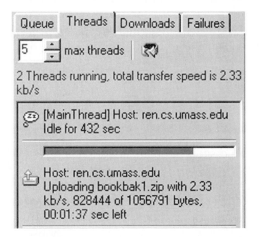

As an example, Figure 1.5 shows a status window from an Internet application called **LeechFTP**. This application transfers files between computers via the Internet. At the time of this snapshot, LeechFTP was transferring data at an average rate of 2.33 kbps.

The Windows Dial-Up Networking™ window in Figure 1.6 shows a connection made over a 56K modem which is operating at a maximal speed of 44 kbps.

Downloading and Uploading Files

The terms *download* and *upload* refer to file transfers across a network. You **download** a file when you move a copy of a file from a computer at a remote location to your local computer. You **upload** a file when you move a copy of a file on your local computer to a computer at a remote location.

The amount of data that can be moved through a digital device during a fixed period of time is called **bandwidth**. The greater the bandwidth, the faster the data exchange. A file in one computer will travel to another, remote, computer over various communication channels, ranging from copper telephone wires to optical fiber. **Broadband channels—**

Figure 1.6:
The Maximal Speed
of an Internet
Connection

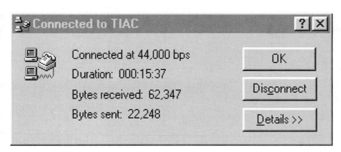

that is, *high bandwidth* channels—might move the file at 1 billion bits per second, but that doesn't mean that they will arrive at the same rate. Data transfer on the Internet is ruled by the dictum "hurry up and wait." A 1MB file can cross the United States in only seconds. However, it will hit a major bottleneck when it meets a 56K modem, which can transfer 1MB in, at best, 3 minutes. This is why it takes the average home personal computer at least an hour to download a 20MB file such as Microsoft Internet Explorer™ (MSIE).

Traffic patterns on the Net vary from time to time and place to place. To view current traffic conditions, you can visit **The Internet Weather Report** (see Figure 1.7). There, you can choose from the available maps either a global view or a more detailed regional view. A large circle indicates where servers are showing slower response times—these times are also called **latencies**. Nested circles indicate more congestion than does a single circle. Such maps show that the most favorable traffic conditions are at 6 A.M. Eastern Standard Time (EST).

1.5 ■ THE INTERNET

The earlier discussion of speed spoke casually about computers exchanging data over the Internet. Thus one might imagine that the Internet is a massive network similar to that used for telephone communications, except with computer-to-computer connections instead of telephone-to-telephone connections. Any two computers connected to the Internet can establish a communication link between them via telephone lines. However, a look at the nature of Internet communication shows that Internet connections are fundamentally different from telephone-to-telephone connections even when the computers involved access the Internet via telephone lines. If this sounds confusing, read on—it takes a little explaining.

The **Internet** is more than a network of computers. It actually is a network of networks. *Internet* stands for **inter**networked **net**works. Computer networks have been around for decades. The first were geographically close to one another, often within a single building. Called a **local area network** (**LAN**), these networks were used by large companies for in-house data processing long before the arrival of the Internet. Universities used LANs for administrative, educational, and research purposes. Libraries used LANs to hold their card catalogs. In time, university research LANs and commercial research LANs began to create communication links so that computers in different LANs could share information. Then government networks and corporate networks joined the mix. Eventually, commercial networks were created for the sole purpose of giving consumers access to this rapidly expanding infrastructure, this Internet, of computer-based communication. The Internet now reaches into more than 185 countries, connects more than seventy thousand computer networks, and is used by over three hundred million people worldwide.

Figure 1.7:
A "Weather Report"
for the Internet

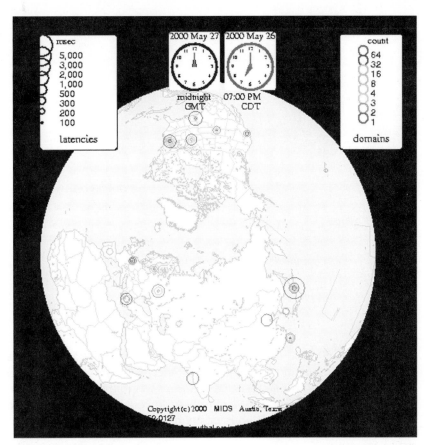

The Internet's structure is largely heterarchical (the correct word is probably "heterogenous" but computer scientists insist on saying "heterarchical"). In a **heterarchical network**, the members, or *nodes*, of the network are interconnected randomly, with no node occupying a position of greater importance than any other node. This is done to ensure robust communication. By contrast, some communication networks are designed as a **hierarchy**. A hierarchical network is organized in the shape of a pyramid and always includes a unique *root node* that is superior over all other nodes. Two nodes that want to exchange data within a hierarchy must use a path that passes through some node that is superior to them. The shortest such path is unique and will always be a part of any path between the same two nodes. In other words, to get from one location to another inside of a hierarchy there is always one critical path for doing so (see Figure 1.8).

A hierarchical network is much less robust than a heterarchical network. This is because removing the root node from a hierarchy destroys the only communication paths available to nodes that are not close to each other within the hierarchy. The more nodes that are removed from the top regions of the hierarchy, the more communication that is disrupted. In a heterarchy, by contrast, many ways are possible to get from one node to another. You can reduce the speed of communication within a heterarchy by removing nodes; however, you would have to remove a great many nodes in order to disrupt communications completely.

The original research that formed the foundation for today's Internet was motivated by concern for robust network communications: If one part of the network failed, the rest would continue to function. This could be accomplished only if more than one way was available for information to get from point A to point B. Network designers decided that the standard means of moving data across the Internet would be **dynamic routing**. A

Figure 1.8:
Heterarchies and
Hierarchies.

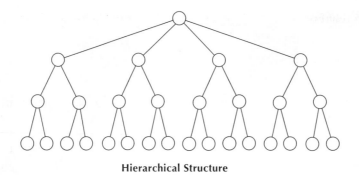

Hierarchical Structure

Heterarchical Structure

dynamic route is a route that is selected at the time of transmission and based on current network conditions. The ability to select such a route is distributed throughout the network so that no one essential site is responsible for the operation of the entire network. The computers that decide how to route data across the Internet are called **routers**. The Internet has thousands of routers.

1.6 HOST MACHINES AND HOST NAMES

Each computer on the Internet is called an **Internet host**, or a **host machine**. Each host machine has a special *Internet protocol address*, called an **IP address**, that identifies that host uniquely. IP addresses were never designed for human eyes; they were created by computer programmers for the sake of computer programs. Computers handle numbers well, so each IP address consists of numbers, four integers separated by periods. For example, one host machine at the University of Massachusetts at Amherst has the IP address 128.119.240.41. Some Internet hosts have their own permanent IP addresses, whereas others "borrow" IP addresses for use temporarily. For example, when you connect to the Internet over a telephone line, your home computer is assigned a temporary IP number for the duration of that Internet session.

Although IP addresses are fine for computer communications, most people can't easily remember long strings of numbers. To make life easier for people, most host machines have a symbolic **Domain Name Service (DNS) address** in addition to their IP address. Following are some examples of IP host addresses and their corresponding DNS addresses.

IP Host Address	IP Host DNS Address
128.119.240.41	freya.cs.umass.edu
18.92.0.3	mitvma.mit.edu
204.71.200.33	ns1.yahoo.com

Each DNS address contains a **host name** followed by a **domain name**, as illustrated in the following chart.

DNS Address	Host Name	Domain Name
`freya.cs.umass.edu`	`freya`	`cs.umass.edu`
`mitvma.mit.edu`	`mitvma`	`mit.edu`
`ns1.yahoo.com`	`ns1`	`yahoo.com`

Each domain name consists of two parts: the **institutional site name** and the **Top-Level Domain name** (**TLD**). For example, `cs.umass` is an institutional site name that represents the Department of Computer Science at the University of Massachusetts and `mit` represents the Massachusetts Institute of Technology. An example of a TLD name is `edu`, which refers to an *educational* site. The TLD name identifies the type of site at which the host machine resides. The most common TLD names are given in the following chart.

TLD Name	Type of Organization
`.com`	A commercial organization
`.edu`	An educational site in the United States
`.gov`	A government agency in the United States
`.mil`	A military site in the United States
`.net`	A network site
`.org`	A nonprofit organization

Other TLD names identify geographical locations by country, as illustrated in the following partial list.

TLD Name	Country
`.au`	Australia
`.ca`	Canada
`.dk`	Denmark
`.fr`	France
`.de`	Germany
`.uk`	Great Britain
`.hk`	Hong Kong
`.hu`	Hungary
`.ie`	Ireland
`.il`	Israel
`.es`	Spain
`.lk`	Sri Lanka

TLD names have been the subject of much discussion in recent years. The current names will continue to be used, but they will probably be augmented by names that represent a set of new domains that better describe the various types of commercial (`.com`) sites. Likely contenders include `.firm`, `.shop`, `.web`, `.arts`, `.rec`, `.info`, and `.nom`. Once you've learned some institutional acronyms, you'll be able to recognize and unravel DNS addresses quickly on your own.

Although each host machine has a unique IP address, some hosts have more than one DNS address. An alternative name for a host machine is an **alias**. Heavily used host machines are often assigned an alias. A host may have any number of aliases.

No one polices the aliases that a machine can use or the selection of DNS names beyond making sure that each DNS address is unique. Anyone can register a host machine under any, unclaimed, address. Be cautious about making assumptions based on a host machine's DNS address. For example, Figure 1.9(b) shows the Web page at the address `http://www.gwbush.com`. This page looks like it could have been the address for the official George W. Bush campaign Web site for the 2000 presidential election. Actually, it was set up by a counterfeit operation that had posted a satirical Web page. The legitimate Bush campaign site was found at the address `http://www.georgewbush.com`, as shown in Figure 1.9(a).

Figure 1.9:
Which Is the Legitimate Site and Which Is the Spoof?

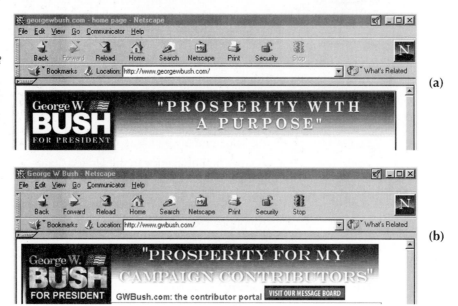

(a)

(b)

An official-sounding DNS address might be what you think it is, or it might not. If you're not sure what you are looking at, proceed with caution.

DNS addresses need to be translated into IP addresses. This essential function in the Internet's operation is handled by **domain name servers** (also shortened to DNS). If the database used by a DNS is corrupted, all Internet service moving through that server will be affected. DNS's are managed with great care, have many levels of redundancy, and have carefully designed fallback plans.

1.7   THE CLIENT/SERVER SOFTWARE MODEL

When you read about Internet software, you inevitably will encounter the terms *client* and *server*. The **client/server software model** is the basic design for all Internet applications. It is based on a simple idea. That is, a host machine can act as either a client or a server. Client/server interactions underlie all communication on the Internet and the model is a de facto standard for network-oriented computing.

Generally, a host acting as a client is an information consumer and when acting as a server is an information provider. The server acts as a resource for all of its clients and provides a service for those clients. For example, a **Web server** provides information on the Internet by housing publicly accessible Web pages. A host running a **Web browser** acts as a client that is capable of moving from one server to another based on a single mouse click.

A host acting as a server typically interacts with multiple clients at one time (see Figure 1.10). As a result, heavily utilized servers are sometimes overwhelmed by client requests. For example, when the Starr Report was initially released on the Internet in 1998, a Cable News Network (CNN) Web server that posted the report handled more than 30,000 client requests per minute—a lot of traffic for a single server. However, even this did not set a record. Some DNS's routinely receive an average of 42,000 requests per minute.

Figure 1.10:
One Server
Interacting with
Many Clients

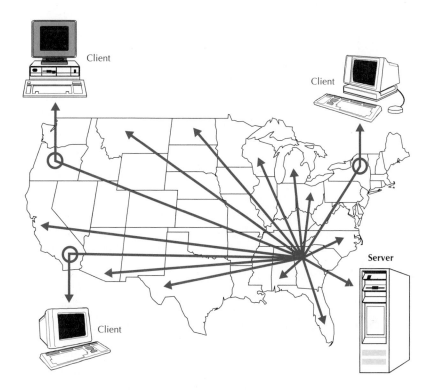

In a client/server interaction, client software interacts with server software so that both the client's host machine and the server's host machine share the total computing load. Clients and servers are designed to form a seamless computing environment. Thus the user typically has no idea which machine is performing which operations, and, indeed, the exact division of labor is irrelevant to the user.

1.7.1 Web-Based Software Hosting

Sometimes proprietary software is made available to the public through the client/server model. For example, a keyword search engine for the Web might reside on a server that can be accessed on demand by many remote clients. Therefore many people can use the server's software without having to install copies of that software on their own host machines.

Several companies currently are exploring commercial markets for *Web-based software hosting*. Standard office applications such as spreadsheet and word processing programs are being made available on Web servers by **Application Service Providers** (**ASPs**). Subscribers to an ASP will not need to install software applications on their own computers and will not have to upgrade or patch that software in order to keep it up to date. They will simply "rent" the applications that they need and let the ASP handle everything else.

If a suitable selection of ASP software were available, more of the online computing load would shift from the client side of the client/server equation to the server side. Such a shift would require more-powerful servers while reducing the amount of computational muscle needed for client machines. The ASP model also depends on very fast, reliable Internet connections. Although it's too early to predict the future size of the ASP market, AT&T announced plans in 2000 to build 26 data hosting centers worldwide. The relationship between clients and servers is constantly changing as people create new business models for distributed computing on the Internet.

Versionless Software

In 1999, **McAfee.com** released a suite of services that gives users access to various personal computer utilities via the Web. Called McAfee Clinic, it allows subscribers to scan their local drives for viruses, tune system settings, and rid directories of unneeded files, simply by clicking a few buttons on a Web page. Additional services support online collaborations, a "smart" Web navigation toolbar, and online shopping. Minimal software downloads are required to support the service, and subscribers automatically access the most recent software releases each time that they log on. McAfee was one of the first ASPs to pioneer *versionless software*. As a result, their site is the second most-visited software site on the Web (Microsoft is number one).

The client/server model is a very powerful framework for sharing computational resources over a computer network. By making the computational power of a host available for public use, a software designer can maximize the number of users of the software (who might also be paying customers), while retaining maximal control over the software.

1.8   THE WORLD WIDE WEB AND WEB BROWSERS

The **World Wide Web**—or, simply, the **Web**—is the premier Internet application. It has made the Internet widely accessible to millions of people, from children to senior citizens. Its most remarkable feature is the ease of working with it. Many people think that the Web is the same as the Internet. This is not true, although the confusion is understandable. The Web is only one software application that uses the Internet. It actually is a newcomer to the Internet. However, it is the application that integrates resources from other Internet applications. This contributes to some confusion about where the Web stops and everything else begins.

A **Web browser** is a piece of software that enables users to view information on the Web. The essential mechanics of all Web browsers are very simple—learn two or three navigational commands, and you are off and running. Because a Web browser can support other Internet activities in addition to Web browsing, it is an excellent starting point for Internet exploration. The most popular Web browsers can handle the most commonly used Internet resources. Even though the Web is not the same as the Internet, many users will find that all their Internet needs can be adequately addressed by using the right Web browser.

The Web consists of hypertext interspersed with multimedia elements such as graphics, sound clips, and video clips. **Hypertext** is a dynamic variation on traditional text that allows you to digress as you read to view related documents. A hypertext document contains *pointers* to other hypertext documents, called **hyperlinks**, or **links**, that you click with your mouse. Hyperlinks on a Web page might be underlined, boldfaced, or a different color (traditionally blue) so that you can easily see them. Different browsers use different display conventions. Clicking hyperlinks allows you to easily weave through multiple documents according to your interests and preferences. You decide whether you want to digress and visit related documents. In fact, you can jump from document to document and never return to the original at the start of the chain. Figure 1.11 shows a Web page of interest to authors of Internet books.

Figure 1.11:
A Web Page That
Requires Frequent
Updates

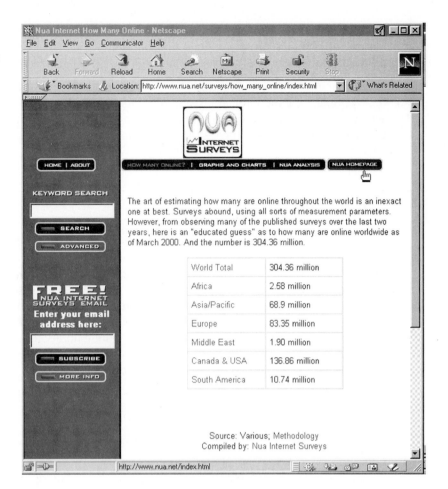

A **Web page** is an online document that is viewed with a Web browser. A Web page may contain any number of words. When a page is long, you can scroll it up and down, typically by pointing to arrows on the scroll bar that runs vertically along the right-hand side of the page. Most documents on the Web contain hyperlinks to other Web pages. The process of reading Web pages and traversing links to more Web pages is called **browsing**. You can browse Web pages casually for entertainment or with a serious goal in mind. Either way, when you don't know beforehand exactly where a link is going to take you, then you are browsing. Browsing is an exploratory process. It's a lot like daydreaming: You simply go where your interests lead you.

You can traverse many links in only a few minutes of browsing. If you want to return to a Web page that you left twenty links ago, you might find this difficult to do. Fortunately, all Web browsers make it easy for you to return to earlier pages by maintaining a **history list** of all visited pages. You simply ask the browser to pop up the history list. Then you can retrace your steps—it's a little like following a trail of breadcrumbs that you left along the way. Or, you can use the browser's **Back button** to retrace the pages in the history list one step at a time. Also, you can use the **View History command** to view the complete history list and the links to any pages that you may have put on hold while you were distracted by promising links and other Web pages. The history command is especially useful when you've wandered far from familiar territory and you just want to return to an earlier starting page without having to revisit each visited page.

Each time that you start your Web browser, you begin from a **default home page**. Your Web browser probably came configured with a default home page, such as **Netscape**

Navigator's NetCenter. You can change this default Web page, selecting any Web page that you want. The most useful choice is one that shows you links to places that you like to visit each time that you get onto the Web.

Each Web page is located at a unique global address called a **uniform resource locator** (**URL**). By referencing the URL, you can jump directly to that page at that URL no matter where you currently are on the Web. All Web browsers let you jump directly to a URL. In Netscape Navigator (Navigator), for example, you type a URL in a Location text box and hit Enter or Return to jump to the desired page.

1.9   HOW TO GET ONLINE

Before you can do anything online, you must have access to the Internet. Students at colleges and universities can usually obtain an educational account. Check whether your school has an Office of Information Technology or a Computer Services Office that maintains educational accounts for students. If you do not have access to an educational computing facility, you will need to use a commercial **Internet service provider** (**ISP**), a company that provides access to the Internet. To find directories of ISPs to help you research the available options, go online at a local public library (or a friend's house or your place of work) and visit **The List** or **ISPs.com** (see Figure 1.12). Some points to consider when selecting an ISP are discussed in Appendix A.

Figure 1.12:
Directories to Help
You Shop for an ISP

When you work from an educational computing lab, all of the necessary software to get online will be in place and ready to go. To use your own personal computer for Internet access, you will need to install some special software. Your ISP can recommend preferred system configurations, including memory requirements. They will set up a personal user identification (**userid**) and password for you and give you a telephone number to dial to connect your computer to the Internet. Your ISP also will help you to obtain and install the software that you need. Many provide conveniently bundled software that has step-by-step instructions for installation and start-up. If you are fairly new to computers (most Internet users are beginners), follow the ISP's recommendations. It's the ISP's job to get its customers up and running as quickly and easily as possible.

When you have difficulties with your Internet software, ask the service provider's **technical support staff** for assistance. If you are using an ISP, technical support is one of its services that you pay for. If you are a student at a university or college using an educational account, look for a **Help Desk** service where you first signed up for your account. *Do not* go to your school's Computer Science Department for technical support. These departments are not responsible for campuswide computing facilities; their technical staffs are paid to handle other problems. While it's important to know that you can ask for help when you need it, be sure that you're talking to the right people. (See Appendix B for more tips on how to talk to technical support staff when you have a problem.)

1.10 BROWSER TIPS AND TRICKS

Web browsers are very easy to use with only a small amount of instruction. However, some simple tips can make your browsing sessions more productive and less time-consuming. This section focuses on some key browser features and includes specific instructions for Navigator. Additional tips and tricks, as well as instructions for MSIE, can be found at **CNet's Browser Help Center**. This section discusses the following tips.

- Select your own default home page.
- Use the Find command.
- Use your history list.
- Use bookmarks.
- Add bookmarks with care.
- Abort a download if you get stuck.
- Turn off graphics.
- Don't let a "404 Not Found" stop you dead
- Avoid peak hours.

1.10.1 Select Your Own Default Home Page

Each browser is configured to display a default home page every time that you start the browser. Very likely, that default home page is not the best for you. A better alternative is a Web page that contains many links to places that you like to visit each time that you get on the Web.

To change your default home page in Navigator, follow these steps:

1. From the Options menu, click General Preferences.
2. Click the Appearance tab, and then click Home Page Location.
3. Click the Home Page Location text button, and type the URL of the page that you want to use.
4. Close the dialog box by clicking OK.

1.10.2 Use the Find Command

If you know exactly where you want to go, you often can use the Find command to take you there immediately. Most browsers have a Find command that lets you enter a text string and go directly to the first instance of that string on the current Web page.

The Find command can be useful on long Web pages when you are interested in a specific topic and want to read only about that topic. In addition, some browsers have a Find Next command, which will take you to the next occurrence of that same text string.

Keyboard Shortcuts

These shortcuts work for both Navigator and MSIE.

What You Want to Do	What to Type
Pop up the dialog box for a Find command	Ctrl + F
Jump to the end of a Web page	Ctrl + End
Jump to the top of a Web page	Ctrl + Home
Open a new browser window	Ctrl + N
Close the current browser window	Ctrl + W

Note: Macintosh users, type the Command key (⌘) instead of Ctrl.

1.10.3 Use Your History List

To save time while on the Web, you need to master some navigational tricks associated with hyperlinks. For example, you might find that you easily wander down a path of links on some digression that takes you deeper into a region of the Web that is irrelevant to your original topic. Eventually, you decide to return to business and need to retrace a lot of links back to some page that you were on 10 or 20 minutes ago (possibly an hour ago, if you have no sense of time). You could do this by hitting the Back button a dozen times. Or, you could look at your history list. All browsers have a History command that takes you to a list of all the pages that you visited. Consult this list, and click an address to return to an earlier page. Experiment with your history list and get into the habit of using it whenever you need to retrace a lot of steps. It might save you from getting distracted all over again on your way home.

1.10.4 Use Bookmarks

If you spend much time on the Web, you'll likely find many Web pages that you'll want to revisit regularly. You could start a listing of their URLs and some notes about each one. Or, you can take advantage of your browser's *bookmark feature*. A **bookmark** is pointer to a Web page that you expect to revisit. You can add a bookmark whenever you are viewing the page that you want to mark.

Setting up a bookmark in Navigator takes two steps:

1. Visit the page that you want to mark.
2. From the Communicator menu, select Bookmarks and then select Add Bookmark (or type Cmd + D).

Your bookmark file will display each entry along with a link to its URL. Once a bookmark has been added to the bookmark file, you simply click the bookmark entry whenever you want to return to that particular page.

You also can edit bookmark entries. Follows these steps to edit a bookmark entry in Navigator:

1. From the Windows menu, click Bookmarks.
2. Highlight the bookmark entry.
3. From the Item menu, click Edit Bookmark. A window will appear showing the name of the bookmark, its URL, when you added it to your bookmark file, and when you last visited it.
4. Add a more detailed description of the site or change its name, as desired.

The bookmark file can grow very quickly and get out of control. Your browser should allow you to delete bookmark entries. You should periodically review your bookmark file and weed out entries that you no longer use. A good browser also will let you organize and categorize your bookmarks in a hierarchy for easier reference. To do this in Navigator, follow these steps:

1. From the Bookmark window, click Item/Insert Folder. A dialog window opens.
2. In the window, name the new folder. The name will be inserted at the top level of your bookmark list.

You can place bookmarks in the folder or put the folder inside of another folder by using drag-and-drop operations inside of the bookmark window. If you collect a lot of bookmarks, your bookmark window will become an extensive URL directory. Keep it well-organized, and don't hesitate to prune it as your information needs change.

1.10.5 Add Bookmarks with Care

You might be tempted to save in your bookmark file everything that could ever be of interest to you. However, doing this will result in an unwieldy bookmark file. Decide if a Web page deserves to be in your bookmark file because you really do intend to revisit the page. If a pointer is good to save but you expect it to be useful only for infrequent visits, then it is better to store it elsewhere.

Keyboard Shortcuts

These shortcuts work for both Navigator and MSIE.

What You Want to Do	What to Type
Display your bookmarks	Ctrl + B
Add the current page to your bookmark file	Ctrl + D
View the history window	Ctrl + H
Quit the browser session (close the application)	Ctrl + Q

Note: Macintosh users, type the Command key (⌘) instead of Ctrl.

1.10.6 Abort a Download If You Get Stuck

Sometimes, your browser might appear to stick during the downloading of a page. If your browser has a status line showing the progress of the download, you will sometimes see it freeze and appear to be dead. Stuck downloads happen for various reasons, and they happen with all browsers. Check your browser for a command button that aborts downloads. In Navigator, it is the Stop button. With some browsers, issuing this abort command will make the page mysteriously appear (as if it had been waiting for you to ask). With Navigator, the page will sometimes pop up if you click the same link again right after aborting.

Browser Checklist: Get to Know Your Browser

1. Change your default home page to something new. When does it make sense to change your default home page?

2. Locate your history list. Does it contain entries for only the current browsing session or also entries from previous browsing sessions? How much control do you have over your history list? (Check your preference settings to see what preferences you can change.)

3. Locate your bookmarks. Add a new bookmark. Create a new folder for only that bookmark, and move the bookmark into the new folder. Can you add a comment to this bookmark? Delete the new bookmark and the new folder. Where does your browser store your bookmarks? Can you back up your bookmark file for safekeeping?

4. Try out five keyboard shortcuts that you like. Do they all work? Is it hard to remember them? Work with them for a session or two until you can use them easily. Do they save you time?

If you don't know how to do everything on this checklist, consult your browser's Help menu. Different browsers will have slightly different procedures, but all support these standard features.

1.10.7 Turn Off Graphics

When the Web gets pokey, you'll find that pages with lots of graphics are always the slowest to load. This is because graphics files are relatively large and consume a fair amount of bandwidth. If you don't have a fast modem or enough memory on your machine or if the Internet is very busy, you might find yourself too often waiting for some Web pages. This is no fun if you are accustomed to faster performance or you are in a hurry. You can speed up things by trading in the graphics for faster downloads. Sometimes you don't need to see the graphics; they might be purely cosmetic. Or you might have already seen a page a number of times, and the graphics are no longer important to you.

All browsers enable you to turn off graphics. Because your browser never requests the graphic's file, you don't have to wait for that graphic to appear. When graphics are turned off, a page is displayed with a *placeholder* for each graphic on the page to indicate where the graphic would have been displayed. In Navigator, follow these steps to turn off graphics:

1. In the Edit menu, select Preferences.

2. Click Advanced in the Categories list, and uncheck the check box entitled "Automatically load images."

If you later decide that you want to see a specific graphic, click its placeholder on the Web page; Navigator will download that one graphic file. Most browsers support graphic file downloads-on-demand in this way.

1.10.8 Don't Let a "404 Not Found" Stop You Dead

From time to time, everyone sees this error message: **404 Not Found**. It means that the requested URL was not found on the specified server. When you see this error, first make sure that the URL is correct. If it is, then the error message appeared for other reasons. For example, the page might have been removed from the server. Or, it might have been moved, in which case, you might be able to find it at its new location (if you know that new location). Sometimes, a site's author will rearrange its files and directories; this can cause obsolete URLs. Before you give up all hope of ever seeing the lost page, here are some tricks that you can try in order to retrieve it.

Suppose that you try linking to `http://www.unc.edu/lib/launcch/oct96n.htm` and you get the 404 Not Found error message.

1. Start by examining the URL to see whether the Web page might be accessible from a related Web page. Look at the diagram of the following URL.

$$\underbrace{\texttt{http://www.unc.edu/lib/launcch/}}_{\text{WEB SERVER}}\underbrace{\texttt{oct96n.htm}}_{\text{FILE NAME}}$$

The first segment gives the name of the Web server, and the last segment is the name of the file in which the page resides. Everything in between are the names of subdirectories, in this case `lib` and `launcch`. If this link previously was operational, you don't need to worry about the possibility of typing errors. Otherwise, try the URL with "launch" instead of "launcch," in case there's a typographical error in your typed URL.

2. If the URL is correct, try to backtrack to a related Web page. Sometimes, you can find a home page or page index by going to a subdirectory. In this case, try these two subdirectories: the top directory `lib` and the subdirectory `launcch` that resides inside `lib`. To visit these, use these URLs:

   `http://www.unc.edu/lib/`

   `http://www.unc.edu/lib/launcch/`

   One of these might give you a link or a path to the old Web page. This often works on large institutional sites or a site that houses many Web pages. The contents of large Web sites are periodically reorganized into new subdirectories, thereby causing some URLs to become obsolete.

3. When all else fails, see whether the server has a Web page at the root address, in this case,

   `http://www.unc.edu`

   With a little luck, you'll find a high-level home page at this address that can point you in the right direction.

Keyboard Shortcuts

These shortcuts work for both Navigator and MSIE.

What You Want to Do	What to Do Instead
Press the Back button	Press ⬅ (or Backspace)
Press the Forward button	Press ➡ (or Enter)
Scroll down a little	Press Spacebar
Scroll up a little	Hold down Shift and press Spacebar

1.10.9 Avoid Peak Hours

Just as you probably want to avoid rush hour on major highways, you will be wise to avoid peak usage periods on the Internet. In the United States, peak periods are generally the middle of the day and early evenings on weekdays (see Figure 1.13). Many people do recreational browsing from their workplace during the lunch hour. Try to hit the Web early in the morning or late at night. You'll be surprised how much faster your response times can be. To experience the Internet at its fastest, surf at 6 A.M. EST on weekdays or anytime on a Sunday morning.

Figure 1.13:
Internet Traffic
Patterns Online

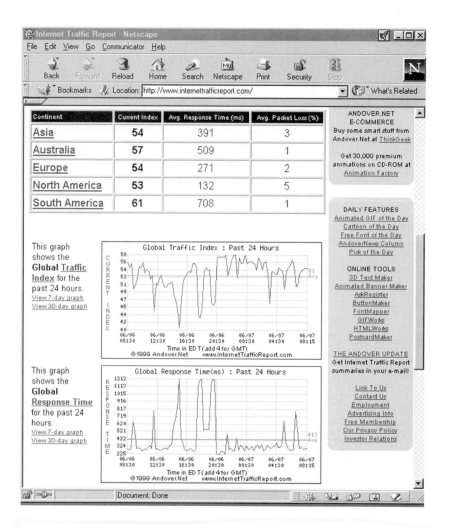

Things to Remember

- An Internet connection is only as fast as its weakest link.
- Additional RAM might speed up your computer; a larger hard drive will not.
- Each character in the ASCII character set requires one 8-bit byte of memory.
- On average, audio files consume more memory than graphics files and graphics files consume more memory than text files.
- Computer memory is measured in bytes, kilobytes, megabytes, and gigabytes.
- Bandwidth is measured in bits per second.
- When your browser displays the error message 404 Not Found, you might still be able to find the page sought.
- You can save time while browsing by using keyboard shortcuts instead of your mouse.

Important Concepts

bandwidth—the maximal rate of data transmission over a given communication channel.

client—an Internet host that consumes information from the Net.

DNS address—a symbolic name for an Internet host.

dynamic routing—a strategy for finding the best pathway between two hosts, when given current conditions on the Net.

heterarchical structure—a connected structure in which no nodes are more central or more important than any other nodes.

hierarchical structure—a connected structure in which all nodes have a common ancestor (the root node).

host—a computer connected to the Internet.

IP address—a numerical name for an Internet host.

server—an Internet host that serves information on the Net.

Web browser—software for viewing Web pages found on Web servers.

Web server—an Internet host that offers Web pages for public consumption.

Where Can I Learn More?

Webopedia—http://www.webopedia.com/

PC Pitstop—http://www.pcpitstop.com/

Internet Traffic Report—http://www.internettrafficreport.com/

NUA Internet Surveys—http://www.nua.net/surveys/

CNet's Browser Help Center—http://www.help.com (Click "Internet" and then "Browsers.")

Internet Errors Explained—http://coverage.cnet.com/Resources/Tech/Advisers/Error/

How MP3 Files Work—http://www.howstuffworks.com/mp3.htm

Problems and Exercises

1. In 1993, an Intel 486 CPU ran at 40MHz. and by the end of 1999, the fastest Intel Pentium III chips were running at 733MHz. Are these CPU speeds consistent with Moore's Law? Assume that the cost of a personal computer was constant during the 1990s.

2. Does clicking a link on a Web page begin a file download or upload? Can you see the Web page on your computer monitor before the file transfer is complete? Explain your answer.

3. If a kilo means 1,000, why doesn't 10KB equal 10,000 bytes? When does "K" mean 1,000, and when does "K" mean something else?

4. If you connect to the Internet with a 56K modem, what is the fastest transmission rate that you can expect?

5. Is the Internet heterarchical or hierarchical in its overall design? Explain the difference between a heterarchical network and a hierarchical network. Why was the Internet's networking design adopted?

6. What is dynamic routing, and how is it used on the Internet?

7. If you connect to the Internet over a telephone line, what can you say about your computer's IP address?

8. Match up the items in the left-hand column with their most likely memory requirements in the right-hand column.

1.	one floppy disk	a.	700KB
2.	one sentence	b.	10GB
3.	one small drawing	c.	1 byte
4.	one large photograph	d.	10KB
5.	one zip disk	e.	4 bytes
6.	200 audio CDs	f.	640MB
7.	the MSIE browser	g.	100MB
8.	one CD-ROM	h.	65 bytes
9.	32 bits	i.	1.44MB
10.	the letter "A"	j.	20MB

9. How many bits are needed to represent an alphabet that contains 300 different characters?

10. Explain the difference between an IP address and a DNS address.

11. List six top-level domain names, and explain what they mean.

12. When music is recorded on a CD, a digital recording device samples the sound 44,100 times per second. Each sample is 2 bytes (16 bits) long, and a separate sample is taken for each of the two speakers in a stereo system. Therefore each second of sound on the CD requires $44,100 \times 2 \times 2 = 176,400$ bytes of memory. How much memory is this in bits? Using these figures, determine how many megabytes of memory are needed to store a 3-minute song. If you could attain the maximal MP3 file reduction of 93%, how much memory would this 3-minute song consume as an MP3 file?

13. What does a domain name server do?

14. Which of the following are clients, and which are servers?

    a. A Web browser

    b. A Web site where you can access a general search engine

    c. A Web site that tells you the correct time

    d. A program that displays news headlines on your desktop

    e. A Web site that tells you the speed of your Internet connection

    f. A program that tracks stock prices and displays a customized stock ticker for you

15. Who initiates a client/server interaction: the client or the server?

16. How many client requests per second do the busiest Web servers handle?

17. What is an Application Service Provider? Who might want to use one? What advantages does using one offer?

18. Explain the difference between a history list and a bookmark file. When do you use the history list? When do you use a bookmark?

19. What is the first thing that you should do when you see a 404 Not Found error message? What can you try after that?

20. Do you notice different response times when you are on the Net? Which times of day tend to give you the fastest file downloads? Which times are the worst? If you haven't noticed any patterns, try logging on at different times of the day, watch for fast connections and slow connections, and see if you can find any patterns. You might find it useful to keep a log on which you can record the times of day and one or two actual download times that you can monitor each time that you log on.

CHAPTER TWO

Personal Safety Online

CHAPTER**GOALS**

- Understand the importance of acceptable use policies, passwords, and constant vigilance while online.

- Learn how your computer is not secure on the Internet unless you make it secure.

- Discover what you can do to protect your computer and personal data while you are online.

- Know when your own online activities violate copyright or software piracy laws.

- Become aware of privacy issues, and learn what you can do to protect your personal privacy.

- Find out how to separate fact from fiction when you see warnings and advice on the Net.

2.1 | TAKING CHARGE

The Internet gives you access to a very public space. It might not feel particularly public when you dial in from the privacy of your own home. However, each time that you connect you enter a public space. This means that your conduct will be visible to others, as well as monitored by various network administrators (and others) who may be invisible to you. You have rights as well as responsibilities. To be a good *Netizen* of the Internet, you need to act responsibly. And because of aggressive data collection, intrusive advertisers, underhanded business practices, and malicious miscreants, you need to protect your rights.

Being online is not so very different from being offline. When you visit a large city, you plan your trip, tuck your wallet in a safe pocket, obey the law, and use common sense. Going online is much the same. When you log on to the Internet, you need to understand and follow the behavioral codes that are specific to the Net, and you need to minimize your personal risk. The same laws that constrain your behavior in real life still apply when you are on the Internet. However, the extremely public nature of the Internet can amplify and broadcast your actions to a potentially large audience. Some rules (the cyberspace equivalent of parking tickets) can be broken with little or no consequence. Others (the ones that protect the rights of others) might arouse the attention of law enforcement agents. Just as in real life, some actions will have consequences for only you. In any case, it is always wise to anticipate the potential consequences of your actions. Your taking the time to read this book will help: we cover everything you need to know to be a good Netizen.

Note that the technology that enables you to access the Internet assumes no moral or legal responsibility regarding how you use that technology. Simply because some software enables a person to easily reproduce an image or distribute a document does not mean that anyone has the legal, or moral right to do so. Many newcomers to the Internet, sometimes called **newbies**, mistakenly assume they have this right. Such assumptions derive from unrealistic expectations about software. Read the licensing agreement that accompanies your software. You'll discover that the software manufacturer assumes no responsibility for any consequences that might arise from the use of its software (see Figure 2.1). Only you can be responsible for your actions. ***Software doesn't break laws; people break laws.***

Figure 2.1:
Sample Software
Manufacturers
Licensing
Agreement

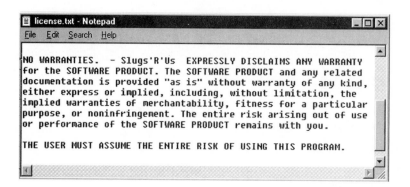

2.2   ACCEPTABLE USE POLICIES

All computer accounts and some public Internet servers are subject to an **acceptable use policy** (**AUP**), a policy that outlines appropriate use of the Internet and that is enforced by system administrators. Your Internet access privileges can be withdrawn if you violate the rules and restrictions specified by the AUP. AUPs are posted on the Web and should be easy to locate.

The restrictions that pertain to ISP accounts are often called **terms of service** (**ToS**). Whenever you open a computer account or join an online discussion group, take the time to locate and read the AUP that governs your use of those facilities. University AUPs typically prohibit the use of university resources for commercial profit, any form of academic dishonesty, and ongoing communications with other individuals that are deemed to be harassment. Some schools might also prohibit the use of specific Internet services, such as **Napster**, a software program designed to facilitate audio file sharing among Internet users (see Section 2.12), because they do not have enough bandwidth to support the demand for the service. Check your AUP periodically to see if any new restrictions have been added. ***You are expected to know your AUP and any of its restrictions that apply to your online activities.***

2.3   PASSWORD SECURITY

Your first line of defense against all kinds of mischief and misery is your password. You probably don't have a password for your personal computer, and that's fine. It's the password on your Internet access account that needs to be handled with care. Someone who breaks into your university account or ISP account is probably hoping to break into more than only your account. Starting from your account, a digital trespasser might be able to break into other accounts and acquire access privileges normally reserved for system administrators. You must protect your computer account not only for your own sake but also for that of everyone in your immediate computing environment.

In a secure computing environment, passwords are stored by using special techniques so that no one, including the most powerful system administrator, can retrieve a password for a given account. No system administrator will ever need to know your password for the sake of legitimate system maintenance and will never ask for it. Privileged administrators can bypass the usual password protocol if an appropriate circumstance justifies it. Any stranger who asks you for your password is up to no good. No matter what someone tells you, no matter how forceful their argument, don't buy it.

Further, if you ever receive an e-mail message from some official-sounding person, with an official-looking return address, that includes a request for your password, realize this is a ruse. Hackers who want to break into computer accounts often use elaborate scenarios in an effort to take advantage of the unwary. This is called **social engineering**. Never give your password to *anyone*, including your own mother. As soon as you share your password with another person, that person also becomes a potential target for social engineering, and you are no longer in control of your own computer account.

Beware of Social Engineering

Any request for your password from a stranger should be reported to a system administrator as soon as possible. If it comes to you via e-mail, forward the message to your system postmaster with the Subject: field containing URGENT: PASSWORD THEFT ATTEMPT.

People can also steal passwords without resorting to social engineering. Computer programs can run through a full dictionary of the English language in an effort to "guess" your password. Dictionaries of common names are also used for the same purpose. You can foil these programs by carefully creating passwords that are not words in a dictionary or proper names. Examples of bad passwords are "television" and "Jessica." An example of a good password is "fiNallY93."

Finally, never use the same password at more than one Web site.

A safe, secure password always contains the following elements:

- At least six characters (eight is better)
- Both lowercase and uppercase letters
- At least one numeric character

Passwords and Underwear

Passwords are like underwear. Change them often. Don't share them with anyone. Not even friends.

—Seen on Usenet

Regardless of how carefully you create your passwords, you still should change them every month or two. Passwords can be "sniffed out" by software that is designed to eavesdrop on your Internet communications.

Tips for Good Password Security

- Never tell anyone your password. Ever.
- Don't write your password where someone can find it.
- Change your password about every month or two.
- Don't use the same password in many different places.

2.4 VIRUSES, TROJANS, AND WORMS

Computer security experts worry about software that can be used maliciously to put computer users at risk. Over the years, they have found it useful to distinguish different classes of software that are often associated with security problems. Mainstream news outlets tend to call such software a *virus*. However, many fast-spreading troublemakers are actually *worms*, and one of the most insidious forms of software attack is the *Trojan horse*.

Is Your Front Door Open?

As soon as you connect your home computer to the Internet, financial records and other personal information stored on your computer become potential targets of cyber-attacks. All computers are at some risk if appropriate steps have not been taken to limit access to them. Computers operating over broadband connections are especially susceptible to attack.

Failure to take steps to secure your computer and its most sensitive files is like leaving the front door of your home wide open.

A **virus** is an executable program that attaches itself to a host program and whose purpose is to replicate itself via files that are transferred from one computer to another. They can propagate via shared floppies or other media and need a host program in order to propagate. Some viruses are benign, doing nothing more than leaving the equivalent of their initials on a file somewhere. Others, however, are extremely destructive, capable of destroying files or even entire file systems.

A **Trojan horse** is an executable program that slips into a system under the guise of another program. To qualify as a Trojan horse, the program must do something that is undocumented and intended by the programmer that the user would not approve of. Deception is a key characteristic of all Trojan horses. You think that you've installed only a particular program, but you end up getting more than you expected. Some Trojan horses are designed to record every key that you hit, including the credit card account number that you use when online shopping. Your keystrokes might be monitored by the program's author in real time, or they might be saved to a log file which can be sent back to the program's author at a later time. Other Trojan horses allow a stranger to take control of your computer and issue commands remotely. If this is done cleverly, sensitive files can be uploaded to a remote host without your knowledge.

A **worm** is very similar to a virus but differs in its reproductive habits. Whereas viruses propagate via shared floppies or other media and need a host program in order to propagate, a worm depends on active network connections in order to multiply and needs many different hosts that are running the same software. Sophisticated worms can have multiple parts, or segments, that run on different machines, do different things, and communicate with each other over a network. Some are programmed to act maliciously, whereas others are merely resource hogs that pull down entire networks by tying up too much memory or too many CPU cycles.

If you can't remember how these three differ from each other, just remember that everyone who uses computers is vulnerable to attack and must take precautions. There are some that you can take to protect your system. Once you know the ropes, good computer security doesn't have to take a lot of your time.

The Price of Malicious Code

A 1997 study reported that computer viruses had been discovered at 99% of all medium-sized and large organizations in North America and that 33% of those sites fell victim to a costly computer virus incident. During 1999, malicious code attacks on business computers cost an estimated $12 billion in damaged data and lost productivity.

- **Use antivirus software.** Antivirus software should contain a virus scanner which has a memory-resident option that runs in the background, checking every new file that enters your computer no matter where it comes from (whether a floppy drive, a CD-ROM drive, an Internet download, or elsewhere). Set the software to scan all program files on your computer whenever you turn it on, and make sure that it is always running in the background. You might have to turn off the scanner during a software installation. If so, make sure that you turn it back on again after the installation is complete.

- **Update your antivirus software regularly.** You should update at least once a month the data files that contain information about particular viruses, Trojan horses, and worms (see Figure 2.2). If you can't do this regularly, use versionless antivirus software instead, which is updated for you automatically over the Internet (see Section 1.7.1).

- **Keep floppy diskettes out of your floppy drive unless you are actively working with the files on a floppy.** Boot sector viruses hide on floppies. They are triggered when your machine routinely checks to see whether it should run its start-up sequence from the floppy drive. If the floppy's boot sector is infected, its virus will kick into action.

If you need to work without a virus scanner running continuously in the background, then you must remember to manually scan each file before opening or executing it. Don't take someone else's word that a file is safe. Always check for yourself.

Figure 2.2:
Updating Antivirus
Software

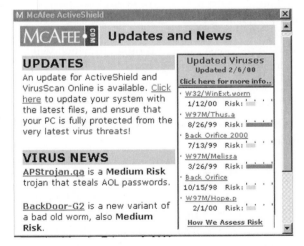

- **If you are not running a virus scanner in the background, disable Java and JavaScript in your Web browser** (see Figure 2.3). Java and JavaScript both can contain **applets**, small executable programs that can be attached to a Web page. By disabling Java and JavaScript, you prevent malicious applets from infecting your system.

Figure 2.3:
Uncheck the
Appropriate
Preferences to
Disable Java and
JavaScript

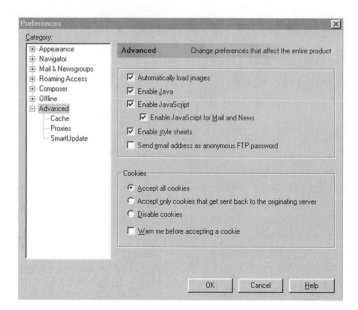

- **For maximal safety, *encrypt* all files that contain sensitive information or store them offline on floppies or other removable media.**
- **Do not leave your computer connected to the Internet any longer than necessary.** A computer connected to the Internet via a 56K modem is not an attractive target for unauthorized file access. This is because breaking into systems that have faster Net connections is easier. However, your computer could still be compromised, especially if you leave it connected to the Net for long intervals of time. Disconnect whenever you don't need to access online resources. In general, the longer you stay online, the easier it is for someone to break into your system over your Internet connection. The amount of time that you spend connected to the Net is more of a risk factor than the speed of your Net connection.

Sophisticated Web pages are another avenue of attack that must be scanned by antivirus software that is configured to check all downloaded Web pages. Some Web pages contain small computer programs that are automatically executed by a Java-enabled or Javascript-enabled Web browser. Most of these programs are harmless, but it is possible to visit a Web page that contains a malicious program which will be automatically executed upon download. Treat *all* incoming files with suspicion, no matter their source.

Running with Scissors

Automatically executed content is like running with scissors; it may be fun, but sooner or later someone's going to get hurt.

—Peter Ciccarelli

You might have heard that Macs are safe from viruses and therefore don't need antivirus software. This is partly true because most viruses "in the wild" (see "Viruses in the Wild") are designed to attack Windows installations and 90% of personal computers run Windows. However, the most commonly found viruses today are *macro viruses*. A

macro is a small computer program that executes in response to a specific combination of keystrokes or clicking a particular icon. Macros allow power users to customize personalized keyboard commands, and they can also be set up to automatically execute whenever a document is opened. A **macro virus** is a virus written inside a macro, which typically executes as soon as the document containing the macro is opened. Of all virus incidents reported in 1997, 80% were the work of macro viruses. Further, macro viruses are platform-independent—a macro virus will strike a Mac as easily as a Windows-based machine.

Computers running the UNIX or Linux OS generally are safe from viruses. If you decide to install Linux on your personal computer, ensure that you know what you're doing, as a proper Linux installation is a significant undertaking. Recall that Linux is an offshoot of UNIX, and UNIX was designed with professional system administrators in mind; it was never intended for computer novices.

Viruses in the Wild

Virus specialists have identified more than 16,000 computer viruses, but most of these exist only in research laboratories. Currently, fewer than 300 computer viruses are **in the wild**, that is, on computers not associated with virus research.

If you have installed a memory-resident virus scanner on your machine, you can determine if your scanner is working correctly by testing what it does when it finds a virus. Do this by introducing on your computer a harmless test virus called EICAR. With a text editor, type the following line into a file:

```
X5O!P%@AP[4\PZX54(P^)7CC)7}$EICAR-STANDARD-ANTIVIRUS-TEST-FILE!$H+H*
```

Make sure that this is the file's first, and only, line and that the line contains no blanks or tabs. Then save the file anywhere you want, naming it `eicar.com`. Next, use your antivirus program to scan your system. It should recognize the EICAR virus when it scans `eicar.com` and display a virus alert, as McAfee's antivirus software does, depicted in Figure 2.4.

Figure 2.4:
A Virus Scanner Passing the EICAR Virus Test

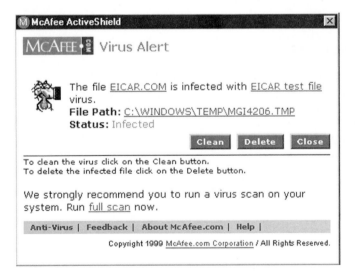

Under certain circumstances, when *file sharing*—giving others access to your files—is turned on, sensitive files on your hard drive can be made publicly available to anyone on the Internet. On a personal computer that runs Windows, you can protect yourself from a relatively trivial attack by ensuring that the File and Printer Sharing setting is turned off. To turn this off, follow these steps:

1. From the Start menu, select Settings, and then the Control Panel.

2. Double-click the Network icon.

3. Under the Configuration tab, click the File and Print Sharing button. Make sure that the two checkboxes displayed in the top of the next window are *not* checked (see Figure 2.5).

Figure 2.5:
Turning Off File and Printer Sharing on a Windows Personal Computer

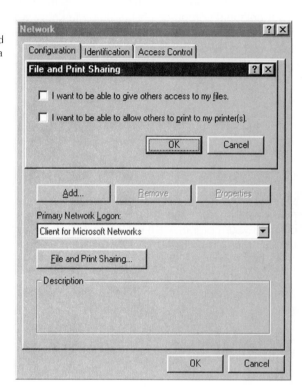

Antivirus Software Facts

Here are some tips to use your antivirus software effectively:

■ Good commercial antivirus software watches for Trojan horses, worms, and malicious applets, as well as viruses.

■ Multiple virus scanners can interfere with one another. Don't install more than one.

■ No virus scanner can guarantee 100% safety, but keeping your scanner up-to-date will minimize your risk.

■ Don't take unnecessary chances. Avoid suspicious executables from unknown sources.

2.5   E-MAIL VIRUSES

Periodically, you'll see warnings on the Internet about viruses in e-mail messages. The most famous one is the Good Times virus, but many others exist. These warnings typically tell you to never read anything with a specific Subject: field content (such as Good Times or Pen Pal Greetings) and to be sure to pass this warning along to everyone you know. ***Such warnings are hoaxes. You cannot get a computer virus from reading a plain text mail message.*** If you see such a virus warning, you can check whether it is a known hoax by visiting the **Vmyths.com** Web site. Whatever you do, don't forward the message to all of your friends and coworkers. If there is a real virus on the loose, leave it to the professionals in technical support to distribute appropriate warnings.

E-mail messages that contain *mail attachments* are a different story. ***Mail attachments can carry viruses, and reading a mail attachment can cause a virus to swing into action.*** If you read your mail on a UNIX or Linux host, don't worry about viruses in mail attachments. However, if you are reading your e-mail on a Mac or a Windows machine (or any other platform with Windows software installed), be careful about mail attachments. You should first save the file to your hard drive *before* you open it (see Figure 2.6) and then check it with a virus scanner before you read it. If an up-to-date scanner detects no viruses, then the file is 99.99% safe to open. (You still might receive a new virus before the antivirus software vendor has had a chance to add it to its scanner's data files.) For 100% safety, read on.

Figure 2.6:
Saving an
Attachment to the
Hard Drive from
Outlook Express

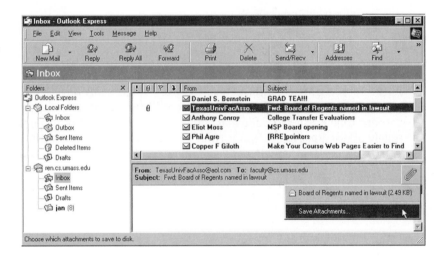

Mail attachments are a problem because they are not always only data files. Some mail attachments contain executable code in the form of scripts. A **script** is a small computer program written in a scripting language such as Microsoft's Visual Basic™ (VB). Other mail attachments contain executable code in the form of *macros.* Your first line of defense against malicious mail attachments is to make sure that your e-mail client, also called a mailer, is not configured to open one of these files for you automatically.

Making Sure That No Mail Attachments Are Opened without Your Consent

If you use Outlook:

Follow these steps to turn off the auto-execution of attachments. Doing this will not only prevent auto-execution of most attachments, including VB scripts (such as the LoveLetter), but also warn you when you try to open the attachment.

1. Select Tools menu, the Options menu item, and then the Security tab.
2. In the Secure Content section, click the Attachment Security button.
3. Set the security to High.

If you use Outlook Express:

Outlook Express doesn't provide a simple mechanism for preventing auto-execution of attachments. Consider upgrading to Outlook.

If you use Netscape Communicator:

1. Select Edit menu and then Preferences.
2. From the Navigation menu, select Navigator and then Applications (see Figure 2.7a).
3. Scroll down to the Winword File entry that specifies a `.doc` file extension (see Figure 2.7a).
4. Click the Edit button, and in the Handled By section, select Save to Disk (see Figure 2.7b).

If you use Eudora Pro:

1. Select Tools menu, the Options menu item, and then the Viewing Mail (icon).
2. In the "HTML content" section, uncheck "Allow executables."
3. Edit your `eudora.ini` file to add (or modify) the following lines:

```
WarnLaunchProgram=1
WarnLaunchExtensions=exe|com|bat|cmd|pif|htm|do|xl|reg|lnk|
```

2.5.1 Macro Viruses

In recent years, macros in Microsoft Word™ documents have been the single greatest source of computer viruses; Microsoft Excel™ spreadsheet documents are also frequent carriers. Opening a Word file that comes to your mailbox from an unknown party is definitely asking for trouble. But it is not enough to know and trust the person who sends you the attachment. ***Word and Excel users can pass a macro virus on to friends and co-workers without realizing it.***

The Melissa Virus

(The Melissa virus was the first e-mail attachment virus designed to exploit the user's e-mail address book in order to propagate itself.)

On Friday, March 26, 2000, CERT/CC received initial reports of a fast-spreading new MS Word macro virus called Melissa. Once loaded, it used the victim's MAPI-standard e-mail address book to send copies of itself to the first 50 people on the list. The virus attached an infected document to an e-mail message bearing the subject line, "Important Message From <name>," with <name> that of the inadvertent sender. The e-mail message read, "Here is that document you asked for … don't show anyone else ;-)," and included an infected MS Word file as an attachment. The original infected document, list.doc, was a compilation of URLs for pornographic Web sites.

—1999 Infosecurity Year-in-Review

Trusting recipients recognized the return address on the Melissa mail and let down their guard, just as Melissa's author intended. The message was not what it appeared to be, even though it did come from the indicated source.

Determine whether your mail program includes an option that allows you to save Word file attachments to your hard drive. Then you can scan them before opening them with Word. Figure 2.7 shows this preference setting for Netscape Communicator's e-mail client. In addition, **never configure your mail program to automatically open a Word**

attachment for you. See Section 2.5 for more details on how to use antivirus software. Many macro viruses are relatively subtle and can easily go unnoticed by a casual user. This allows the virus to migrate freely within a large population of relatively inexperienced e-mail users.

Avoiding Macros by using RTF

Macros cannot be saved in a **Rich Text Format (RTF)** file. RTF files consist of ASCII text, so they can be inserted *into* e-mail message bodies as an alternative to attaching a file.

Word documents can be saved as RTF files. To convert an RTF file back into a Word document, save the RTF file to your hard disk and then open it in Word. Opening an RTF file that is inside of a plain text message body is always safe.

If everyone saved their Word files in RTF format and never opened Word documents that were not in RTF format, macro viruses in Word documents would go away. Figure 2.8 shows a document saved in both RTF and Word's `.doc` formats. Files that contain graphics, however, are much larger in RTF than in Word's `.doc` format. So reserve the RTF format for documents that contain only text or mostly text.

Figure 2.7:
Setting Software
Preferences for
Word Documents

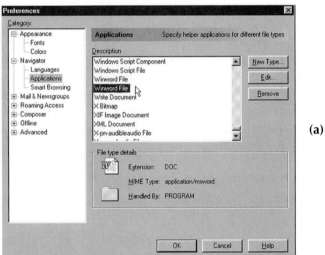

(a)

(b)

Figure 2.8:
Files Saved in RTF
and .doc Formats

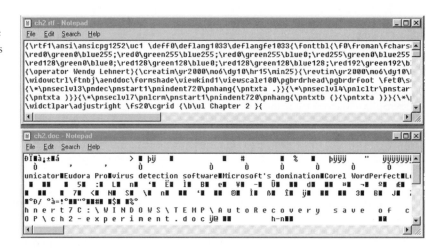

Macro viruses affect primarily Word users and spread rapidly for two reasons.

1. Microsoft's domination of the office application market results in many users (potential victims) who share documents that are in a common format.

2. Microsoft's decision to allow powerful programming instructions, in the form of macros, to be *embedded* within documents. Other software manufacturers that support macro capabilities store their macros in separate files, for example Corel WordPerfect and Lotus WordPro. However, 90% of all home computers run Windows, and a large percentage of those run Word. (Word is also available for the Mac, where it enjoys a substantial user community as well.)

Because of Word's widespread popularity, combined with the routine use of e-mail attachments for document distribution by largely naive newbies, a highly successful class of computer viruses has emerged. We can blame those who create the viruses, questionable software design decisions, or the users who embrace sophisticated software without adequate training or preparation. In fact, a macro virus needs all three of these in order to create widespread chaos.

How Word Macro Viruses Infect a Computer

Word templates allow users to customize various settings for different types of documents. A number of predefined templates for business letters, faxes, professional resumes, and other document types are available. To see these templates, select File and then New and then click the various tabs in the pop-up window. Most people who use Word rely on its default template, `normal.dot`, for most documents. Word uses this template when you create a new document using Ctrl + N or the new document icon in Word.

Recall that a crucial feature of macros is that they can be set up to execute automatically whenever a document is opened. Anyone can create a Word macro by recording a sequence of Word commands using Word's *macro recorder*. Programmers who know VB can create Word macros that are not limited to operations available as Word commands. User-defined macros are associated with specific templates. A Word document moved from one computer to another takes its template with it, along with any macros associated with that template. When you open a Word file whose template is new to your system, Word installs the new template for you. This usually means overwriting an existing template file to make new macros available to you.

Macro viruses most often are passed to new systems by their overwriting of the `normal.dot` template. A macro virus in the `normal.dot` template will be attached to all of your Word files that use `normal.dot`, both new and old. If you pass on a Word file that uses this template to someone else, it will overwrite that person's version of `normal.dot`—and the macro virus will have claimed another computer. The `normal.dot` template is the foundation template for all other Word templates, so you can't stop a macro virus by using a different template for your Word documents. In addition, a macro added to the `normal.dot` template will infect all of your Word documents.

Virus protection measures are effective against macro viruses for the most part. However, a computer programmer can easily take an existing macro virus and alter it so that virus scanners will no longer recognize it. Some users protect themselves simply by refusing to open any documents that contain macros. If you use Word 97 or 2000, you can set an option so that Word will warn you whenever you attempt to open a document that contains a macro (see Figure 2.9) and thereby give you the opportunity to disable it. To set up the macro alert, follow these steps:

1. Select Tools, Options, and then the General tab.
2. Make sure that the "Macro virus protection" check box is checked.

Figure 2.9:
Instructing Word to Warn You When a Document Contains a Macro

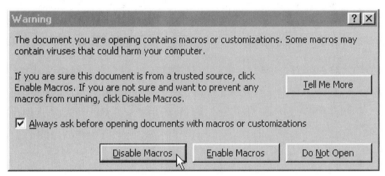

In addition, Word 2000 introduced new security options that check for *trusted digital signatures* whenever a document contains a macro. If everyone sending e-mail placed a digital signature on their outgoing mail, then you could simply ignore any e-mail attachments that don't have a signature. Until that happens, however, you can disable all macros that do not come from a trusted source by setting the macro security option to "High." This will protect you from viruses in documents from unknown or untrusted sources. Of course, a trusted source that is already infected can unknowingly pass on a macro virus to you, so you still must be watchful.

Deception and Trickery

6.11.99 The Explore.Zip worm appeared as an attachment to e-mail masquerading as an innocuous compressed WinZip file. The executable file used the icon from WinZip to fool people into double-clicking it, at which time it began destroying files on disk.
9.20.99 A couple of new Y2K-related virus/worms were discovered in September. One e-mail Trojan, called Y2Kcount.exe, claimed that its attachment was a Y2K-countdown clock; actually, it sent user IDs and passwords out into the 'Net by e-mail. Microsoft reported finding eight different versions of the e-mail in circulation.
The other Y2K virus, named W32/ Fix2001, came as an attachment (ostensibly from the system administrator) and urged victims to install the "fix" to prevent Internet problems related to the Y2K transition. Actually, the virus/worm would replicate through attachments to all outbound e-mail messages from the infected system.
—1999 Infosecurity Year-in-Review

What to Do When You Receive an E-mail Attachment

1. If you receive an unsolicited e-mail attachment from an unknown person, delete it without opening it first.

2. If you receive an e-mail attachment accompanied by an empty message body, delete it. Even if you recognize the return address, the absence of a message is very suspicious (or, given the potential dangers associated with e-mail attachments, very rude).

3. If you receive an unexpected e-mail attachment from someone you know and the message body looks generic, contact the sender to make sure that the sender sent the e-mail message to you.

4. If you do decide to open any mail attachment, make sure that you scan it with antivirus software first, even if you have confirmed its authorship and you trust the source.

5. To be 100% safe, disable all macros before opening any Microsoft Office™ document.

When possible, avoid using e-mail attachments in your outgoing e-mail messages.

What to Do When You Have to Send an E-mail Attachment

If you must attach a file to an e-mail message, be considerate of your recipient.

- Include a personalized message body that only you could send. If your message body looks too generic, your recipient will be (should be) suspicious.

- Describe the purpose and content of your attachment in the message body.

- If the file you are attaching contains no graphics, save it as an RTF file. A knowledgeable recipient will know that RTF files do not need to be scanned.

2.5.2 Script Attacks

Although attachments are the primary source of e-mail risk, e-mail clients that render message bodies into Web-like page displays (complete with clickable links and graphics) can also be susceptible to malicious attacks. This happens if the content of a message body is allowed to trigger scripts.

BubbleBoy

11.08.99 In early November, a worrisome new worm called BubbleBoy appeared on the scene. This proof-of-concept worm was sent to Network Associates, which immediately posted a free software patch and alerted the FBI of the danger. The problem with this worm was that it would infect a host if an MS-Outlook user merely highlighted the subject line of the carrier e-mail message—no double-clicking was required. The worm's payload was mild—changes to the Registry and a simple display screen—but experts warned that the same techniques could carry much more dangerous payloads in future variations. The worm spread by mailing itself to every e-mail address on the infected system's address list, thus posing an even greater potential danger than the Melissa virus. This attack again demonstrates the foolishness of allowing automatic execution of code by e-mail and word-processing packages.

—1999 Infosecurity Year-in-Review

In 2000, two new e-mail attachment attacks targeted users of Outlook and Outlook Express. The LoveLetter and NewLove viruses—technically speaking, these were worms, not viruses—were spread via VB scripts passed along as e-mail attachments. Each script deleted files on the target host and then sent itself on to new targets, using addresses in the Outlook address book. Users who knew to scan all e-mail attachments before opening them and to keep their antivirus software up-to-date should have been safe. However, in the case of the LoveLetter virus it spread too quickly and the damage that it caused was not immediately obvious, so the antivirus protection software companies were slow to catch it and alert their customers about it. The effects of the NewLove virus were more immediately obvious; this kept it from spreading too far, too fast.

Microsoft and Security Patches

If you use Outlook or Outlook Express, be on the lookout for software patches and system upgrades whenever a new security hole is discovered. Patches and upgrades for all Microsoft products are available from the **Microsoft Download Center**. Microsoft has repeatedly refused to add stronger security safeguards to its e-mail clients. However, it does issue patches for specific problems as they arise (which is fairly often). To avoid having to deal with frequent software updates, shop around for a different e-mail client.

2.6 ■ SHOPPING ONLINE

Purchasing merchandise online does pose some risk, but you can take precautions to protect yourself. For example, be aware that *using credit cards is safer than using personal checks and money orders*. When you send someone a check or money order as payment, you might have no recourse if your order is damaged, not as requested, or lost in transit. When you use a credit card, you can always complain to the credit card issuer for help with an unresolved dispute with the vendor. Credit card issuers are required by the federal Fair Credit Billing Act to limit your potential loss to $50 when disputed charges are made on your credit card, provided that you report such charges in a timely manner. Retailers and credit card issuers absorb the bulk of any losses incurred resulting from theft of a credit card or its account number.

Note that bank debit cards *do not* afford you the same protections as do credit cards. Be careful not to confuse the two. Credit cards are much safer than debit cards for online transactions.

Risks Are Everywhere

Over the past four years, there has been an enormous amount of publicity about the dangers of credit card fraud on the Net . . . . Yet, as many savvy Internet shoppers now know, the reality is that it's actually much safer to enter your credit card number on a secure online order form than it is to give your credit card to a waiter at a restaurant. After all, what's to stop the waiter from writing down your credit card number and placing orders on the phone with it later? And research shows that the rate of fraudulent purchases made by cell phones is much higher than credit card fraud on the Net.

—*Internet ScamBusters*

If you want to buy something online, make sure that the address of the page on which you are to enter your credit card account information begins with `https://`. The "s" means that the page is **secure**, that is, protected by the **Secure Sockets Layer (SSL)** encryption protocol—an effective safeguard against anyone who might want to steal your card information in transit.

In addition, your browser should display a special icon to indicate whether the Web page is secure, either a key or a padlock. Look in the lower left-hand corner of your browser window for this icon. An unbroken key or unlocked padlock indicates that the page is secure. Figure 2.10(a) shows a locked padlock—the page is secure—and Figure 2.10(b) shows an unlocked padlock—the page is not secure.

Figure 2.10:
Padlock Icon That Indicates Whether a Web Page Is Secure or Unsecure

(a)   (b)

Although you can examine a Web page to see if it is secure, you unfortunately have no way of knowing how secure the computers are that store your order history and billing data. If your order is *encrypted* during transit, but then stored without encryption on a public server that is not properly maintained, your order history and billing data might be at risk long after your transaction has been completed.

Maintaining a secure server and monitoring network activity for possible security breaches requires the services of a professional system administrator. If an e-store out-sources their storefront operation to a reputable, professionally managed e-commerce service, they are paying that service to manage their storefront security. But some e-stores try to handle their storefront operation inhouse. In that case, a full-time professional system administrator represents a non-trivial payroll expenditure, and many small business operators may not realize that this is a necessary business expense. Smaller companies that cannot afford experienced system administrators pose the greatest risk. However, even large corporations with no prior experience in e-commerce will go through a settling-in period where mistakes may be made. Most companies try to cut corners wherever possible, and some view the costs associated with top-rate system security as unnecessary. Unfortunately, consumers can't know if any given e-store operation is being managed by professionals who are knowledgeable about computer security. A large corporation with a thriving e-commerce operation is more likely to hire the necessary technical personnel to keep its servers safe from cyberattacks. A small or medium-sized company that is trying out Web-based sales for the first time may be much less secure. But before you get too caught up in risk assessments, remember to put these risks in their proper perspective. Whenever you use a credit card in a restaurant or over the phone, you are subjecting yourself to comparable risks. The only difference is that you are probably not worrying about it in those more familiar contexts.

Acceptable Levels of Risk

Before you enter your credit card account number on a Web page, check whether the Web page is secure. If it is, your risk is very small. If you feel safe placing a credit card order over the telephone or if you allow store clerks to discard credit card impression carbons without their tearing them up in front of you first, you have no reason to worry about using Navigator and MSIE for credit card transactions. All of these scenarios carry some amount of risk, but most people live with such risks in exchange for the convenience of fast transactions.

If you do a lot of shopping online, you'll end up with accounts at different sites so that you can track your orders. Some sites support the convenience of **one-click shopping** for repeat customers. This is a convenient service designed to speed you through your purchase, and your account information is protected by a password. Most people pick the same userid and the same password for each new e-commerce site with which they do business. This is like using the same key for your home, your office, your car, and your safe deposit box. It might be more convenient, but you stand to lose a lot if someone steals that key. You should always select a new password for each site. You can easily manage multiple passwords for various online merchants if you install a *password manager* to help you out. A good password manager is easy to use and can be obtained online for free.

When You Shop Online, Remember These Tips

1. Use a credit card instead of checks, money orders, or debit cards.

2. Examine the URL for the beginning `https://`, and check for a locked padlock or unbroken key icon before entering any credit card account information.

3. Do business with reputable companies that have been selling online for at least a year.

4. Do not use the same password for all of your e-commerce accounts.

5. Save a copy of all purchase orders and confirmation numbers for your records.

6. Review your credit card billing statement each month, and report any questionable charges immediately to the credit card issuer.

2.7 PROTECTING YOUR PRIVACY

Sometimes people don't appreciate what they have until it's gone. Privacy is like that. Consumer data has always been valuable for marketing purposes, but the Internet has created opportunities for data collection on a scale never before encountered. Imagine a man following you around all day, taking notes. He jots down which television shows you watch and how many times you leave the room while the television set is on. He pays attention to how much time you spend on the telephone and to whom you talk. He follows you when you go shopping, recording which stores you visit, how much time you spend looking at specific items, and which items you purchased. He notes which magazines and newspapers you read, as well as exactly which articles catch your eye. He knows when you wake up and when you go to bed. He does this every day—and then he sells this information to anyone who wants it!

This level of surveillance might seem an unthinkable invasion of privacy, but this is what can happen each time that you take your Web browser for a spin. Any Web page can be programmed to collect information about, for example, when you visited the page and how many times, which links you clicked on the page, and how long it took before you clicked them. Consumer privacy is not protected by the U.S. Constitution or by federal law, so it's up to each of us to protect ourselves, if we care about keeping our private lives private.

Never fill out a form on a Web page that asks for personal information unless that information is required for a credit card transaction; for example, your home address is needed for shipping purposes. **Under no circumstances should you divulge your social security number, age, income, or other sensitive information.** This information is used only for profiling purposes and should not be required by any company, online or offline.

Before you complete a site's form as part of a credit card transaction, check the site's **privacy policy** (see below). Companies are required by law to divulge computer records under court order and need not obtain your permission before releasing your personal data to law enforcement agencies. However, they are not required by U.S. law to obtain your permission in order to sell your personal data. So, read the policy to find out if the company plans to sell or distribute your personal information to third parties or its business partners.

Privacy Policies

A responsible e-commerce site points to its privacy policy via a link at the bottom of its home page. Many sites display a **TRUSTe** icon; click the TRUSTe icon to see the site's privacy policy. If a company does not make finding its privacy policy easy, or it hasn't posted a privacy statement, assume the worst. This is one case in which no news is bad news. Sites that take your privacy seriously will go out of their way to reassure you that your data is safe.

Sometimes a company will offer you a customized service of some sort in exchange for information about your interests and other background information. This is a big feature for portal sites and online news delivery services. You might feel that a personalized Web page is exactly what you need. In such cases, collecting personal information might be necessary. For example, to receive a regional weather report, you must reveal where you live. However, be aware that the same information needed to customize a service for you can also be used by banner advertisers, junk e-mail operations, and direct mail companies, if the site chooses to sell that information. In these cases, be especially careful to check for a privacy policy and weigh the pros and cons before giving away your personal information. Once it goes up for grabs, you will not be able to call it back.

Few privacy laws have been passed to protect personal data. The proposed privacy legislation in the United States that does exist is being drafted slowly and piecemeal. However, thanks to the Child Online Protection Act, information collected from children on the Internet requires prior parental permission.

In addition, the 1999 Electronic Privacy Bill of Rights Act attempts to establish more comprehensive guidelines that are on par with the more stringent European regulations. Yet as of this writing, this legislation is still pending and might never make it through Congress. For the most part, U.S. companies are self-regulating regarding consumer privacy policies. That is, they can do as they please with the information that they collect.

You need to protect your personal information; no one else will do that for you.

2.8   INTERNET SCAMS

The famous saying "There's a sucker born every minute" dates from 1869 and was never actually said by the famous P. T. Barnum (it was said by someone named David Hannum, but that's another story). However, since the advent of the Internet, it might be more accurate to say, "There are 1,000 suckers born every minute." Scam artists are nothing new. The Internet has simply made it easier than ever for them to reach a huge pool of potential pigeons. The **Internet Fraud Watch** site has compiled a complete index of commonly encountered Internet frauds and scams. You can also read the **Internet ScamBusters** newsletter or research classic scams in the **ScamBusters archive** of back issues.

If something sounds too good to be true, it probably is—and if you saw it on the Internet, you can be sure of that. Here are some tips for avoiding scams on the Net.

- Beware of get rich quick offers, especially if they show up in your e-mail inbox as unsolicited e-mail messages.
- Don't trust an operation only because it offers a slick-looking Web site.
- Be wary of anyone who pressures you to respond fast.
- Never send cash. When buying something from a private individual over the Net, try to arrange for a cash on delivery (COD) payment to protect yourself. Any operation that lists only a P.O. box address could disappear tomorrow without a trace. If you must send someone a check or money order, don't spend more than you are prepared to lose.

Further, watch out for any e-mail offer that promises you any of the following:

- Money by pulling in additional "investors"
- Money by stuffing envelopes at home
- Money playing the currency exchange markets
- Free goods once you pay a membership fee
- Miracle health cures and diet formulas
- Your credit record repaired for a fee
- Insider investment advice for a fee
- Free cable service by using a descrambler (these are illegal)
- Guaranteed loans or credit
- Vacations as a prize

Con artists and criminals have greater reach and more opportunities than ever before. As more people go online, the potential audience for scams and rip-offs grows as well. A scam artist can set up shop in cyberspace and then quickly vanish to stay clear of the law. However, law enforcement agencies are getting wise to online crime. If you believe that a scam artist or fraudulent business has victimized you or you become aware of any suspicious communications or criminal activities, contact the **National Fraud Information Center**. It might not be able to resolve your complaint, but it will forward your report to a relevant law enforcement agency that can initiate an investigation.

2.9 ONLINE AUCTIONS

Online auctions link buyers with sellers who might never find each other any other way. Hard-to-find items might be no further away than the right search query, and prices are subject to the simple rules of supply and demand. When all goes well, the seller is happy, the buyer is happy, and everyone will tell you how a particular online auction site, such as eBay, has changed their lives. Millions of transactions take place at online auctions every day.

Participating in online auctions also involves risk. Online auction sites have topped **Internet Fraud Watch**'s list of popular Internet scams since its inception in 1997. In 1999, the Federal Trade Commission (FTC) received almost 11,000 complaints about Internet auctions, a dramatic increase from only 107 in 1997. The FTC, Justice Department, U.S. Postal Inspection Service, and other federal agencies have filed almost three dozen law enforcement actions concerning online auction fraud.

Watch Out for Highly Popular Items

Popular collectibles attract a lot of bidders at online auction sites. They also attract a lot of scam artists. In the typical set up, a buyer pays for an item that is never delivered. Documented complaints have exposed operators who have collected as much as $50,000 from victims without delivering merchandise to any. The top three states for reported cyberfraud operations are California, Florida, and Texas. Personal checks are the most common method of payment in fraudulent Internet transactions, with money orders ranking second.

Before buying an item at an online auction, do some homework first and proceed with caution. On your first visit to an auction site, browse to find out how it operates. Most sites are just fancy bulletin boards for public notices. The site assumes no responsibility for the accuracy of its posts or the integrity of its sellers. Look for sites that post fraud warnings and offer the following features:

- Escrow services (see later in the chapter)
- Feedback areas
- Easy-to-follow complaint procedures
- A policy to remove problem vendors

If you see an item that interests you, find out anything you can about the seller. If it's a company, contact the **Better Business Bureau** (BBB) and see if any complaints have been filed. Be aware, however, that not all legitimate companies are members of a BBB. Also, no record at the BBB means only that no one has filed a complaint against a company; it doesn't mean that no complaints exist against that company. If the auction site offers online feedback from other customers, check out what they say. Note, however, that feedback comments come with no guarantees; for example, a seller can post bogus messages to bolster the seller's image. Further, a seller who has never sold items at that site will have no track record.

Sales by private sellers are riskier than are sales by companies. Consumer protection laws apply only to commercial businesses, so if you have problems with a private seller, you are on your own. A legitimate private seller should be happy to provide you with his or her name, street address (don't accept a P.O. box address), and telephone number. Avoid transactions that can't be backed up with this much information.

Never pay for an item in cash unless you can first examine the item. Paying with a credit card gives you the greatest protection should you need to return the item. However, many sellers at an online auction are not merchants and therefore can't process a credit card transaction. In this case, use an **escrow service**, which will withhold your payment from the seller until you've received your item and deemed it acceptable. You might also be able to arrange for a COD shipment.

Some Sellers Are Honest

On March 6, 1998, I threw caution to the wind and sent off a $27 check to someone selling Beanie Baby™ toys online. This was at the height of the Beanie Baby™ feeding frenzy, with people lining up outside of stores for hours when new shipments of the toy were expected. I was happy to take a chance buying two of the toys from a seller on the Net. However, I had had no prior contact with the seller and I found no recommendations from any other satisfied customers. So I was pleased, and mildly surprised, when Iggy and Gobbles actually arrived at my house on March 14. They had been sent via insured U.S. Postal Service Priority Mail and were in excellent condition (see Figure 2.11). Despite the risks, I felt reassured by two facts.

1. The seller replied to me from a `.edu` mail address. This told me that the mail account had not been set up primarily for an Internet scam. I would have been much more suspicious of a free Web-based mail account.

2. I was given a residential mailing address to which to send payment. Had the address been a P. O. box, I probably would have backed off.

However, I still knew I could get burned. Negotiating with unknown individuals over the Internet is always a gamble, despite precautions.

Figure 2.11:
Iggy and Gobbles, Delivered Promptly and in Excellent Condition

Until you become better educated about how online auctions work, follow these tips:

- Begin with inexpensive items.
- Work with large well-known auction sites.
- Deal with sellers who are willing to give you their telephone numbers.
- For expensive items, always use an escrow service.

If you have trouble with a transaction, report the incident to the **National Fraud Information Center**, which will relay the report to appropriate federal, state, or local law enforcement agencies.

2.10 | LIBEL AND LAWSUITS

Libel is any written or pictorial statement that damages a person or organization. Posting libelous statements on the Net can result in legal actions against the poster. Some large corporations monitor Web pages and online discussions in public forums in an effort to discover potentially damaging statements about corporate services or products. Libel is not a criminal offense, so you can't be sent to jail for it. However, you can be sued for damages in civil court.

Statements about a company's products or services could be considered libelous if they result in lost revenues for the company. The Internet offers ample opportunity for people to make damaging misrepresentations that could have widespread negative consequences. ***A person who disseminates information that is deemed harmful to a company***

can be the target of a lawsuit even if the information is accurate. If the claims can be verified, the lawsuit will fail, but the ensuing legal process can be very costly and time-consuming. Most people do not want to risk a lawsuit even if they know their defense is solid.

Statements about individuals can also be considered libelous, under certain conditions, although individuals are less likely to initiate lawsuits. However, if the person libeled is a public figure, no lawsuit is likely. This is because in 1988, the U.S. Supreme Court held that public figures can be publicly ridiculed, even if that ridicule borders on libel. For example, Bill Gates, the founder and former CEO of Microsoft, is considered to be a public figure and therefore a safe target. If Bill Gates won a civil suit each time that someone said something nasty about him on the Internet, he could probably collect enough money to buy out all of his company's shareholders. However, care should be taken regarding people who are less famous. In a libel dispute, a private individual who has not opted for public life has stronger rights than does a public figure.

Information is difficult to contain on the Internet. All digital communication can be easily reproduced and distributed without your permission, so you can't be sure that a private e-mail communication will remain private. Before you send anything out onto the Internet, ask yourself how you would feel if your message turned up on the front page of the local newspaper. If that thought makes you sweat, reconsider posting your message. ***Any online communication can be easily transformed into a very public document,*** either by its intended recipient or by someone who has broken system security and has covertly intercepted your outgoing e-mail.

2.11   THREATS AND HARASSMENT

Children used to scream "I'm going to kill you!" on playgrounds and schoolyards all over the country, and with total impunity. However, that was before grade-school children started carrying handguns—and following through on their threats. Our society takes threats of deadly force more seriously these days.

Threats posted to chat rooms or contained in e-mail messages are likely to arouse serious attention. There is no such thing as a casual threat on the Internet, even when said in jest and between close friends. Online stalking and hate mail incidents are a reality. One chilling Web site detailed the emotional breakdown of a teenage user who eventually carried out his murderous fantasies about a 15-year-old girl who had spurned his advances.

The Internet fosters online attacks in which anonymity and geographical distance seem to turn some seemingly normal people into raving lunatics, engaging in flame wars. A **flame** is an e-mail or newsgroup message in which the writer attacks another person with uninhibited hostility. A **flame war** is an exchange of flames between two or more participants. It can be very easy to write off any online display of rage as just another flame. Who can say when the rage is pathological and when it's just another flame? This makes many people nervous, since it's impossible to know much about the people behind the words in an Internet communication.

Regardless of the social climate, U.S. criminal laws make issuing threats on or off the Internet illegal. Anyone who threatens the President of the United States will be investigated by the Secret Service and can be both fined and jailed for the offense (18 USC Sec. 871). Any threat of kidnapping or causing bodily harm that crosses state lines can be punished with a $250,000 fine and five years in jail (18 USC Sec. 875). How do state lines apply to the Net? A packet moving through an out-of-state server might qualify even if it contains an e-mail message that has a source address and destination address in the same state.

Consider as an example the eighteen-year-old Florida student who made threatening remarks to a student in an Internet chat room in December 1999 (see Figure 2.12). The second student attended Columbine High School in Littleton, Colorado. Those threats resulted in Columbine High School's closing down for two days while the FBI investigated the threat and tracked down the author. In April 1999, two Columbine students, Eric Harris and Dylan Klebold, killed 12 fellow students and a teacher at their school, before killing themselves. Once identified, the Florida youth publicly apologized for his chat room fantasy play. No firearms were found in his possession, and there was no evidence that he intended to carry out his threats. His words were nevertheless a felony offense worthy of an FBI investigation and subsequent arrest under the Interstate Communications statute (18 USC Sec. 875).

Figure 2.12:
A Chat Session That Prompted an FBI Investigation

Soup81: Listen, I can't tell you who I am because you know me... Do me a favor, don't go to school tomorrow.

Student: Why?

Soup81: Please, I trust in you and confide in you.

Student: I have to go. I can't miss school.

Soup81: I need to finish what begun and if you go I don't want blood on your hands.

Student: Please don't do this. You are really scaring me.

Soup81: There is nothing to be scared about, just don't go to school and don't tell anyone. If anyone finds out, you'll be the first to go.

Student: Please don't do this.

Soup81: Time magazine has brought more chaos and I need to strengthen this. This is what they wanted and people need to know what is really going on here. Don't go to school.

Student: What am I going to tell my parents when they wonder why I didn't go to school?

Soup81: Pretend you're sick! But don't tell anyone because you and only one person knows now. I had to tell someone before the big day.

Student: Well, what about my two best friends?

Soup81: It was nice to know you. I only wish I could tell you who I really was and to let you know how much I liked you. But I'm a nobody, and soon everyone will know who I am. Goodbye. Good to evil and evil to good.

Student: Please don't do this. You are really scaring me.

Harassment in the workplace is another potential trouble area for Internet users. Title VII of the 1964 Civil Rights Act changed the workplace dramatically. Since Title VII, you can't hang up a Penthouse calendar in your office and you can't make a racist joke with impunity. Similarly, offensive materials available on the Internet have no business in the workplace. If an employee is looking at a Web page that contains sexually (or religiously or racially) offensive material, and a coworker happens to see it while walking by, the employer could be cited for harassment. An employee who receives an e-mail that contains religiously or sexually or racially offensive jokes and forwards the e-mail to the whole department could be the target of a lawsuit.

Companies have become increasingly vigilant about Title VII infractions because they are legally liable if an employee chooses to initiate a lawsuit based on a civil rights violation in the workplace. In an effort to avoid lawsuits, many companies have installed pornography filters on their Web browsers and mail monitors on their e-mail servers. Employees are subject to stringent AUPs and can be terminated for noncompliance of them (see Section 2.2). Free speech in the workplace takes a back seat to Title VII. Employees must understand that an employer who is trying to comply with Title VII can curb their freedom.

It is often said that e-mail communications are more like postcards than letters: Anyone can read the writing on a postcard that is in transit. It's safer to think of e-mail in the workplace like posting a notice on a billboard. Not only is your e-mail very visible to anyone who wants to look, but you can be fairly sure that someone is looking regularly. Similarly, your employer might be keeping a log of all of your browser activities in an effort to maintain a proper workplace environment. If you want to exercise your First Amendment rights on the Internet, do it on your own time, from your own personal computer, using a commercial ISP. When it comes to the workplace, you are subject to a different set of behavioral codes than the ones that apply after hours (see also Section 2.13).

Students are similarly constrained by the AUPs of their educational institution, although colleges and universities are somewhat more reluctant to enforce rules that could interfere with the free expression of ideas. Schools nevertheless can be fined for Title VII violations and therefore must walk a fine line regarding what is considered to be offensive material in student e-mail and graphical displays on computers in public areas.

2.12   SOFTWARE PIRACY AND COPYRIGHT INFRINGEMENTS

Software piracy is the willful reproduction or distribution of one or more copies of one or more copyrighted works that collectively have a total retail value of more than $1,000. It is a criminal offense punishable by a jail term and a fine. Newcomers to the Internet often mistakenly think that copyright violations can be prosecuted only if the materials being distributed are sold for profit. This is not true; the person performing the piracy need not profit from the action in order to be found guilty of software piracy. The seriousness of a copyright violation is measured by how much the copyright owner's potential income has been harmed.

When you purchase commercial software, you do not become the owner of that software. Rather, you purchase only *licensee rights* to that software. Software licenses grant you only the right to *use* the software, subject to specific restrictions. It is your responsibility to understand the applicable licensing restrictions of the commercial software that you use. For more information about software piracy and answers to commonly asked questions, visit **Microsoft's Anti-Piracy Web site**.

Be especially careful about software that is distributed over the Internet. Legitimate software is always accompanied by a licensing agreement, even when distributed for free. *If you obtain any software that does not come with a licensing agreement, discard the software.*

Software Piracy Is Big Business

From *1999 Infosecurity Year-in-Review*:

- Worldwide, software piracy costs industry $11 billion a year.
- More than 90% of all software used in Bulgaria, China, Indonesia, Lebanon, Oman, and Russia is pirated software.
- 60% of the software sold via online auctions is sold illegally.

In August 1999, a 22-year-old University of Oregon senior became the first person convicted under the 1997 No Electronic Theft (NET) Act for software piracy and other copyright violations on the Internet. This student used his university computer account to publicly post on the Web a large number of MP3 files, as well as software applications, games, and movies. Under this law, acts of software piracy are either felonies or misdemeanors, depending on the value of the materials distributed. A felony conviction is punishable by up to three years in prison and a $250,000 fine.

While the U.S. Justice Department is poised to make Internet piracy a law enforcement priority under NET, the **Recording Industry Association of America (RIAA)** is taking matters into its own hands when it comes to illegal MP3 file distributions. RIAA is a trade association whose members create, manufacture, or distribute approximately 90% of all audio recordings produced in the United States. The Anti-Piracy division of the RIAA investigates the illegal production and distribution of these recordings. According to the RIAA, increased access to CD-R (Compact Disk-Recordable) drives are responsible for the surge in the number of illegal audio CDs created during 1999. The RIAA reports that in the first six months of 1999, 165,981 counterfeit audio CDs were seized by law enforcement agents. This compares to only 23,858 in all of 1998.

RIAA Bounty Hunters

In 1999, RIAA announced the CDReward program against CD-R pirates. Under this controversial policy, the RIAA will award up to $10,000 to an individual who provides the RIAA with information regarding illegal CD-R drive manufacturing locations.

RIAA is presumably looking for the big fish—the people who run large MP3 distribution sites on the Web or who manufacture CDs on order. However, anyone who downloads illegal MP3s from the Internet is also engaging in a criminal activity. The RIAA could stage a well-publicized lynching of a lowly user just to make a point.

The routine distribution of illegal MP3 files on the Internet presents an ethical dilemma for college students. Some universities are stepping in to protect themselves when copyright infringements are brought to their attention. For example, in 1999, university officials at Carnegie-Mellon University shut down Internet access accounts for 71 students who posted music files and other copyrighted material on the campus computer system.

When Is It Against the Law to Copy a Music File?

Some music files on the Internet are freely available from artists and record companies that are looking for maximal exposure. Downloading these files for personal use is legal. Other music, however, typically music recorded by major record companies, cannot be downloaded from the Internet without violating copyright protections. Many commercial MP3 sites are careful to post only legal MP3 files for public downloads. Other sites, usually private sites run by students or hackers, post MP3 files illegally. *If you download an audio file that is being distributed illegally, you are guilty of copyright infringement.*

Your legal status is somewhat more complicated if you have purchased the music in question on a CD (however, bootlegged CDs are not legitimate). The Copyright Act of 1971 prohibits anyone but the copyright owner from making a copy of a recording. However, the Audio Home Recording Act of 1992 protects consumers from lawsuits by record companies when they make copies of personal recordings for their own use. Under this act, people may copy cassette tapes and CDs onto computer files as long as the original source material was acquired legally and the copies are made for personal use only. Is it illegal to download a file from an Internet site if you have a legal right to create that file on your own through other means? The courts have not yet had an opportunity to rule on this issue. RIAA is not likely to prosecute anyone who legitimately paid for the right to enjoy a piece of music produced and distributed by RIAA member companies. RIAA is more concerned with blatant copyright infringements, since those activities pose a serious threat to the recording industry.

Converting CD Tracks to MP3 Files

The 1992 Audio Home Recording Act gives you the legal right to convert CD tracks to MP3 files as long as you are the legitimate owner of the CD that you want to copy. Converting the tracks depends on your having the right software. You need a CD ripper to copy the tracks into a `.wav` file format and an MP3 converter to translate the `.wav` file into an MP3 file. Details, as well as pointers to freeware for doing this, can be found on the Internet. mp3.com has good tutorials for beginners (if the RIAA hasn't shut it down by the time that you read this).

2.13 PORNOGRAPHY AND OTHER LAPSES IN GOOD TASTE

For those who enjoy off-color jokes or have an interest in "blue" material (pornography), the Internet might appear to be a haven in which anything goes. This is not quite true. The FBI has launched many successful sting operations on the Internet to trap child pornography rings, while in 1999, 22 employees of *The New York Times* newspaper were fired for sending offensive e-mail messages from work.

The First Amendment protects against the censorship of pornography and prosecution of those who create or distribute pornography. These protections also extend to pornography on the Internet. As a result, attempts to outlaw "bad" language online have so far been unsuccessful. For example, the well-publicized federal law, the Communications Decency Act of 1996, was overturned by the U.S. Supreme Court in 1998 for violating the First Amendment. Although the First Amendment does limit the powers of government, exclusions to it apply. For example, pornography involving adults is generally protected (as long as it doesn't cross a mysterious line that separates the merely pornographic from the genuinely obscene), but owning or distributing child pornography in the United States is a felony.

When Your Personal Computer Is Not

Ronald F. Thiemann, Dean of the Harvard Divinity School, resigned from his post in 1998 "for conduct unbecoming a dean." Apparently, Thiemann had a healthy collection of explicit pornography on his personal computer—equipment that actually was the property of Harvard University. When he asked university technical support personnel to transfer his files to a larger hard drive, the collection was discovered and brought to the attention of Harvard's president, Neil L. Rudenstine.

Although Thiemann had done nothing illegal, his resignation was accepted presumably to minimize public embarrassment for Harvard. Thiemann still holds a tenured faculty position at the university.

Chances are, your proclivities are more mainstream. Who hasn't passed along a raunchy joke or made a sexist statement (in jest, if not in earnest), perhaps in an e-mail message to a friend or relative from work? Be aware that personal e-mail on a company computer is less private than a personal telephone call on an office telephone. Employers cannot legally monitor personal calls on company telephones, but they can monitor e-mail messages that pass through company computers. If company policy prohibits offensive materials on office computers, a raunchy joke or a sexist statement could cost you your job. The First Amendment affords you no protection in such situations.

Workplace Rules

Computer communications must be consistent with conventional standards of ethical and proper conduct, behavior and manners and are not to be used to create, forward or display any offensive or disruptive messages, including photographs, graphics and audio materials.
—From a policy document for employees of *The New York Times*

Your employer determines your rights and freedoms in the workplace. Even though *The New York Times* allows its employees "reasonable" personal use of company e-mail, its management fired 22 workers for sending offensive e-mail messages. The *Times* justified the firings as necessary in order to minimize its legal liability in the face of potential harassment lawsuits.

When it comes to offensive materials in the workplace, legal liability is the bottom line. In 1995, offensive e-mail played a key role in a case involving a subsidiary of Chevron Corp. An e-mail message entitled "25 reasons beer is better than women" was used as supporting evidence in a sexual harassment claim that cost the company a $2.2 million settlement. Given this legal climate, some companies use sophisticated software to spy on employee e-mail. Although employees might feel that they deserve more privacy in the workplace, the courts generally find that companies are justified in monitoring the use of their computer equipment. The right to free expression is squaring off against the right to a harassment-free workplace—and free expression is losing. If you must be off-color, save it for after work hours and keep it out of your office e-mail. Note that if the computer in your home is owned by your employer, you should treat it as you would any computer in the office. The same company policies apply at 2 A.M. in your own bedroom if the computer that you are using is company property (see Section 2.11).

Search engines make finding adult content online easy, and all sorts of kinky characters can be found in chat rooms devoted to pornography. Indulge if you must, but if you want to stay out of trouble you need to understand what lines you can and cannot cross.

2.14 HOAXES AND LEGENDS

The Internet is a source of valuable information and, unfortunately, much misinformation. This section discusses the long-standing tradition of Internet hoaxes and urban legends that never fail to snare innocent new victims year after year.

Don't Be Naive

You can't believe everything that you read, especially if you read it on the Internet.

The Internet is particularly effective at propagating misinformation designed to alarm people and generate panic among the uninitiated. Once you start getting e-mail, you might begin to see earnest computer virus alerts and chain letters that promise to turn your life into a living hell (or possibly heaven on Earth) if you don't send the letter on to other people. These notices always ask you pass the information along to all of your friends, relatives, and coworkers. Since there are always enough newbies on the Net who helpfully comply out of ignorance and goodwill, the Net will probably never be rid of these things. The virus warnings tend to come and go, and come again, whenever enough collective ignorance is available to breathe life into them one more time. This problem will go away only when everyone becomes educated about the Internet. You can do your part by checking out the **Vmyths.com** Web site.

Although the Internet is a fertile breeding ground for frauds, scams, and misinformation, some information on the Net is not necessarily malicious—it's just false. If you see something on the Net that sounds not quite right, visit the **Urban Legends and Folklore** Web site and conduct a keyword search for the item. If it's an Internet classic, you'll find it here. In time, you'll learn to spot an Internet hoax a mile away.

Things to Remember

- Read the terms of all AUPs that apply to you.
- Never tell anyone your password.
- Change your passwords periodically.
- E-mail is not private, and chat room participants can be traced.
- Do not offer personal information on a site before seeing and agreeing with the site's privacy policy.
- Handle e-mail attachments with great care, and use antivirus software.
- If you are running Windows, turn off the File and Printer Sharing feature.
- Do not give out credit card account information on an insecure Web page.
- Computers in a workplace might be monitored for offensive materials.
- Just because something is easy to do doesn't make it legal.
- It is your responsibility to know the laws that pertain to your activities (both online and offline).

Important Concepts

acceptable use policy (AUP)—usage restrictions for computer accounts, Internet access accounts, and many other Internet-related services.

computer virus—potentially destructive code hidden inside of a host program and distributed to a large number of computers.

copyright infringement—the unauthorized distribution of material protected by copyright restrictions.

e-mail virus—a worm (erroneously called a virus) that is spread by e-mail attachments or scripts associated with HTML-enabled e-mail.

harassment—offensive, unwanted, and unavoidable communications or content, usually characterized by multiple or habitual incidents.

libel—damaging statements about a company or individual.

password security—your first and most powerful line of defense against hackers.

secure Web page—a Web page where it is safe to enter sensitive data such as credit card account numbers.

software piracy—the unauthorized distribution of commercial software.

terms of service (ToS)—same as an acceptable use policy.

Trojan horse—unauthorized code, often designed to enable remote control over your computer at a later date.

worm—potentially destructive code that depends on networked communications and commonly used software in order to propagate.

Where Can I Learn More?

Vmyths.com `http://www.kumite.com/myths/`

Symantec Security Updates `http://www.symantec.com/avcenter`

Widespread Virus Myths `http://www.stiller.com/myths.htm`

Urban Legends and Folklore `http://urbanlegends.about.com/`

File and Printer Sharing (NetBIOS) Fact and Fiction
  `http://cable-dsl.home.att.net/netbios.htm`

PFIR—People for Internet Responsibility `http://www.pfir.org/`

Electronic Frontier Foundation `http://www.eff.org/`

Privacy Rights Clearinghouse `http://www.privacyrights.org/`

Electronic Privacy Information Center `http://www.epic.org/`

Center for Democracy and Technology `http://www.cdt.org/`

First Amendment Cyber-Tribune `http://w3.trib.com/FACT/`

Problems and Exercises

1. What is an acceptable use policy (AUP)? Find the AUP for your Internet access account, and study it carefully. Have you ever violated the terms of your AUP without realizing it at the time? Are there any restrictions that you do not understand or to which you object?

2. Explain how a computer virus, a Trojan horse, and a worm differ from each other.

3. The Melissa virus used an innovative strategy for tricking people into opening e-mail attachments. How did Melissa fool users?

4. What is an RTF file? Can an RTF file contain a macro virus? Should Microsoft make RTF the default file format for Word? Explain your answer.

5. What is `normal.dot`? Explain how `normal.dot` is used to spread macro viruses.

6. Explain how HTML-enabled e-mail clients can spread worms without the use of e-mail attachments.

7. Which is safer to use online: a check, a credit card, or a money order? Explain your answer.

8. What two things should you look for before you enter any personal information on a Web page?

9. What laws protect the privacy of American consumers? Is personal privacy protected by the U.S. Constitution?

10. According to Internet Fraud Watch, what online activity is responsible for the largest number of consumer complaints?

11. If you are thinking of participating in an online auction, what four safeguards should you look for at the auction site?

12. When can someone be sued for libel? Why is it relatively safe to criticize a politician?

13. Is it safe to criticize a person or company in a personal e-mail message to a friend? Is it safer to make the same statements in a personal telephone call? Or a written letter? How about posting the statements on a Web site if you don't give out the URL to anyone? Discuss the relative risks and worst-case scenarios in each of these cases.

14. What is the maximal penalty for making a threat of bodily harm that crosses state lines?

15. What law makes a business liable for harassment in the workplace? What steps are companies taking to protect themselves against harassment lawsuits?

16. What is the legal definition of software piracy? Do you have to profit from your activities in order to be guilty of software piracy?

17. When is it legal for a private individual to make a copy of an audio CD? Is it illegal to make copies of audio CDs by using a CD-R drive?

18. What is the Recording Industry Association of America, and what is it doing to combat the illegal distribution of MP3 files?

19. Is it illegal to download pornography? Can your employer legally override your First Amendment rights in its AUP? Can your employer legally monitor all of your online activities? Can it censor objectionable Web sites on workplace computers?

20. Why do so many virus hoaxes exist on the Net, and why don't they ever die out?

CHAPTER THREE

E-Mail Management

CHAPTER**GOALS**

- Become familiar with the basic operations of your mail client.
- Understand the basic differences among the SMTP, HTTP, POP, and IMAP mail protocols.
- Learn how the MIME protocol and HTML-enabled mail clients have changed e-mail.
- Find out how to augment your primary mail service with a Web-based e-mail account.
- Learn to use mail filters to save time and combat information overload.

3.1 | TAKING CHARGE

E-mail is here to stay, and a lot of people have a love-hate relationship with it. E-mail has become an indispensable tool for business communication and a speedy, inexpensive alternative to *snail mail*. People of all ages use it to stay in touch with friends and relatives. Virtual communities blossom via e-mail, and virtual relationships transcend geography because of e-mail.

However, e-mail also has a dark side. As convenient as it is, it can still be time-consuming, and there is no escape from it if your workplace requires frequent e-mail contact. Indeed, e-mail has undermined the concept of "normal working hours" for those who check their workplace mail from home. A message that begs for an urgent reply might be difficult to set aside, no matter when you read it. It is downright impossible to estimate how much time will be needed to deal with a pile of new e-mail. Ten mail messages might look like something that should require no more than 15 minutes of your time, but if just one of those messages compels you to investigate a URL or compose a thoughtful reply, those 15 minutes can easily expand into 30 minutes or more. This can mean the difference between a boiling pot of water and a very hot but empty pot that is beginning to crackle because you let all of the water boil away. (I have ruined a lot of cookware because of e-mail.) It also can make you late for an appointment, a dinner date, or a class, if you were silly enough to check your e-mail just before you had to go somewhere. If you are reading e-mail a few times a day, you might have noticed how your e-mail habit can rob you of those little blocks of time that used to be used for other things (a water cooler break, a quick game of fetch with the dog, or a quiet moment of contemplation). Everyone seems to feel pressed for time these days, and e-mail might be one reason why.

If you have just started to use e-mail and you are only getting ten or twenty messages a week, you probably don't have much of an e-mail problem. The challenges mount with the amount of e-mail in your mailbox. More and more people are receiving at least a hundred messages a day, and that's when you really need to look at the amount of time you are spending with e-mail. You might not be at this level now, but there's a good chance you will join the "100 Club" sometime in the near future. Even if you are not yet flooded with e-mail, but you do need to check your e-mail once a day, you will find useful information in this chapter.

E-mail is a compelling siren that claims our time and can lure us away from lots of little things that we used to do. It can become an addiction, especially when it masquerades as a work requirement or an enjoyable social activity. The activities that we drop in order to accommodate an e-mail habit might not seem important enough to mourn. However, if a large number of these unimportant activities are abandoned with little or no thought, the long-term effects of an e-mail habit might creep up on us in unexpected ways. Many people who telecommute or who augment their normal workday with "overtime" e-mail sessions begin to resent their work. When no clean division exists between working hours and personal time, the feeling of being constantly "on call" can be very stressful for some people (not to mention their families). The ubiquitous availability of e-mail access seems like a wonderful convenience at first but can result in "e-mail burn-out" when people let the technology run them, instead of the other way around.

As compulsive behaviors go, an e-mail habit is relatively easy to modify and manage. If you want to spend less time on e-mail (or perhaps just more time on other things), it's really not that difficult. You just need to understand your options. This chapter describes time-saving software options, along with software tips to help you manage your e-mail more productively.

3.2 ■ BASIC E-MAIL CLIENT OPERATIONS

Before learning about e-mail management strategies, you need to understand the basic functions of an e-mail client. If you have been using e-mail for a year or more, you probably know everything in this section; simply skim the next few pages to make sure. If you are new to e-mail , this is the place to start. Read this section carefully, and do the e-mail checklist exercises to make sure that you have these operations under control. Each e-mail client works a little differently, but all support the basic e-mail operations. If you aren't sure how to do something with your specific e-mail client, visit the **Checklist Solutions** on the Web or browse the resources under **Where Can I Learn More** to find tutorials and online help.

If you do consult a tutorial for your client, don't worry about all of the preference settings for now. Many advanced features are available, and you don't have to understand them all now. Your software comes preconfigured with default preference settings; these will be fine while you are learning.

3.2.1 Anatomy of an E-Mail Message

An e-mail message is very similar to an office memo, sharing the following characteristics:

- E-mail messages are usually fairly short.
- Each message usually addresses a single topic.

- Most messages rely on plain text (no graphics or fancy fonts), although this is changing.
- Messages are usually written in an informal style.
- Some messages are replies to previous messages.
- Messages can be sent to one person or many people.
- Messages can be forwarded to many other people.
- E-mail is often timely.
- A reckless e-mail message might someday come back to haunt you.

Although these are typical features of e-mail messages, the technology can be pushed in different directions. You could send an entire book manuscript to someone via e-mail (although there are better ways to send large documents). You can send files through e-mail that are not text files (for example, photographs). You can also have an e-mail dialog with someone about all sorts of highly personal matters, despite the fact that e-mail is neither secure nor truly private.

Each e-mail message contains two parts:

- Header
- Message body

The header contains addressing information, such as who the message is from and who the message is being sent to, the time that the message was sent, and a subject line describing the content of the message. Figure 3.1 shows a short e-mail message.

Figure 3.1:
A Typical E-Mail Message

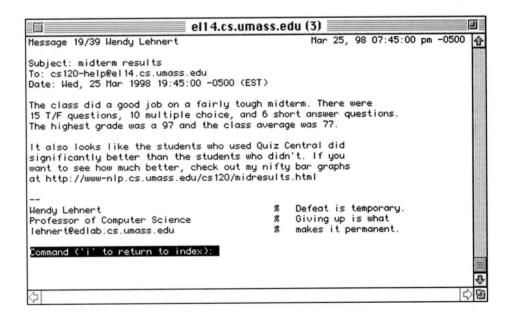

The first four lines of the message are part of the header, and the rest is the message body. When you create an e-mail message, the From: and the Date: fields of the header are always filled in automatically for you by the mail program. You complete the To: and the Subject:. You *must* complete the To: field, but you can leave the Subject: field blank. You can even leave the message body empty and still have a legitimate e-mail message. However, if you leave the To: field unfilled, your message will have no place to go.

When completing the To: field, you must specify an e-mail address. A *valid* **e-mail address** consists of a **userid** and a **host address** separated by the @ character. If the address contains any typographical errors, your message typically will be returned to you along with an error message. However, a typographical error might send your mail to a legitimate address—only not the one that you intended. In that case, no error message will alert you. If the accidental recipient does not respond, you may never know that something went wrong. So be careful when you complete the To: field.

Here are some examples of valid e-mail addresses.:

Userid	Host Address	E-mail Address
`ajones`	`apple.orchard.com`	`ajones@apple.orchard.com`
`deadbug`	`antfarm.net`	`deadbug@antfarm.net`
`kgranite`	`context.wccm.org`	`kgranite@context.wccm.org`

If you don't know the address of the person that you want to contact, you'll have to track it down. Many online directories can help you find e-mail addresses. You can take a guess, but only if you don't care that your mail might go to a wrong person. Some userids are not particularly formulaic. For example, if you know that Dave Brown is an AOL subscriber, you will have only the host address, aol.com. It would be impossible to guess at a userid like `DRBMC986`.

Shortcuts for E-Mail Addresses

If you send a lot of e-mail to the same person, most mail programs will let you refer to that person's full e-mail address by using a shortcut abbreviation, or a *nickname*. Check your mail client for an *address book feature*. When an e-mail address is very long or hard to remember, put it in your address book and assign a nickname for that entry. Then you need to remember only the nickname, and whenever you enter the nickname in a mail header, your mail client will automatically substitute the full e-mail address.

A system of first names followed by a last initial is easy to remember. If the names of two people collide by using this system, you can add another letter from their last names. Whatever system you use, use it consistently. Nicknames can save you a lot of time, but only if you can get the address you need on the first try.

Although you type in only a few header fields when you send e-mail, the header that your mail software uses is a bit more involved. Figure 3.1 showed only a short version of the full mail header. Figure 3.2 shows a full e-mail header.

The header in this message contains routing information and various time stamps that indicate when the message was received by different hosts along the route from your machine to the recipient's (note all of the different Received: fields). Most users don't need to see this information, so most mailers hide it. However, it should always be available on request because sometimes the full version is useful.

Each e-mail message that you receive is stored in a plain text file. The full header appears at the top of the file, and the message body follows. Your mail program is responsible for scanning this file and deciding how much of it you probably want to see. Don't confuse a mail message with the way that the mail message is being displayed. There might be more to your mail than meets the eye.

Other address fields are available to use when you send an e-mail message. The most commonly used optional field is Cc: (carbon copy). When you put an e-mail address in this field, a copy of your message is sent to that person. Some people always Cc: themselves so that they can have a copy of all of the messages that they send. This is called

Figure 3.2:
A Full E-Mail Header

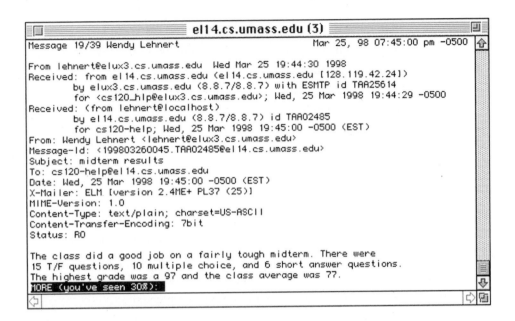

```
┌─────────────────── el14.cs.umass.edu (3) ──────────────────┐
│ Message 19/39 Wendy Lehnert          Mar 25, 98 07:45:00 pm -0500 │
│                                                            │
│ From lehnert@elux3.cs.umass.edu  Wed Mar 25 19:44:30 1998  │
│ Received: from el14.cs.umass.edu (el14.cs.umass.edu [128.119.42.24]) │
│          by elux3.cs.umass.edu (8.8.7/8.8.7) with ESMTP id TAA25614 │
│          for <cs120_hlp@elux3.cs.umass.edu>; Wed, 25 Mar 1998 19:44:29 -0500 │
│ Received: (from lehnert@localhost)                         │
│          by el14.cs.umass.edu (8.8.7/8.8.7) id TAA02485    │
│          for cs120-help; Wed, 25 Mar 1998 19:45:00 -0500 (EST) │
│ From: Wendy Lehnert <lehnert@elux3.cs.umass.edu>           │
│ Message-Id: <199803260045.TAA02485@el14.cs.umass.edu>      │
│ Subject: midterm results                                   │
│ To: cs120-help@el14.cs.umass.edu                           │
│ Date: Wed, 25 Mar 1998 19:45:00 -0500 (EST)               │
│ X-Mailer: ELM [version 2.4ME+ PL37 (25)]                   │
│ MIME-Version: 1.0                                          │
│ Content-Type: text/plain; charset=US-ASCII                 │
│ Content-Transfer-Encoding: 7bit                            │
│ Status: RO                                                 │
│                                                            │
│ The class did a good job on a fairly tough midterm. There were │
│ 15 T/F questions, 10 multiple choice, and 6 short answer questions. │
│ The highest grade was a 97 and the class average was 77.   │
│ MORE (you've seen 30%):                                    │
└────────────────────────────────────────────────────────────┘
```

a self-Cc:. Some mailers give you a switch that you can set to make self-Cc: copies automatically. If a message is intended primarily for one person but also would be useful to other people, use the Cc: field for the other addresses. However, if your message is intended for more than one person, all of whom are equally important as recipients, put their addresses in the To: field.

The Bcc: field is similar to Cc: but is a *blind* carbon copy. When you include an address in this field, the message is sent to that recipient, but the recipient's address is not visible in the header received by other recipients. Blind carbon copies are used when you want to preserve someone's privacy or not broadcast that person's e-mail address.

How to Create a Distribution List

If you send mail to the same group of people regularly (for example, you all are members of the same committee), you can use the address book feature to create a *mail distribution list*. To do this, follow these steps:

1. Create a new address book entry.
2. Enter the list of e-mail addresses, separated by blanks or commas.
3. Give the list a nickname.
4. Use the nickname as you would any other address book entry.

A distribution list will save you from a lot of tedious typing and possible typographical errors.

3.2.2 What to Expect from Your Mail Client

Many different e-mail clients (also called *mailers*) are available, and their operations and features are all quite similar. Once you've seen one mail client, you'll know what to expect from another. This means that you don't have to worry too much about which mailer to adopt. Moreover, if you ever need to switch mail clients, you won't have to learn how to work with it from scratch. A few basic commands are enough to make you operational. If you're accustomed to some special features in your former mailer, you should be able to find equivalent features in your new mailer.

All mailers will enable you to do the following.

- Send a message that you have written yourself.
- Read any message that has been sent to you.
- Reply to any message that has been sent to you.
- Forward a message to a third party.
- Save or delete messages sent to you.
- Scan the Subject: and From: fields of all of your new mail.

A good e-mail client also supports other features, such as:

- The ability to sort mail and save it in different locations.
- The ability to tag unread mail messages for easy identification.
- An address book to hold frequently used e-mail addresses.
- A reply option that allows you to edit the original message.
- A customizable mail filter that sorts and routes incoming mail.
- The ability to include a *signature* automatically.

If you're working on a Windows-based personal computer or a Mac and have Internet access through an ISP or university, the Eudora mail program is a popular option. It includes many advanced features and has an intuitive interface. However, you also can manage your mail with the mail clients that are bundled with the Navigator and MSIE Web browsers.

A good mail program will give you the most commonly used commands in convenient toolbar buttons and pull-down menus. In addition, if you can't remember all of the details of your particular mailer, looking up something in the online documentation is usually easy.

Which Mailer?

If you can't spell, look for a mailer with a spelling checker. If you expect to handle a lot of e-mail, look for a mailer that offers automated filtering and routing. For some users, a single crucial feature might be enough to decide which mailer to use. For example, most modern mailers recognize URLs inside of mail message bodies. If someone sends a URL in a mail message, the mailer will recognize it as a hyperlink, underline it in the display, and make it an operational hot link that you can click if you want to visit the Web page right then. For people who get a lot of Web pointers in their mail, this might be the most wonderful feature in the world. For others, it might not matter. Only you can decide what features are important to you.

3.2.3 Viewing Your Inbox

Typically, the first thing that people do when they open their mailer is to check for new mail. New mail is stored in your inbox upon downloading. The **inbox** is very much like a mailbox, in which new mail awaits your retrieval. Many mailers take you directly to the inbox at start-up. Others might require you to load the inbox in order to see your new mail.

The inbox displays a list of each piece of mail received and not deleted, with a single descriptive line for each mail message. This line displays the Subject: and the From: fields so that you can see what each message is about and who sent it to you. Most also show the message's date of arrival. Figure 3.3 shows Navigator's mail client, with a display of the inbox headers in the upper right-hand corner.

Figure 3.3:
A Mail Inbox
Display

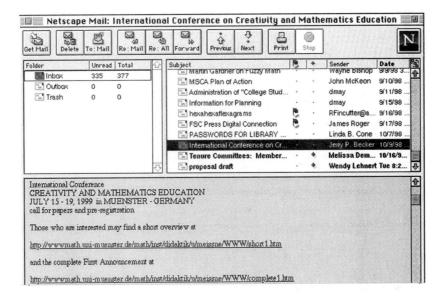

Each message in this inbox display is given a header line that indicates

- the subject header for the message,
- whether the user has marked the message for deletion,
- whether the message has been read,
- the name of the author, and
- the date received.

In most inbox displays, a message listed without an icon or marker next to it usually means that the message has been read. All of these messages in Figure 3.3 have been sorted by their dates. A preference setting can be reset if you prefer to have them sorted by another criteria, such a the senders' names, the subject headers, or the lengths of the messages. A subject header or a sender's name that is too long is *truncated* (shortened) in the display; however, you can resize these fields within the fixed dimensions of the message header display window in order to show more information. Keep this in mind when you write your own subject headers. If you give a mail message a long subject header, only the first few words may be visible in the recipient's inbox display.

Note that some of the sender entries are actual e-mail addresses, whereas others are names of people. Whenever you send mail, your From: field is filled with both your e-mail address and an **alias**, or alternative identifier, for yourself. Most mail programs give you an opportunity to enter your full name in one of your configuration or preference settings. If it does, whatever you enter becomes your e-mail alias and that alias will be added automatically to the From: field (along with your return address) whenever you send mail. Other mail programs that receive your mail often display aliases in addition to or in place of e-mail addresses. You can specify any alias that you want; most people use their real names.

E-Mail Checklist—1

Study your mailer's documentation to be sure that you know how to do the following.

1. View your inbox and identify all your new mail.
2. Know how to distinguish read messages from unread messages.
3. Navigate multiple pages in a large inbox (both forward and backward).

Sometimes your inbox contains more messages than your screen can display in one window. In that case, you can scroll to the next block of messages and move back and forth across different segments of your inbox. Be sure to view all of the headers in your inbox so that you can see everything that's in there.

3.2.4 Viewing Individual Mail Messages

When you view your inbox, you see only a short header for each mail message. To see the body of a message, click the message header to open the message. You'll then see a screen display that contains an abbreviated version of the full message header followed by the message body. A very long message body won't fit in a single screen display. However, you can navigate both forward and backward by using the vertical scroll bar on the right border of the window.

All mailers offer many options that you can set, along with many advanced commands that you might find useful. Start by learning the settings and commands that you need in order to complete the e-mail checklists in this chapter. Whenever you need to learn a new command, use your Help menu or visit the **Checklist Solutions** for various mail clients online.

E-Mail Checklist—2

Study your mail program's documentation to be sure that you know how to do the following.

1. Select a specific message in your inbox.
2. Open a single mail message in order to view its message body.
3. Page forward and backward through a long message body.
4. Exit a mail message display, and return to the inbox.
5. Display the long version of a message header.

3.2.5 Sending a New Mail Message

All mailers have a command that puts you in a mode for creating and sending a mail message. Look for a New Message command in a pull-down menu or a special "new message" icon on a toolbar. Once in that mode, you enter information in the To: field, the Subject: field, and, optionally, the Cc: field. The From: field will be filled in for you automatically. You will probably be given a window display in which all of the information can be entered by clicking the field that you want to complete. If you don't want to put something in a given field, press the Return or Enter key to leave it blank. Remember, the only field that you must complete is the To: field. Note, if you're new to sending messages, you can experiment by sending a message to yourself before sending one to someone else. Simply put your own userid in the To: field, and the mail will be sent to you.

In most mailers, a blank window is reserved for the message body. Type your message in it and edit it as needed, and then you're ready to send it. All mailers are designed to make the most basic operations highly intuitive, so editing an e-mail message isn't likely to require much beyond the most basic editing commands.

What Can You Send?

Some mailers can display text in different fonts or with special effects such as color. Outlook and Outlook Express make it easy to create messages with these features. While composing a new message, go to the Tools menu and select Rich Text (HTML) to bring up a toolbar that offers access to such text effects as boldface, colors, italics, and indented lists.

You also can create hyperlinks or insert graphics from files. Some mailers, such as Outlook and Outlook Express, can do this in a message body and even create operational hyperlinks (as shown in Figure 3.7). This makes the message body resemble a Web page. A mailer that can do this is called an **HTML-enabled mail client**. HTML-enabled mail is fun when you want to send someone a colorful greeting or a photograph. However, not everybody else has it. For various reasons, many people still use mailers that are not HTML-enabled.

Enter the text for your message body, review it to be sure that it says what you think it says, and prepare to send your message. If you have a spell checker, use it (especially if you are a poor speller). Then click the Send button.

All mailers also allow you to scrap the message if you decide you don't want to send it. You simply close the window that contains your message without saving or sending it.

Now that you've learned the basics of sending a mail message, it's time to add two more features to your repertoire. Earlier this chapter discussed the nickname feature as a short-cut device for handling long or difficult to remember e-mail addresses. Now is a good time to start an address book that you can update as needed. Set up an address book entry for someone you know that you'll be writing to often (perhaps your Internet instructor!). Then the next time that you send e-mail to this person, use that person's nickname instead of the full e-mail address. This powerful feature can save you a lot of time.

3.2.6 Signatures

Another time-saver is the **signature file** (or **sig file**). People who send a lot of e-mail have signature files that they append to the end of the message body. A sig file identifies the sender in some way. It personalizes your e-mail and saves you the tedious task of retyping the same identifying lines for each message. For business communications, it should contain your name, title, organization, mailing address, telephone number, fax number, and e-mail address. For casual e-mail, it could include a name and e-mail address, with perhaps a favorite quotation to add a little personality to an e-mail message. Figure 3.4 shows some sig files that I use.

Some mailers automatically add your sig file to the end of your message body, whereas others add it only on command. You might or might not be able to see your sig file at the end of your outgoing mail message. If you can't, that doesn't mean it isn't being included in your outgoing messages (send yourself a test message to see). Some mailers also let you set up and select from multiple sig files to convey different online personas. You might want to use a straightforward signature until you've been online for a while and have seen a lot of different signatures.

Some people will see your signature repeatedly. An unobtrusive sig file wears well after repeated exposures. Extremely lengthy signatures become annoying after a few encounters. Generally, keep your sig file to no more than four lines. By using all of the available horizontal space, you can pack a lot of information into those four lines.

Message Body Do's and Don't's

Beginners often make some common mistakes regarding their e-mail. Because you're reading this book, you can avoid the most common Newbie errors.

- Avoid inserting carriage returns into your message body. If you must insert them, then limit the width of each line to no more than 72 characters—65 characters is better.

- Keep your sig file short and sweet. Generally, use no more than four lines for it.
- Always include a signature in the message body that contains your full name and return e-mail address.
- Reread the complete message body before sending your mail. Be sure that it says what you think it says, and correct any errors. Careless errors can be embarrassing, especially if the message goes to many people. Be extra careful when people are relying on you for accurate information.

Figure 3.4:

Sample Signature Files

```
| Prof. Wendy Lehnert          Office hours: Mon. 11-12 and Wed 2:30-3:30
| lehnert@elux3.cs.umass.edu   LGRC A327 (the lowrise)
| (413) 545-3639               http://www-edlab.cs.umass.edu/cs120/
| ICQ #4909018                 http://www-nlp.cs.umass.edu/aw/home.html




| Prof. Wendy Lehnert          Get my public PGP key from:                |
| lehnert@cs.umass.edu         http://pgp5.ai.mit.edu/pks-commands-beta.html |



--
Wendy Lehnert                    %
Professor of Computer Science    %   "640K ought to be enough for anybody."
University of Massachusetts      %
lehnert@edlab.cs.umass.edu       %                       -Bill Gates, 1981




      Wendy Lehnert, dachshund owner and member of the world famous
                   Dachshund Underground Railroad
                  ( - We Go The Extra Lengths - )
          http://www.geocities.com/Heartland/Prairie/5370/index.html
```

3.2.7 Importing Text into Messages

Importing text from an existing file into an e-mail message body is often useful. If the text fragment is small, you can easily insert into your message body using copy-and-paste. Text insertion comes in handy when you want to set up stock replies to frequently encountered requests or situations. You essentially create a form letter in a file and then when you need to send it to someone, you insert it into your message body, change it here and there as needed, and you're done.

Form letters are most often needed in work environments, but you might find them useful for certain casual communication as well.

3.2.8 Importance of Good Writing

Practice sending e-mail to a friend until you feel comfortable and confident about your mailer. Once you have the hang of it, the mechanics of sending e-mail will be second nature and you can concentrate on content.

Be aware that on the Internet, you are what you type. A message filled with misspelled words and ungrammatical sentences does not reflect well on the sender. The quality of your writing is particularly important when you're writing to people who have no other contact with you. Some people take creative liberties with e-mail, devising their own quirky writing styles. While this might be appropriate in some contexts, it probably will not be appreciated in the business world. Think about who you're writing to, how busy that person is, how well you know that person, and the point of your message. Each message that you send takes time to read it. Try not to waste anyone's time. Think carefully about what you write. The rules of e-mail *Netiquette* are discussed in more detail in Section 3.4.

E-Mail Checklist—3

Study your mail program's documentation to be sure that you know how to do the following.

1. Set up an address book entry with a nickname for someone.
2. Begin a new message.
3. Enter information in the message header and the message body.
4. Change the message header and message body as needed.
5. Cancel a message before you send it.
6. Run the spell checker (if the mailer offers one).
7. Set up a sig file (if your mailer supports that feature).
8. Insert text from a file into a message body.
9. Send a message after you've completed the message body.

3.2.9 Replying To and Forwarding E-Mail Messages

Many e-mail conversations begin when someone replies to a message. By using the Reply command, you can conduct one-on-one discussions in a series of replies to previous messages, as well as conversations involving a large group of people.

Before replying to anyone, first be sure that you know the difference between two variations on the Reply command: the **sender-only reply** and the **group reply** (sometimes called **reply-to-all**). In the first case, your message is sent only to the original author of the current message. In the second case, your message is sent to the original author, as well as everyone included in the To: field and everyone included in the Cc: and Bcc: fields. The first type of reply is private; the second type, however, might be very public. Sometimes, you might want to use a group reply, but you'll probably more often use the sender-only reply.

One of the most helpful features of mailers is the inclusion of the original mail message in the reply message body. All the better mailers give you the option of either including the original message to which you are replying in your message body or starting from scratch with an empty message body. In addition, if you include the original message in your reply, you don't have to preserve it all. You can keep only the parts that you need in order to make your reply coherent by using your editor to delete anything that doesn't need to be seen again. This courtesy is especially important if your reply is going to many people who have already seen the original. No one wants to scroll through a long message that they've already read.

Each mailer uses a convention for distinguishing the text of an original message from the text that you add in the reply. An example is indenting of each line preceded by caret (>) character, as shown in Figure 3.5.

Figure 3.5:
An E-Mail Reply
with an Indented
Original Message

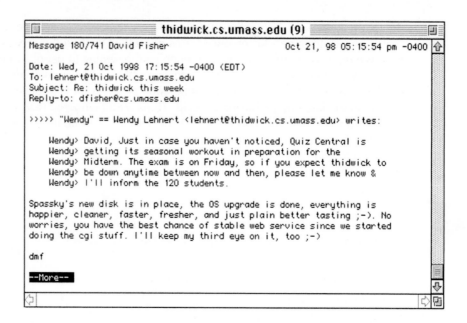

```
┌─────────────────────────────────────────────────────────────────┐
│ ▢        ▦▦▦▦▦▦    thidwick.cs.umass.edu (9)    ▦▦▦▦▦▦        ▤  │
├─────────────────────────────────────────────────────────────────┤
│ Message 180/741 David Fisher            Oct 21, 98 05:15:54 pm -0400 ⬆│
│                                                                   │
│ Date: Wed, 21 Oct 1998 17:15:54 -0400 (EDT)                       │
│ To: lehnert@thidwick.cs.umass.edu                                 │
│ Subject: Re: thidwick this week                                   │
│ Reply-to: dfisher@cs.umass.edu                                    │
│                                                                   │
│ >>>>> "Wendy" == Wendy Lehnert <lehnert@thidwick.cs.umass.edu> writes: │
│                                                                   │
│     Wendy> David, Just in case you haven't noticed, Quiz Central is │
│     Wendy> getting its seasonal workout in preparation for the    │
│     Wendy> Midterm. The exam is on Friday, so if you expect thidwick to │
│     Wendy> be down anytime between now and then, please let me know & │
│     Wendy> I'll inform the 120 students.                          │
│                                                                   │
│ Spassky's new disk is in place, the OS upgrade is done, everything is │
│ happier, cleaner, faster, fresher, and just plain better tasting ;-). No │
│ worries, you have the best chance of stable web service since we started │
│ doing the cgi stuff. I'll keep my third eye on it, too ;-)         │
│                                                                   │
│ dmf                                                               │
│                                                                   │
│ ┌─────────┐                                                     ▦ │
│ │ --More-- │                                                     ⬇ │
│ └─────────┘                                                       │
├─────────────────────────────────────────────────────────────────┤
│ ◁▯                                                            ▷▯ │
└─────────────────────────────────────────────────────────────────┘
```

A reply to a reply shows two levels of indentation, a reply to that shows three levels, and so on. You can make a dialog more readable by using blank lines to separate different speakers. Use your editor freely.

E-Mail Reply Do's and Don't's

Here are some more mistakes that beginners make and that you'll want to avoid.

- Know the difference between the sender-only reply and the group reply. If you use the group reply for a message intended for the original sender only, you might embarrass yourself by broadcasting something unintentionally.

- If you get into a lengthy dialog with someone, take the time to replace the subject in the Subject: field with a new subject when the original no longer describes the topic of your conversation. It's easy to keep the original subject content, but after exchanged replies, your mailbox might contain many messages that have the same subject. If you ever need to return to one of these messages, you won't know where to look.

- If you find yourself responding emotionally to a piece of e-mail, cool off a bit before replying, especially if you feel angry. Although your feelings might be justified, take some time to think about what you want to say before responding.

- Be selective when you include text from the original message in your reply. Don't duplicate the original message in its entirety unless it is absolutely necessary. However, do include enough so your reply will make sense to someone who can't remember the message that preceded yours.

When you reply to a message, your mailer might or might not include your sig file automatically. It might include a preference setting to control this default. If all of your e-mail replies go to people who already know you, it makes sense to forgo a sig file; friends and colleagues don't need to see your signature repeatedly. In addition, many people who have been using e-mail since its beginning tend not to use sig files because they grew up in an e-mail culture in which they sent messages only to people whom they knew. Sig files make more sense when your mail is going to people who don't know you.

Forwarding e-mail is like replying to e-mail, except that you send the message to a third party. Most mailers will let you edit the message body when you forward a message, a useful feature when you want to insert your own comments. You can forward anything to anyone; however, be aware that you might be dealing with sensitive information or information given to you in confidence. Betraying a confidence can hurt someone who trusted you, as well as make you look untrustworthy. Just because a program makes something easy to do doesn't necessarily make doing it a good idea.

E-Mail Checklist—4

Study your mailer's documentation to be sure that you know how to do the following.

1. Send a reply only to the original author of the current message.
2. Send a group reply to everyone associated with the current message.
3. Include the text of the current message in your reply.
4. Reply by using a blank message body (no old text included).
5. Change the subject header for your reply.
6. Forward a message to a third party with or without your comments.

3.3   MIME ATTACHMENTS AND HTML-ENABLED MAILERS

Once upon a time, all mailers expected to see plain ASCII text in their message bodies, and life was simple. No one had to worry about e-mail viruses (although some bogus virus warnings tried to convince the uninitiated otherwise), and no one had to spend much time beautifying their messages because there's only so much that can be done with plain ASCII text. However, people are rarely happy with what they have, and so it was with e-mail. Why be limited to plain ASCII text? Wouldn't it be nice to be able send binary files?

For a long time, users got around the text-only message body constraint by converting binary files into *ASCII-encoded binary files*. These converted files could then be inserted into plain ASCII text message bodies and sent via e-mail. Mailers needed to make no changes to handle these files, although extra work was required to encode the file before sending it and to decode after it was received. It worked well enough, but it was a little clumsy.

As more people began using e-mail, demand grew for more sophisticated e-mail programs. E-mail software programmers decided to make the software smarter about handling binary files by having it do all of the encoding and decoding automatically? The process wasn't that difficult to automate, and it would save everyone a lot of time. To do this, a new protocol was needed.

3.3.1 The MIME Protocol

To encode and unencode binary files automatically, a special mail protocol was created in 1991: the **Multi-Purpose Internet Mail Extension (MIME)**. Today, the MIME protocol is a globally recognized standard. If you have ever sent or received an e-mail attachment, you have used MIME. Thanks to MIME, modern mailers now make sending any file as a mail attachment easy to do. You either click a toolbar button for adding an attachment (often marked by a paperclip icon) or an "add attachment" command in a pull-down menu. Then you use a dialog box to navigate your way to the local file that you want to include as an attachment, select the file, and return to your message (see Figure 3.6). You can add more than one attachment to a single message, and you can include a file in any file format.

MIME is clearly an improvement over the old way of doing e-mail. New users need to be aware about possible dangers whenever they received an e-mail attachment (see Section 2.5).

Figure 3.6:
Including a File in a
Message as a MIME
Attachment

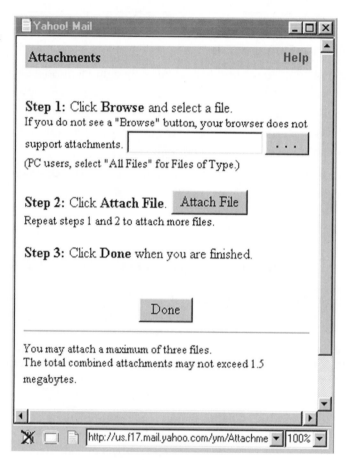

Before You Send That Attachment, Read This!

As explained in Section 2.5, people receiving e-mail attachments must protect themselves from e-mail viruses. You should never send an e-mail attachment unnecessarily. There is almost always some way around sending e-mail attachments. An attachment that is a plain text file can be inserted directly into the message body by using copy-and-paste. A Word file can be saved in RTF format and the resulting text inserted into the message body, again, by using copy-and-paste. A photograph can be posted at a Web site for public photo albums and a URL pointing to it there sent to friends instead of an attachment.

However, if you absolutely must send an attachment, be careful to include some personal information in the message body so that your recipient will know that the message really is from you (rather than some devious e-mail worm who appropriated your mailer after infecting your computer). Always identify the attachment by name, format, and file size.

3.3.2 HTML-Enabled Mailers

Soon after MIME was created, the Internet was opened up to commercial ISPs and the general public. Commercial software vendors saw an opportunity to make the Internet as user-friendly as possible, and e-mail was one popular application in which improvements could be made. The result was the HTML-enabled mailer. Suppose that you want to send a hyperlink to someone. If you send it in a plain ASCII text message body, the recipient will have to copy and paste it into a browser window. It would be better if it could simply show up in the message body as a clickable hyperlink. Then the user will need only click the link in order to be linked automatically to the referenced Web page. Embedding hyperlinks inside of the message body would be fast, convenient, and easy to understand.

The first HTML-enabled mailers were programmed to recognize URLs and render them as clickable hyperlinks, as they would be on a Web page. Navigator's mailer sent its URLs to Navigator, and MSIE's mailer sent its links to Explorer. A few independent mailers (for example, Eudora) let the user decide which browser to use in a preference setting.

Clickable hyperlinks were only the first step. If a mailer could recognize a URL, why not have it render entire Web pages like a Web browser would? Web pages are simply ASCII text files, so a Web page could be sent as an e-mail message body without any alterations to existing mail protocols. All that was needed were mailers that could make message bodies look like Web pages. Then e-mail could be as flashy and as much fun as a Web page (see Figure 3.7).

Figure 3.7:
Viewing Mail with
an HTML-Enabled
Mail Client

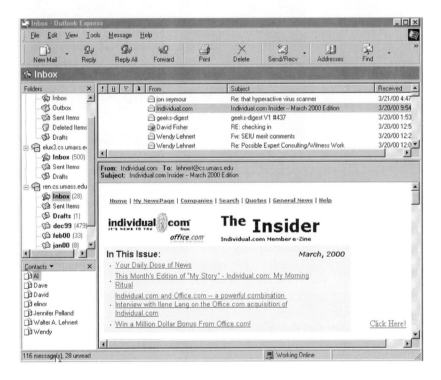

Of course, most people don't want to have to author Web pages in order to send a simple e-mail message to a friend. Sometimes, all you need is plain ASCII text. However, advertisers were quick to jump on the idea of HTML-enabled e-mail. This new form of e-mail meant the difference between sending out a black-and-white typed paragraph and sending out a slick color brochure. In addition, Web-based e-mail and free e-mail services on the Web had begun to catch on. If you're using your Web browser to read mail on the Web, why not see some mail that looks like it belongs on the Web? Of course, graphics files are still binary files. However, they can be retrieved from a Web server by using the HTTP protocol, which is a more efficient way to moving a graphics file than e-mail (see Section 4.6).

Users who simply want to send a picture to a friend need not create an HTML file or post the picture on a Web server. They can just send the picture as a MIME attachment and trust the receiving mailer to handle the attachment appropriately. Most Web-based mail accounts (see Section 3.8) automatically display graphical attachments in a Web page display, as one would expect an HTML-enabled mail client to do (see Figure 3.8).

Figure 3.8:
A Web-Based Mail Client Automatically Displaying a Graphical MIME Attachment

Use of HTML-enabled mailers does entail some risk. Some mailers run executable scripts in order to render Web pages more effectively. This enables a new breed of e-mail virus based on malicious scripts embedded in e-mail messages. The BubbleBoy virus, which surfaced in 1999, was the first scripting virus. It attacked Outlook and Outlook Express users and was more theoretical than real. BubbleBoy nonetheless demonstrated that the new breed of mailer could be tricked into running malicious code even when it was reading only a plain text message body. Microsoft solved the BubbleBoy problem by releasing a software patch for that particular type of attack. However, many users remain concerned about the possibility of new scripting viruses.

E-mail remains the most widely used application on the net, surpassing even Web browsers in the size of its user population. Now that e-mail is a commercial concern, the widest possible population must be able to use it as easily as possible. The MIME protocol and HTML-enabled mailers were designed to enhance the e-mail experience without complicating it.

Can I Protect Myself from Malicious E-Mail Scripts?

If you use Outlook or Outlook Express and you are worried about scripting viruses, you can turn off the **Windows Scripting Host option** and you will be safe. It is also a good idea to install any security patches released by the software manufacturers of your Internet applications. Most security breaches could be avoided if everyone kept their software up-to-date in order to prevent known problems. You can visit the **Microsoft Download Center** to find all the available security patches for Microsoft products. Always go back to the original manufacturer's site for any software upgrades, updates, or patches.

3.4 E-MAIL NETIQUETTE AND NETSPEAK

Practicing good e-mail etiquette, or **Netiquette,** is all about respect. Good Netiquette shows respect for people whom you don't know and might never get to know all that well despite long-standing, online conversations. It is especially important because the Internet encourages interactive communication between strangers on such a grand scale. People have never experienced such scale in other public forums, in which the reality of physical distance limits their reach and binds them to familiar communities.

Whenever you send e-mail, remember the following Netiquette guidelines.

- Keep your messages short and to the point.
- Watch your grammar and spelling.
- Be careful with humor; avoid sarcasm.
- Use uppercase words sparingly. UPPERCASE TEXT YELLS AT THE RECIPIENT.
- Never leave the Subject: field blank.
- Include your name and e-mail address in the message body (for example, in your sig file).

If you are new to e-mail, you probably have not experienced its mixed blessings. Some people deal with a hundred or more e-mail messages every day. They are understandably annoyed by any message that wastes their time, especially if the person writing the message doesn't use good Netiquette. Online conversations are not the same as face-to-face or even telephone conversations. When you talk online, no body language cues or vocal intonations are available to help the recipient interpret your message. If you are inexperienced with online dialogs, you might not realize how important and useful all of this "unspoken" communication is. For example, much well-intentioned humor falls flat on the Internet. Or worse, such humor may be completely misinterpreted and end up making someone feel hurt or angry. If you're in the habit of speaking sarcastically, temper that tendency until you have a good feel for how your written words come across to people. What you intend is not always what others perceive.

3.4.1 Emoticons

Some people express themselves by using **emoticons**—combinations of keyboard characters that represent emotions. The most commonly seen emoticon is the **smilee**, shown as :-). A smilee might seem unnecessarily cutesy and perhaps a little annoying :-(if you aren't used to it, but they are useful :-o . A smilee explicitly tells the reader when something is being said in jest or when something shouldn't be taken seriously <grin>.

Messages with smilees are written by people who want to ensure that no one misunderstands :-{ the spirit of their words. I don't think that I've ever seen someone take offense

>:-(at a statement punctuated by a smilee. It's the equivalent of a smile and a wink ;-) or a friendly laugh accompanied by a pat on the back. It works well among people who don't know each other well :-}. In general, emoticons allow people to insert some personality {||:-) into their writing without fear =:-o of being misinterpreted.

3.4.2 Flames, Flaming, and Flame Wars

If you find yourself in an emotional exchange, it's best to cool down before responding. An angry e-mail message is called a **flame**, and people who write them are **flaming**. Flaming is not polite, and if you ever get flamed, you might feel hurt or downright abused. The Internet seems to encourage some people to indulge their pent-up rage by subjecting innocent bystanders to verbal abuse. Two people trading flames are engaged in a **flame war**. This behavior seems to be peculiar to the Internet; it probably wouldn't occur in a face-to-face interaction.

Flames can be contagious. Emotional heat has a way of generating more emotional heat, unless someone is willing to cool off and break the cycle. If a message angers you, wait a while before responding. You might have misinterpreted what was written. A flame war usually isn't worth the elevated blood pressure. Sometimes the best reply is no reply. If you care about good working relationships, you can't be too careful with your online communications. If you're angry or upset about something, deal with it face-to-face. E-mail is not a suitable medium for everything.

3.5   SMTP AND MAIL SERVERS

The *client/server software model* is the foundation for all e-mail service. The mailer that you use to read and send e-mail is an e-mail *client* that depends on a mail *server* each time that you launch it to read mail or send mail. It might depend on two separate servers: one to send outgoing mail and one to read incoming mail. If one host machine is responsible for mail going in both directions, one piece of software will handle the outgoing mail and a different piece will handle the incoming mail. Thus e-mail involves two separate programs, depending on the direction in which the mail is headed.

Mailers are programmed for user convenience so that people can send and receive mail messages using the same software. However, the server side of the picture is always viewed from one direction or the other. When you install and configure a new mailer, you need to know the names of the servers that are responsible for outgoing mail and incoming mail. Figure 3.9 shows the preference settings for Netscape Communicator. Two mail servers are needed to set up e-mail. Your ISP can tell you the required preference settings for a new mailer. This section discusses outgoing mail. Section 3.6 deals with two models for incoming mail.

Mail is sent over the Internet by using the **Simple Mail Transfer Protocol (SMTP)**. SMTP is one of the oldest Internet protocols and is the universal standard for moving mail over the Net. To send e-mail, you need to have access to an SMTP server, the e-mail address of your intended recipient, and a mailer. When you sign up for Internet access, you are given access to an SMTP server, using an account that you can activate with a userid and password. Note that some mailers allow you to access multiple mail servers for incoming mail but only one SMTP server for outgoing mail.

A mailer sending a mail message to a specified address contacts your SMTP server, which passes the DNS address to a DNS name server for verification and translation into an IP address. If an outgoing message bounces back to you with a "host unknown" error message, the DNS name server could not locate the host name in its directory of known DNS addresses. If all goes well with the DNS name server, an IP address is returned for your intended recipient, and the mail message is prepared for transport out over the Net using TCP/IP.

Figure 3.9:
Incoming and
Outgoing Mail
Server Information
Required by the
Mailer

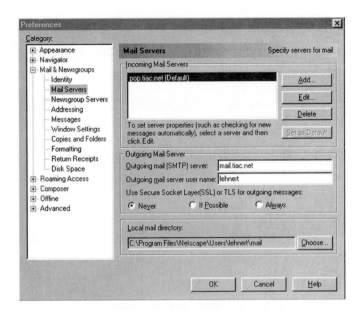

When mail is received at its destination, another mailer catches it and saves it in an inbox for the specified recipient. At that point, SMTP is done with the message. Another server steps in to negotiate the final delivery to the recipient's mail client. This is where things get a bit more complicated.

3.6 ■ HTTP, POP, AND IMAP

Different kinds of mail servers are designed to deliver incoming messages to mail clients. If you are setting up a new mail account, note that not all mailers are compatible with all mail servers. If you are shopping around for a mailer, first check to find out the type of incoming mail service you have, as that will constrain your choice. Currently, the three most popular e-mail protocols (for incoming mail) are

- Hypertext Transfer Protocol (HTTP mail),
- Post Office Protocol 3 (POP mail), and
- Internet Message Access Protocol (IMAP mail).

3.6.1 Hypertext Transfer Protocol

The Hypertext Transfer Protocol (HTTP) might be familiar to you as a Web protocol because it is used to specify URLs for Web browsers. It also can be used as an e-mail protocol by Web sites that provide Web-based e-mail services (see Section 3.8). In this case, the Web browser steps in and acts as the mailer because the mail is being delivered via the Web. If you know that your mail recipient is using an HTTP mail account (for example, a Yahoo! Mail account or a Hotmail account), you can send that recipient a file for a Web page that is viewable just as if it were a Web page (see Figure 3.10). Web-based E-Mail is always HTML-enabled. However, keep in mind an important caveat.

To send a Web page via e-mail, you must reference all of the links on the page (including all links to any image files) by using *absolute URLs* (absolute URLs are described in Section 4.5); otherwise, they will not be operational when your recipient views the page. Most Web pages usually don't reference image files by using absolute URLs. As a result, most Web pages don't travel well via e-mail.

Figure 3.10:
HTML-Enabled
Web-Based E-Mail

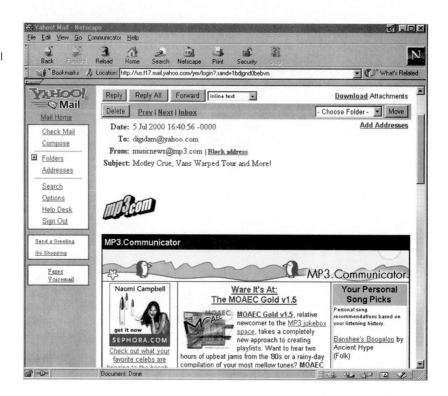

MSIE has a feature that makes sending a Web page to an e-mail address easy (see Figure 3.11). Using this Send Page by E-mail feature works fine, except that the graphics probably won't be visible on the receiving end.

For example, Figure 3.12 is missing the graphical element shown in Figure 3.11 because the Web page was not written with e-mail forwarding in mind (see Section 3.8 for more about forwarding Web pages to e-mail accounts). If viewing the graphics is important, send the URL for the Web page instead of the actual Web page.

Figure 3.11:
MSIE's Send Page
by E-Mail Feature

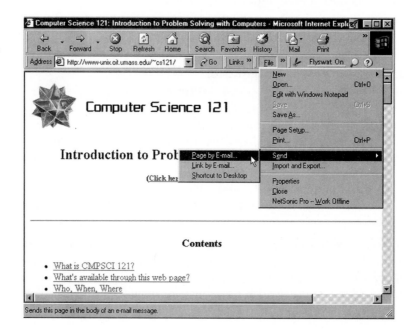

Figure 3.12:
Missing Graphic on
a Web Page Not
Designed for HTTP
Mail

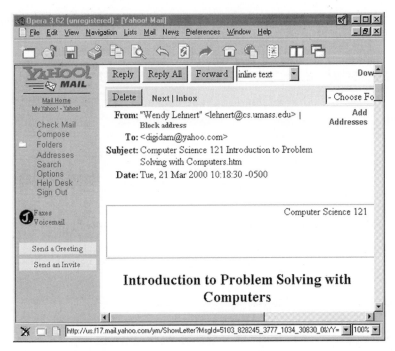

3.6.2 Post Office Protocol 3 and Internet Message Access Protocol

Although Web-based mail has some nice features, people who rely on e-mail for business or other crucial communications opt for either a POP or IMAP mail service. Note however, the choice might not be yours, as most ISPs offer one service or the other but not both (see Figure 3.13).

Figure 3.13:
IMAP, POP, and
SMTP Mail Servers
Move Mail Across
the Internet

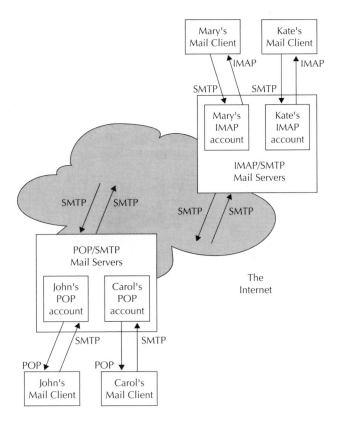

Some mailers can handle both POP and IMAP servers, but you need to know which service you want to use when you install your mailer (see Figure 3.14).

Figure 3.14:
IMAP or POP?
Netscape
Communicator
Needs to Know

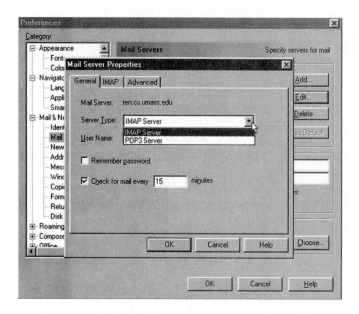

Post Office Protocol 3 If you had an ISP account before 1999, you were probably using a POP mail server. Both Communicator and Internet Explorer came with POP mailers, and Eudora was a popular POP mailer for both Windows-based personal computers and Macs.

POP was designed to support offline mail management, which made great sense when people had to pay for connect time by the hour. Users are in **offline mode** when they work without an active Internet connection. In a POP mail service, the server is basically a drop box in which mail is temporarily stored until the client connects and asks for it. The server then forwards all of the accumulated mail to the client and clears its temporary store to make room for more mail. The user downloads the mail, disconnects from the Net, and deals with the e-mail offline. After reading the messages, the user deletes them or stores them in a local folder. The user also writes messages or replies to messages while offline and sends them all at once the next time that the user connects to the mail server. Thus the most time-consuming work is completed offline, and the Internet connection is reserved for brief mail uploads and downloads. Any mail that is saved is stored on the local host, thereby freeing up the server to accept new mail.

Anyone who has had to access their e-mail from multiple locations understands a major drawback with POP mail. Suppose that you have a computer at work and a computer at home and you want to be able to read your e-mail at both locations. Now suppose that you download 20 messages to the office machine so you can catch up on the day's mail before you go home. However, you never get around to reading the last ten before you leave the office. You'd like to read them at home later, but your home computer cannot access them because they have already been removed from the mail server by your office computer. To get at the mail from your home, you need a connection between your home computer and your office computer so that you can transfer a mail folder from your office machine to your home machine. This is cumbersome, but it can be done. Copying a mail folder enables you to read those messages, but now you have copies of the same mail messages in two places. If you want to save one message and delete the others, you have to figure out where to save the message that you want to keep (on the home machine or the office machine?). You also have to delete all the other messages twice because you have copies of everything in two places now.

This is tedious and time-consuming, not to mention risky because it's easy to make mistakes. (For example, you thought you had saved an important message on one machine, so you deleted it on the other machine, but you were confused about where it was saved, and you deleted your last copy.) POP servers can be instructed to download mail without deleting it, but having multiple copies of every message in multiple computers complicates mail management. Coordinating offline mail in multiple locations is difficult—especially for people who have high volumes of mail and urgent communication requirements. This offline model for e-mail dominated the Internet throughout the 1990s. Increasingly, however, it is being replaced by the Internet Message Access Protocol, a newer, more powerful e-mail service.

Internet Message Access Protocol An alternative to offline mail management is "online" mail management. In **online mode**, the mail client works with the mail server as if it were a program running on the server. The user manipulates mail and mail folders as if they were local, but everything stays on the server. Instead of downloading all the mail messages in a single block, the user can start by downloading just the mail headers. Some mail can be deleted on the basis of the header alone, so it might not be necessary to download all the mail messages to the local host. However, if the user wants to read a message, or search a mail folder for a keyword in the message bodies, then any or all of the mail messages can be downloaded as needed. This is how the IMAP model works. With IMAP, the client and the server work together more interactively in an effort to make mail management more flexible and negotiable.

Depending on how the client is configured, an IMAP mail program can work online, offline, or in a "disconnected" mode. In **disconnected mode**, the client connects to server, creates a local cache of selected messages, and goes offline. The user then has an opportunity to go through the mail, delete some messages, write some replies, and maybe compose some new messages. At any time the client can reconnect with the server to send off new mail or purge a message marked for deletion. When the client and server reconnect, the client automatically resynchronizes its local cache with the server. All mail folders and all mail are left on the IMAP server at all times, making it easier to work with the same mail store from different locations.

IMAP client options are more flexible than POP options because an IMAP client can work in online, offline, or disconnected modes. A POP client only works in offline mode. This can make the preference settings for an IMAP client more complicated, but it is not necessary to master all the settings in order to work with an IMAP server. If you ever need to switch from a POP server to an IMAP server, just remember that the POP server gave you a "store and forward" service. The IMAP server allows you to store messages on the server and manage mail folders on the server through your IMAP client. All of the old familiar mail operations will still be available, but you are working with messages that remain on your mail server until you explicitly (1) mark them for deletion and then (2) purge your deleted messages. You do not need to store mail on a local host, and you do not need to download all of your unread messages in order to read just one. You also don't need to worry about when you are in online mode, offline mode or disconnected mode. Just select the basic mail operations you need to perform and let the client negotiate the client/server communications. You can just concentrate on your mail, and your IMAP client will take care of everything else.

3.7 FILTERING AND ROUTING

People who receive a lot of e-mail find it useful to organize their mail in mail folders. A mail folder is like a file folder for correspondence. Storing mail messages in a system of mail folders makes it easier to find specific messages and to move large blocks of mail into long-term archives (or the trash) when the time comes to thin out the current folders. It takes some thinking and experimentation to come up with a set of folders that will work well: no two people can hope to use the exact same system. If 90% of your mail comes from the same 20 people, you might want to create a folder for each person. If you just want to separate out your personal mail from your business mail and your mailing lists, you could start out with three folders for those three categories. And if your mail is difficult to categorize, you could create a new mail folder once a month in order to store monthly archives chronologically.

Once you settle on a good system of mail folders, you might find it convenient to move mail into certain folders automatically. This can be accomplished with a mail client that supports "filtering" and "routing." E-mail **filtering** is a way of recognizing specific messages based on keywords in their subject headers, from fields, or message bodies. E-mail **routing** is a way of directing mail to a specific folder or subdirectory for later viewing. Filtering and routing are usually combined to help people manage large volumes of e-mail: messages of a certain type can be recognized by filters and then routed to a single folder. Some folders trap important messages that require daily review while others are less urgent and require attention once a week. Many people rely heavily on mail filters and cannot imagine life without them. It is about as close as most of us will ever get to having a personal secretary who faithfully sorts our mail, seven days a week, 24 hours a day.

If your mail client supports mail filters, you will probably find it easy to create any number of filter rules for your own needs. Each filter rule should try to identify mail messages that belong in a particular mail folder, filter them out of the incoming mail stream, and then route them to the appropriate folder. For example, it is usually easy to write a filter rule that routes e-mail from a mailing list to a folder for that mailing list. In Figure 3.15 we see how to create a filter rule for a Yahoo! mail account. This filter rule traps messages from a mailing list newsletter about Unix tips. It recognizes the messages to filter on the basis of the From: field and the Subject: field. We have also told the rule *not* to trap messages that contain the (fictitious) name "Joe WayBeyondMe" just in case I never

Figure 3.15:
Creating Filter Rules for a Yahoo! Mail Account Is Easy

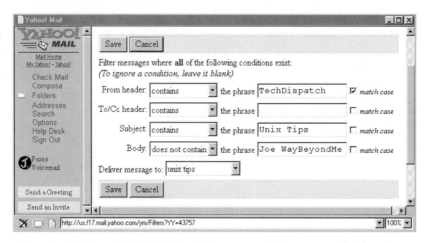

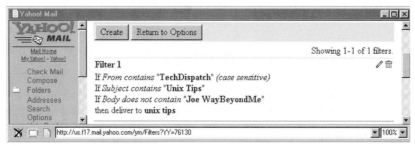

understand anything written by this individual and I've given up trying to read his tips. I could create a separate filter rule to trap anything written by Joe on this mailing list so those messages could be routed to a folder for probable disposal at some later time.

When you see how easy it is to create filter rules, you might be tempted to create filters for everything you can think to trap and route to a folder. It's fine to experiment with lots of filter rules. If one turns out to be a bad idea, you can always delete it. Just watch out for the "out of sight, out of mind" pitfall. When mail is automatically routed to a mail folder, it's very easy to forget about it—totally. So when you first start routing mail into mail folders, remind yourself to take a look at all those folders at least once a week. Then decide if and how you are going to pay attention to those folders. **If anything urgent could be routed into a folder, it's important to check the folder at least once a day.** Also pay attention to how much mail is being routed to each folder: you might have to watch your memory quota. You might also need to make sure that certain messages are *not* being picked up by filters so you will be able to see them as quickly as possible in your inbox.

Automatic mail filters can teach you a lot about how you spend your time and how you might spend your time differently. If you aren't constantly watching over your inbox for new mail, you can better control the time you spend on your mail. Set a time each day to handle work-related mail that's been routed into work folders. Then schedule a block of time once or twice a week for recreational folders. A recreational mailing list might be given one hour twice a week, after more important things have been taken care of.

When used correctly, automatic mail filters can help you stay focused and less distracted by a constant barrage of e-mail. You might even discover that you can drop an entire mailing list that doesn't really interest you that much anymore, now that you aren't seeing the messages all the time. Or you might find out that you just don't want to set aside a dedicated block of time for a specific interest – that interest was actually just an excuse for avoiding work-related messages. If you want to improve your time management, try out some automated mail filters: you might be surprised by what you learn.

3.8 | WEB-BASED MAIL ACCOUNTS

Every major portal on the Web offers free Web-based e-mail in order to maximize repeat visits to the site. These services are usually subsidized by banner ads and they give advertisers easy access to your attention at least once a day or, at worst, maybe once a week. It is usually easy to register for these services—you just have to think of a userid that no one else thought of first, and you may need another e-mail address in order to verify your identity. Some sites require additional personal information, and some don't. Once you've signed up, your account is password protected.

Cookies and Web-Based E-Mail

Some Web-based e-mail services only work when cookies are enabled in your browser. If you have disabled cookies, you might need to manually enable them each time you visit your Web-based mail account. If this becomes annoying, you can download a cookie manager and set it to enable cookies at your mail site, but no where else.

Web-based e-mail has some very nice features. Since you read it with a Web browser, it is always HTML-enabled (see Figure 3.16). It often supports filtering and routing capabilities, and when it does, the process of rule creation tends to be fast and easy. Some of the big portal-related mail services offer an instant messaging client that can monitor your mail account and alert you when a new mail message arrives. Others allow you to consolidate incoming mail from multiple POP accounts so you can read all your POP mail in one place. Different services offer different features so it pays to look around and watch for new features.

Figure 3.16:
Web-Based Mail Can Deliver Mail Messages That Look Like Web Pages

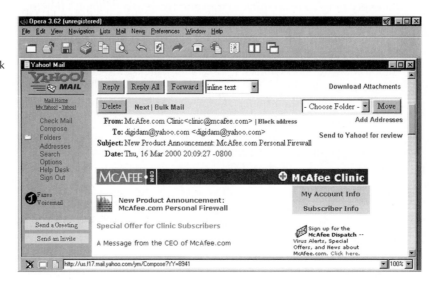

Unfortunately, the quality of service can also vary from service to service, and you might need to shop around for a service you can trust. Some of the most popular mail services struggle to keep up with a rapidly expanding subscriber population. As a result, their servers might be overloaded from time to time. Hotmail has been known to refuse to accept e-mail for hours at a time, when their system load is high. America Online (AOL) is not a free e-mail service, but it often behaves like one. When their systems are overloaded, e-mail can take just as long to be accepted by aol.com as it takes for hotmail.com. In addition, AOL has had mail server failures that have lasted longer than a day, with no e-mail going in or out of aol.com. Many Web-based mail servers are stable, but most experience periodic difficulties (see Figure 3.17). ***If you have to have the most reliable mail service possible, it is best to look for a POP or IMAP mail account instead of an HTTP mail account.***

If you are experienced with e-mail, a Web-based e-mail account should be easy to handle. You might, nevertheless, run into one option that could use a little explanation. Whenever you have an HTML-enabled mail client, you need to think before you for-

Figure 3.17:
HTTP Servers Seem to Experience More Down Time Than Do IMAP or POP Servers

ward an HTML-enhanced mail message to a new recipient. If that recipient reads their mail with Web-based mail client, you can forward the message and it will be rendered faithfully just as it appears in your own inbox. However, some people do not read their e-mail on a Web-based e-mail account. Then the question is whether or not they have an HTML-enabled client. If they have an HTML-enabled client, they will see the same message you do. But, what if your recipient does not have an HTML-enabled client? You can still send them your message as a MIME attachment, but they will have to download it and display it with a Web browser in order to see the same message you do. This might be asking a lot of the person on the receiving end. If they are pressed for time, it might be better to send a plain ASCII text version of the enhanced message (see Figure 3.19). In order to give you control over how you forward HTML-enhanced mail messages, you might see a menu like the one in Figure 3.18.

Figure 3.18:
Forward HTML-
Enhanced E-Mail
with Care

Yahoo! Mail gives us a choice whenever we forward a mail message from our Yahoo! Mail account to another party. If we select the "attachment" option, it will be easy to view the enhanced version of the message with any HTML-enabled mail client. If we select the "inline" option, our recipient will see only a plain text rendering of the original message (see Figure 3.19). This is not a good choice if any multimedia elements are crucial and should not be lost. However, it might be your best choice for users whose mail client cannot handle HTML-enhanced mail messages.

Figure 3.19:
An Inline Version of
the Mail Message in
Figure 3.16

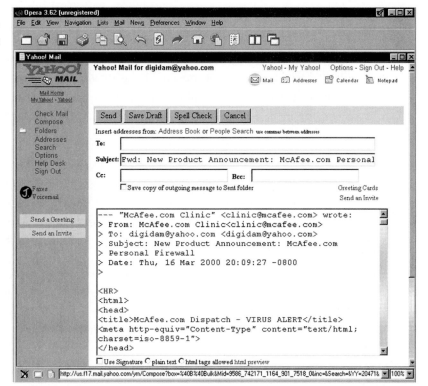

Note that there is a difference between (1) mailing a Web page that you found on the Web, as discussed in Section 3.6, and (2) forwarding an HTML-enhanced mail message that you found in your inbox. In the first case, the Web page probably won't travel well because it was never designed to be moved from its original server. Under those circumstances, it is generally best to send the URL instead of trying to forward the original Web page. However, in the second case, it is safe to assume that any HTML-enhanced mail message was designed for transport across servers: if it looks good in your inbox, it will look good in any inbox. So in this case, you don't have to worry about the document per se, but you still have to think about your intended recipient: are they equipped to view this file without being inconvenienced? Note also that in this case, there is no URL to forward, so forwarding the original message is really your only option.

If you already have a POP or IMAP mail account, you might want to experiment with a few Web-based mail accounts in order to help you segregate certain kinds of e-mail for better mail handling. For example, one Web account might be reserved for commercial transactions. Then all the e-mail receipts and follow-up messages that often follow an online purchase will be found in one place and never get tangled up with other types of e-mail. Another Web account might be reserved for mailing lists and newsletters—any material that does not require immediate attention or fast responses. By reserving entire mail accounts for different types of e-mail, we are really just filtering and routing e-mail on a large scale. However, we might also succeed in segregating a large proportion of the spam that we receive (expect it to show up in the account for commercial transactions if you did not opt out of those "third-party vendor" offers. Just try not to set up too many separate Web accounts. The extra added overhead of having to visit multiple mail accounts might overwhelm any advantage associated with heavily segregated mail. If you push it too hard, excessive mail filtering might generate new problems for you. Only you can know when the cost/benefit ratio of multiple mail accounts has crossed a line.

Things to Remember

- Do not send files larger than 50KB in an e-mail message body.
- POP mail accounts are good for offline mail management.
- IMAP mail accounts support offline, online, and disconnected mail management.
- Free Web-based mail accounts may not be as reliable as POP or IMAP accounts.
- Don't set up a filter to route mail into a mail folder and then forget about it.
- Web-based e-mail accounts may require a cookie-enabled Web browser.

Important Concepts

e-mail client—software that can transfer e-mail messages between a local host and a local e-mail server, as well as display and compose messages on the local host.

e-mail server—software that can send e-mail messages to and receive e-mail messages from other e-mail servers, as well as hold incoming messages for local e-mail clients.

emoticons—a symbolic system for expressing simple emotions in ASCII text.

filtering—a way to recognize specific messages based on keywords in their Subject: fields, From: fields, or message bodies.

flame—an uninhibited display of anger or aggression online.

HTTP—a Web-based e-mail protocol.

IMAP—an e-mail protocol where mail is stored on a mail server.

Netiquette—standard rules of courtesy for online communication.

POP—an e-mail protocol where mail is stored on a local host.

routing—a way to direct mail to a specific folder or subdirectory for later viewing.

SMTP—the original protocol for moving e-mail over the Internet.

Where Can I Learn More?

Everything E-Mail `http://everythingemail.net/`

Harness E-Mail: How It Works `http://www.learnthenet.com/`
   `english/html/20how.htm`

Beginning E-Mail `http://email.tqn.com/internet/email/`
   `msub10.htm`

E-Mail Pet Peeves `http://www.thebee.com/bweb/iinfo43.htm`

Problems and Exercises

1. Name two header fields that are completed for you automatically when you send an e-mail message.

2. What does a signature file contain? What is a good length for a signature file?

3. What is the difference between the Cc: field and the Bcc: field?

4. Why is it a bad idea to compose long Subject: fields?

5. What are emoticons, and why are they useful?

6. Explain the difference between a group reply and a single author reply.

7. When you include the original message in an e-mail reply, should you always include the original message in its entirety? Explain your answer.

8. If you exchange a series of e-mail messages with someone by using the Reply command, what should you remember to do every so often?

9. What is an HTML-enabled mail client?

10. Your best friend has a Hotmail account, and you want her to see a really cool Web site that you just discovered. You use MSIE and know about its send Web page feature. Given the choice of sending your friend the actual Web page that you found or the URL for that Web page, which is better? Explain why.

11. When is it safe to forward an HTML-enhanced mail message to a friend? How does this differ from sending an arbitrary Web page via e-mail? Explain what happens if you use Yahoo's "inline" option for mail forwarding.

12. Explain the main difference between an IMAP mail service and a POP mail service. Which is more powerful? Which was designed to minimize connect time? Which is better for people who need to work with their mail from multiple locations? Which would you want if your hard drive were very full but you still needed to save a lot of mail?

13. What is the MIME protocol used for, and how does it save time?

14. Suppose that you have a Web-based mail account that opens and displays graphical file attachments automatically. Do you need to worry about macro viruses on this account? Explain your answer.

15. Is an HTTP mail account more like a POP mail account or an IMAP mail account? Think about where the mail messages are stored, and then explain your answer.

16. **[Find It Online]** Visit **Everything E-mail** (`http://everythingemail.net/`) and find definitions for the following Netspeak terms in its e-mail glossary: AFAIK, CMIIW, CUL, IAC, IKWUM, IMHO, OTOH, ROTFL, and TIA.

17. **[Find It Online]** Visit Joan Stark's **ASCII Art Gallery** (`http://www.geocities.com/SoHo/7373/`), and find out when typewriter art was first documented. (*Hint*: Look under the History of ASCII Art).

18. **[Hands-on]** Send yourself an e-mail message. Does your mailer default to a full-header display or a short header display? If it defaults to a short header, how many lines are in the header display? Can you find a command that will show you the full header display? How many lines are in the full header? Look at another mail message in your inbox, and check its short and long header displays. Do the short headers for these two messages have the same number of lines? Do the full headers have the same number of lines?

19. **[Hands-on]** Visit **Everything E-mail** (`http://everythingemail.net/`), and send yourself a postcard. What did you have to do to view your postcard? Several postcard services on the Web work like this. Why don't they use e-mail attachments instead?

20. **[Hands-on]** If you subscribe to a mailing list, examine some messages from the list and design a filter rule to trap all incoming mail from your list by using the filter rule options such as the ones in Figure 3.15.

CHAPTER FOUR

Basic Web Page Construction

CHAPTER**GOALS**

- Learn how basic HTML elements are used to create Web pages.

- Understand how to use HTML tags and tag attributes to control a Web page's appearance.

- Learn how to add absolute URLs, relative URLs, and named anchors to your Web pages.

- Find out how to use tables and frames as navigational aids on a Web site.

- Get the answers to all of your questions about copyright law and the Web.

4.1 TAKING CHARGE

Anyone with access to the Internet can post a Web page. Moreover, it doesn't take much expertise to do so. A neophyte can put up a decent Web page in about an hour, using the right resources. More than a few college students are bringing in extra income as freelance Web page designers; some will turn this sideline into a full-time career after graduation. Professional seminars are available for people who want to stay on top of the latest developments in Web design. Beginners, however, can get started right here.

You don't need to major in computer science in order to master Web page design, although the professionals do need to know something about computer programming. Creating sophisticated Web pages is becoming more possible for nontechnical users, thanks to increasingly powerful software tools. This chapter reviews the basics of Web page construction. Chapter 5 covers more-advanced topics, including maintenance issues for large sites, strategies for managing timely information, and ways to add dynamic elements to your Web pages.

To create a Web page, you need only a text editor and a browser. However, you can make the process easier and faster with software designed to expedite Web page development. There are many Web page construction tools available, some designed specifically for beginners, and all are easy to use once you understand the basics. If you want to experiment with an HTML editor or a Web page construction tool, look for the Web Page Construction checklists throughout this chapter and do each exercise using the software of your choice. If you can't figure out how to do something, consult the online documentation for your software.

Many Web page construction tools are designed for people who want to put up a Web page as fast as possible without understanding of the machinery behind the scenes. "*So easy, a child can do it!"* So, why bother with the underlying machinery at all? Why not simply concentrate on how to use a construction tool and be done with it? It's possible to build nice-looking Web pages without any real understanding of what makes a Web page work, but you will have much more control over your Web pages if you know a few basics. Plus, it's not that hard. You do not need to learn a programming language, but you do need to learn a *document mark-up language* (which is similar to but quite a bit easier than any programming language). Then, when you want to make some simple changes to your Web page that your Web page construction software might not make easy, you can duck "behind the curtain" and do it yourself. You can still use specialized software to cut corners and save time, but you won't be limited by that software. When you take charge and learn the basics, you will truly have the best of both worlds.

4.2   WEB PAGE HTML ELEMENTS

Your Web browser is designed to display any ASCII text file that has a filename with the file extension `.htm` or `.html`, even if that file is not formatted for the Web. To experiment, find a file on your hard drive that has a `.txt` file extension (if you're on a Mac, look for a SimpleText file), and make a copy of that file, giving it a new filename that ends with `.htm`. Then, in the File menu of your browser, look for an "Open" or "Open Page" or similar command and select it. The resulting pop-up window will give you different choices, depending on your browser, but all will give you an opportunity to browse your local hard drive for a file (see Figure 4.1).

Learning how to load a local file into your browser is the first step toward becoming a Web page author. You can view any text file of your own creation with a Web browser. The file that you picked for this exercise was probably not written with Web browsing in mind, so it won't look like a page that you would want to post on the Web. However, you've already learned the first lesson of Web page design: Web browsers will display any ASCII text file, even if that file is not formatted for the Web.

View Web Pages Offline during the Design Process

Any ASCII text file with the extension .htm or .html will be recognized as a Web page by any Web browser. You can view your own Web pages locally on your own computer as you develop them. A Web server is not needed during your design phase.

Take a minute to view your local file with your Web browser. You will see that the text has been faithfully preserved, but none of the original formatting remains. Paragraphs and line breaks are gone. If there were any titles or subtitles in the original file, they now run together with the rest of the text. You might also notice that the lines do not break in the same places as previously. This illustrates something very important about Web browsers. Web browsers rework each Web page in an effort to display it in the best way possible for each visitor. Different visitors view the same Web page using different window sizes and screen resolutions depending on the size and power of their computer monitors. Laptops, for example, have smaller screens than desktops. Web browsers must handle all of the resulting display variations.

You can watch your Web browser work for you by resizing its window. If you increase the width of your browser's window, you will see how the browser increases the width of each text line to fill as much of that horizontal space as possible. If you decrease the width of your browser's window, the text lines are shortened accordingly. This is why the original line breaks in your source file are not preserved when you view the file through your Web browser. The Web browser *dynamically reworks* the file in order to fill the display window as best it can. If you want to override the browser, you can control the display in a variety of ways. However, you first need to learn some HTML.

Figure 4.1:
Using Your Browser
to Display Local
Files

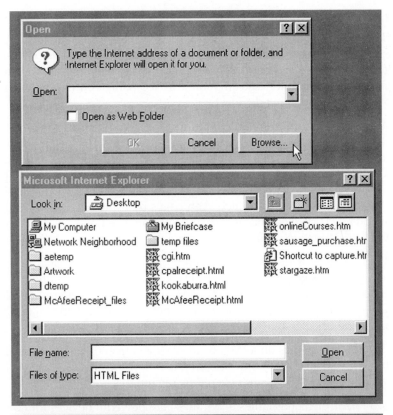

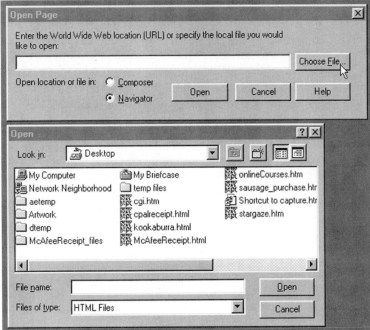

Web Browsers Rework Each Web Page for Each Visitor

The same Web browser will render the same page in different ways for different readers. You can see how the display for a Web page changes when you resize your
browser's window. Web page authors can control how much liberty a Web browser
can take with a Web page, but it is usually not a good idea to take away all of a Web
browser's ability to make dynamic adjustments.

4.2.1 What Is HTML?

Hypertext Markup Language (HTML) is a *mark-up language* that gives Web page authors control over what a Web browser can and can't do when it displays a Web page. It's good to have Web browsers that can dynamically rework Web pages to better suit individual visitors. It's also important to see paragraph breaks as needed, along with other useful formatting devices.

Web page authors communicate formatting commands to Web browsers by inserting HTML *elements* inside of their Web page files. An HTML element can be used to add content to a Web page (as in the case of an image element) or to specify a style for a segment of text (as in the case of a font element). There are many HTML elements, but you don't need to learn them all before you start working on your first Web page. In fact, you can create some very nice Web pages by using only a small number of the more important HTML elements, those used to create line breaks, paragraph breaks, headings, and lists. These are covered in Section 4.3.

Text formatting is just one area of Web page design. The visual impact of a Web page comes from its graphical elements. HTML gives Web page authors a lot of control over the graphical elements of a Web page, including its background color or background pattern; the size, color, and font of the typeface used; and any images that appear on the page. The basic graphical elements of Web page design are covered in Section 4.4.

The addition of links on a Web page gives you hypertext. There are three types of links that visitors can click in order to jump to a new location. The HTML elements associated with hypertext links are covered in Section 4.5.

Two HTML elements, tables and frames, are powerful devices for controlling the layout of a Web page. Web page layouts are challenging because Web page authors must balance what they want and what they need with what the Web browser is prepared to do for individual visitors. If the Web page author is too demanding about the details of the layout, some visitors might not see the best possible layout for their displays. At the same time, there are some demands that nevertheless must be met if a complicated Web page is going to be well-organized and easy to navigate. The use of tables and frames for controlling Web page layouts is discussed in Sections 4.6 and 4.7.

Before discussing the different categories of HTML elements, the chapter presents four basic elements that should always be present on any Web page. You can add these to your experimental page by using a simple text editor in order to move yourself one step closer to being a bona-fide Web page author. Because Web browsers can display any HTML file, even if it contains no HTML elements, no HTML elements are absolutely required. Web browsers are designed to be forgiving about errors in Web page files. However, a well-designed Web page will contain these four elements because they help the Web browser interpret the file more efficiently and effectively.

All Web Pages Should Contain Four Basic HTML Elements

- HTML
- HEAD
- TITLE
- BODY

The next section shows a general Web page template that includes these four elements. All well-designed Web pages should start from this template of four elements.

4.2.2 Editing HTML Files

HTML elements can be added to a text file by using any text editor. If you use Windows, the best editor is Notepad. If you use the Mac, use SimpleText. You can use a more sophisticated editor, such as Word, but there are fewer opportunities for trouble with a simple editor. Even with Notepad, there is one potential snag. When you try to open an existing `.htm` or `.html` file by using Notepad's directory dialog box, you must change the default setting file type from Text Documents to All Files (see Figure 4.2). If you leave the file type on its default value, no HTML files will appear in the directory window.

Figure 4.2:
Adjusting Notepad
to See HTML Files

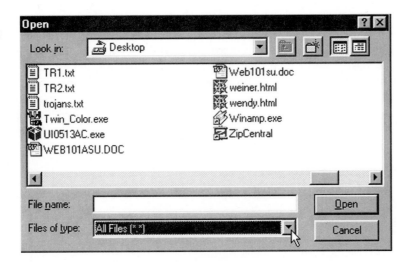

Use a Simple Text Editor for Editing HTML Files

Beginners who are familiar with Word often try to create their first Web page by using Word. Unfortunately, Word can throw you off track when you try to manually edit a simple HTML file. Use Word if you must, but don't say you weren't warned.

First, be careful to save your file by using the Save As command on the File menu. Do not use the Save as HTML command in Word. Save as HTML invokes an *HTML converter*, which is not what you want when you are writing HTML files.

Second, when you use the Save As command, be careful to set the Save option for Text Only with Line Breaks (*.txt). If you do not change the default save option, Word will not save your file as a plain text file. (Word defaults to a binary file format unless you override it.) Your browser will not be able to read the file.

You add an HTML element to a text file by inserting an HTML tag or pair of tags with a text editor. For example, the HTML element requires a pair of tags: `<HTML>` and `</HTML>`. The first tag marks the beginning of the HTML element, and the second marks the end of the element. In general, any HTML tag that starts with a forward slash (/) marks the end of an HTML element. HTML tags tell a Web browser how to render a Web page

HTML tags are used to divide a Web page into segments where different kinds of information belong. Some tag pairs can also be *nested* inside other tag pairs in order to produce a hierarchical structure for each Web page. Figure 4.3 shows the correct structure for all Web pages, along with its text file representation. The indentation of text in this figure is not necessary inside of a Web page file, but it is shown here to emphasize the hierarchical structure of the HTML elements. At the top level we have an HTML element. Inside the HTML element are the HEAD and BODY elements. All Web pages should contain these elements organized in exactly this fashion. The HEAD contains information that is useful behind the scenes, but which is not displayed as part of the Web page display. For example, the TITLE element controls the browser window's title bar. The title bar is not part of the page display per se, so the TITLE element belongs inside the HEAD element. If you do not insert your `<TITLE></TITLE>` tags inside the `<HEAD></HEAD>` tags, the browser will not recognize it and the title bar will not display your title.

Most HTML tags come in pairs, but a few do not (some elements, such as a line break, do not need to be terminated). The most basic HTML elements appear inside of the `BODY` portion of the Web page; this is where the visible elements of the Web page belong. Most Web page authors type their HTML tags in uppercase letters, although Web browsers don't care if the tags are in uppercase or lowercase characters. The uppercase tags stand out better for people viewing the Web page and make it easier to make sense of the Web page. Special HTML editors take this idea a little further by highlighting HTML tags in different colors and adding indentations much like those shown in Figure 4.3.

Figure 4.3:
A General HTML
Template for All
Web Pages

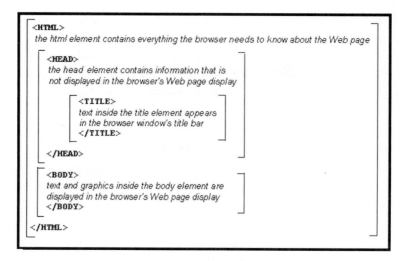

Four-Step Web Page Development Cycle

The Web page development cycle involves four-steps that you repeat until your page looks exactly the way that you want. The cycle begins with an .HTM or .HTML file.

1. Save your file with the Save command.
2. Reload the new file into your Web browser.
3. Review the new Web page to see how it looks.
4. Revise your page as needed using a text editor or an HTML editor.

Be careful to remember Steps 1 and 2, or your browser will not display your last round of revisions.

Some HTML editors can preview your Web page as you edit it so you don't have to switch back and forth between an editor and a browser. This speeds up the development cycle and makes it easier to experiment with different HTML elements while you develop your page. If you expect to do a lot of Web page development, you will come to appreciate any time-saving features that speed up the development process.

Web Page Construction Checklist #1

1. Create a plain text file on your hard drive, and view it with your Web browser.
2. Add the four basic HTML elements to your file, using a simple text editor.
3. Add some text inside of the different elements of the Web page, and view the results with your browser.
4. Resize the browser's window to see how the Web page display is dynamically adjusted.
5. Create a Web page that looks like the one in Figure 4.4 when you resize the window properly. Make sure that your page displays *The Dachshund* on the browser's title bar as shown in Figure 4.4.

4.3 BASIC WEB PAGE FORMATTING

The visible elements of a Web page generally go inside of the BODY of the page. This is where you can control the way that your text looks on a Web page. The next subsections explore the most useful text formatting commands by adding text to the Web page shown in Figure 4.4.

Figure 4.4:
Two Web Browsers
Displaying the
Same Local File
Differently

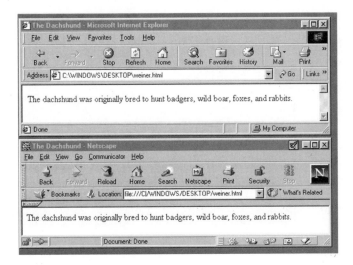

4.3.1 Adding a Heading

As with any written document, it's usually a good idea to tell the reader what the document is all about before launching into a lot of text. This can be done with a title. You've already seen how an HTML element named `TITLE` is used to put identifying information in the title bar for the browser window. However, now you want a title inside of the window, at the top of your Web page display. This can be done with a **heading element** inside of the body of the Web page. Note that heading elements should not be confused with the head element—these are completely different things.

Headings come in six sizes, ranging from `<H1>very large</H1>` to `<H6>very small</H6>` (view these with a browser to see the difference). You can insert a heading anywhere inside of the `BODY` of a Web page, and you can insert as many headings as you want. Large headings are often used for document titles, and smaller headings can be used to mark subsections of long text.

Sometimes, it is useful to fine-tune an HTML element by adding specific *attributes* to the element. For example, you might want to center a heading instead of having it left-justified. An **HTML attribute** is a property of an HTML element, consisting of an attribute name and an attribute value. In fact, many HTML elements use their own, default, attribute values if you don't specify your own. For example, the `H1` element in Figure 4.5 is left-justified because an alignment attribute was not specified inside of the `H1` tag. The default alignment for heading elements is left-justification. However, you can override the default alignment if you prefer something different. Inside the `H1` tag, you can add your own value for the alignment attribute. In Figure 4.6, we added the attribute name ALIGN with the attribute value CENTER to the H1 element, in order to produce a centered heading.

Much of the fine-tuning that goes into a Web page concerns setting attribute values inside of HTML elements. A good HTML reference (you can buy an HTML reference book or find free ones on the Web) will show you all of the attributes and possible attribute values that can be inserted into HTML elements. This book does not attempt to give a comprehensive introduction to all of the attributes (or all of the tags), but it does show you some of the most useful ones.

Figure 4.5:
Adding a Heading
Element

```
<HTML>
<HEAD>
<TITLE> The Dachshund </TITLE>
</HEAD>
<BODY>
<H1>The Dachshund </H1>
The dachshund was originally used to hunt badgers, wild
boar, foxes, and rabbits.
</BODY>
</HTML>
```

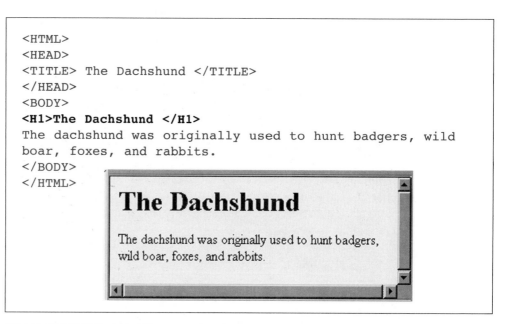

Figure 4.6:
Using the Align
Attribute

```
<HTML>
<HEAD>
<TITLE>The Dachshund</TITLE>
</HEAD>
<BODY>
<H1 ALIGN=CENTER>The Dachshund </H1>
The dachshund was originally used to hunt
badgers, wild boar, foxes, and rabbits.
</BODY>
</HTML>
```

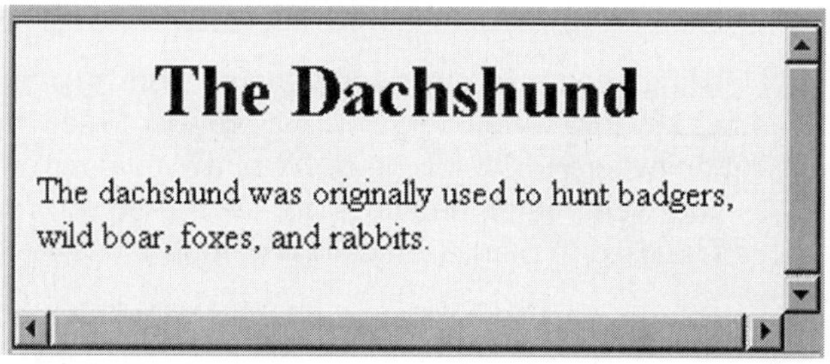

Tag Attributes and Attribute Values

When you add attributes to an HTML tag, make sure that the attribute goes inside of the angle brackets of the leading tag (the first tag if there is a start/stop pair). If an attribute falls outside of the angle brackets, it will not be recognized as an attribute.

Now that you have a title for your Web page, you can add some more text. The HTML paragraph pairs of tags, `<P>` and `</P>`, makes it possible to break up your text into blocks of text set off by blank lines. You won't get an indentation on the first line of the paragraph, but you can at least mark blocks of text when you want to signal topic shifts or break things up a little (see Figure 4.7).

Figure 4.7:
Making Text Easier
to Read by Using
Paragraph Tags

```
<HTML>
<HEAD>
<TITLE> The Dachshund </TITLE>
</HEAD>
<BODY>
<H1 ALIGN=CENTER>The Dachshund </H1>
<P>
The dachshund was originally used to hunt badgers, wild
boar, foxes, and rabbits.
</P><P>
The name "dachshund" means "badger dog" in German, where
these dogs were first bred. Woodcuts and paintings from the
fifteenth century show badgers being hunted by dogs with
short legs, long bodies, and hound-like ears.
</P><P>
To this day, the dachshund's short muscular legs are well
suited for burrowing into tunnels and underground lairs,
although the breed has never been active as a hunting dog
in the United States.As pets, dachshunds are lively, loyal,
and assertive watchdogs.
</P>
</BODY>
</HTML>
```

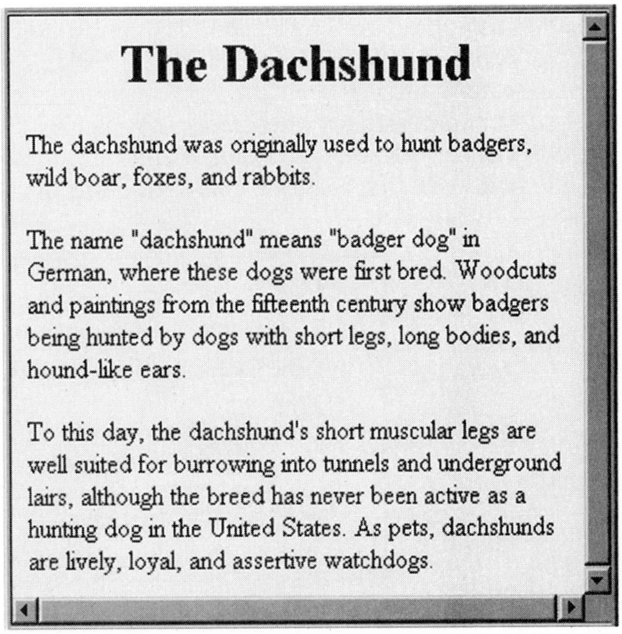

The Dachshund

The dachshund was originally used to hunt badgers, wild boar, foxes, and rabbits.

The name "dachshund" means "badger dog" in German, where these dogs were first bred. Woodcuts and paintings from the fifteenth century show badgers being hunted by dogs with short legs, long bodies, and hound-like ears.

To this day, the dachshund's short muscular legs are well suited for burrowing into tunnels and underground lairs, although the breed has never been active as a hunting dog in the United States. As pets, dachshunds are lively, loyal, and assertive watchdogs.

Most Web page authors like to place each paragraph tag on its own line. This makes the HTML document easier to read and won't change the resulting Web page display. Note that you can close paragraphs with a </P> tag or not—the </P> is optional according to current HTML specifications.

Shooting Blanks

When you put extra whitespace characters or extra blank lines in an HTML file, don't expect to see them on your Web page display. When a Web browser renders a Web page, it normally ignores whitespace (later in the chapter, you'll find out how to make a browser insert whitespace characters and lines). So, feel free to add whitespace or blank lines to make your HTML source file easier to read.

Whereas titles and paragraphs are standard fare for all writers, Web page authors favor lists more than other authors do, and with good reason. Lists of hyperlinks are a common fixture on many Web pages and are useful as navigational devices. For example, a large Web site might start with a list of links that operate as a clickable table of contents. Although you aren't ready to add any links to your Web page, next you'll see how to set up a table of contents by using HTML list elements.

4.3.2 Adding a List

There are two types of lists commonly found on Web pages: the bulleted list (each list item gets a bullet before it) and the enumerated list (the list items are numbered). The tags UL> and </UL> are used to specify an *unordered list*, commonly bulleted lists. The tags <OL> and </OL> are used for an *ordered list*, commonly enumerated (numbered) lists. Figure 4.8 shows how these two types of lists differ.

Each list item inside of a list must be marked with list items tags: <LI> and </LI>. Like the paragraph tag, the list item tag can be used with just the <LI> tag. If you leave out

Figure 4.8:
Two Types of Lists

```
<UL>
<LI>Dachshund Origins</LI>
<LI>Different Kinds of Dachshunds</LI>
<LI>The Dachshund Underground Railroad</LI>
</UL>
<OL>
<LI>Dachshund Origins</LI>
<LI>Different Kinds of Dachshunds</LI>
<LI>The Dachshund Underground Railroad</LI>
</OL>
```

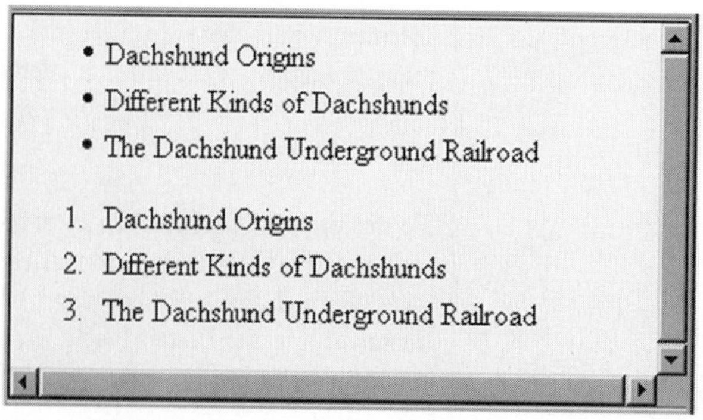

- Dachshund Origins
- Different Kinds of Dachshunds
- The Dachshund Underground Railroad

1. Dachshund Origins
2. Different Kinds of Dachshunds
3. The Dachshund Underground Railroad

all of the corresponding `</LI>` tags, the Web browsers will still format the list properly. Although most of the tags that you've used so far come in pairs, a few are defined only as singletons and do not come in pairs. One very useful one is the line break tag: `<BR>`. If you place this tag at the end of a line of text, your display will insert a line break after that text. The line break works much like a paragraph tag. Unlike the paragraph break, it does not insert a blank line before the next visible page element.

Learning from Examples

You can learn more HTML elements by looking at the HTML files for existing Web pages. If you see something that you like on the Web, you can use your browser's Source command (look for this in the View menu) to view the underlying HTML file.

Copy the tags that you see in the file to duplicate text formatting or other Web page elements in your own Web pages. You can view the HTML version of any Web page in this way. Existing Web pages can be very instructive, and learning from examples is a painless way to master HTML.

4.3.3 Working with Fonts and Type Styles

If you are used to a sophisticated word processing program, you might be surprised to find that your choice of fonts is somewhat problematic in HTML. Font assignment is difficult because different computers will have different fonts available on them and there is no core set of shared fonts that you can count on. Even when the same font is available on two platforms, it might not have the same name. To make matters worse, visitors who have a preference for a specific font can configure their browsers to override the font specifications of a Web page author. Therefore, even when a specific font is available, you can't be sure that it's the font that your Web browser will use.

You can, however, specify a list of font choices in the **FACE** attribute of the **FONT** element. A browser will work through the list from left to right, selecting the first font in the list that is available on the machine on which it wants to display the page. If you use the most common fonts and include a list of the most common fonts found on each platform, then you can exert some control over the fonts seen on your Web pages.

Here are the safest choices for the font face attribute.

- For a sans serif font, choose Arial for Windows, Geneva for Macs, and Helvetica for others:

  `<FONT FACE="Arial, Geneva, Helvetica">`

  This is what Arial/Geneva/Helvetica looks like.

- For a serif font, choose Times New Roman for Windows and Times for Macs:

  `<FONT FACE="Times New Roman, Times">`

  This is what Times New Roman/Times looks like (this is the standard default font for most browsers).

- For a monospaced font, choose Courier New for Windows and Courier for Macs:

  `<FONT FACE="Courier New, Courier">`

  `This is what Courier New/Courier looks like.`

When using fonts, Web page authors must respect the preferences of Web users. Someone with poor vision might have a browser preference set for an easy-to-read font and that preference will override any font attributes specified by the Web page author. It is not wise to design a page that depends on specific type properties, since users can always override those properties if they have their own preferences.

Some useful text effects are nevertheless available to you:

<B>The boldface element darkens any text inside the tag pair. **</B>**

<STRONG> This is like <B> but more general. (good for text-to-voice renderings, etc.) **</STRONG>**

<I> The italic element italicizes any text inside the tag pair. **</I>**

<EM> This is like <I> but more general. (good for text-to-voice renderings, etc.) **</EM>**

<FONT COLOR="red"> This changes the color of the text inside the tag pair. **</FONT>**

<FONT SIZE=+2> This changes the size of the text inside the tag pair. **</FONT>**

Note that any number of these HTML elements can be combined by nesting multiple elements whenever more than one should apply. For example, you can create boldface italics by nesting a pair of <B></B> tags inside a pair of <I></I> tags (or vice-versa—it doesn't matter).

Sometimes, it's useful to add *comments* to your HTML file. Comments are visible to people viewing an HTML source file, but they do not show up as part of the Web page display. Comments can be added to the source file at any point by using the `Comment` tag, `<!--, -->`, as follows:

<!-- Anything inside a Comment tag is ignored by the Web browsers. **-->**

Also, sometimes you'll want the Web browser to recreate some text with the spacing and line breaks exactly the way that you typed them, for example poetry and computer code, when you can't trust a browser to do the right thing with line breaks and indentations. Browsers can be told to preserve text and white space with the `PRE` (preformat) tag pair: <PRE> and </PRE>.

Troubleshooting Your Page

If your Web page won't display properly when viewed through a Web browser, there is probably an HTML error in the file. Here are the most common HTML errors.

- Check all of the HTML elements that require a pair of start/end tags, and verify that both tags are present and don't have any typographical errors.
- Be sure that all of your angle brackets really are angle brackets (not parentheses or some other kind of bracket).
- If you have quotation marks inside an HTML tag, be sure that they are closed off inside of that same tag.

If you create a large file and look at it only when you're done, locating HTML errors might be difficult. Viewing your file periodically as you create it will make it easier to track down errors.

If your Web page is just text, you probably won't have to tinker with it very much. Most of the serious Web page tinkering is associated with graphical elements and layouts for complicated pages that mix text with graphics. That's when things get a bit more challenging (and interesting).

Web Page Construction Checklist #2

1. Explain the difference between a `<P>` tag and a `<BR>` tag.
2. Which is larger, an `<H3>` heading or an `<H2>` heading?
3. Explain the difference between an `<OL>` and a `<UL>` tag. What is the `<LI>` tag used for?
4. Explain how to make a word boldface, italic, and boldface italic.
5. What tag can you use to preserve the whitespace and line breaks in a text block?

4.4   BASIC WEB PAGE GRAPHICS

A Web page without color or graphics is rather dull. The addition of just one or two colored or graphical elements can make a big difference.

4.4.1 Using Color

The easiest way to dress up a page of text is with a background color or pattern. When you tell a Web browser to color the background of a Web page, you have a choice of 16,777,216 colors. If that seems too overwhelming, you can select from any of 216 **Web-safe colors**, colors that can be faithfully reproduced on any computer monitor regardless of OS used.

All Web browsers use a code system for describing colors in **hexadecimal notation**. Each code contains six characters from the 16 possible alphanumeric digits (0123456789 ABCDEF) used to represent numbers in base 16 (hence the name, "hexadecimal"). You can find out which codes to use for various colors on **any number of Web sites** that show color wheels or charts illustrating the 216 Web-safe colors.

If you want to add a background color to a Web page, include a `BGCOLOR` attribute in the `BODY` element, with a code string for the attribute value. For example:

```
<BODY BGCOLOR="#FFFFFF">
```

creates a Web page that has a white background. Always enclose the color code between a pair of double quotation marks, starting the code string with the # character.

Adding a background *pattern* is done very similarly, except that you use a `BACKGROUND` attribute and you must specify a graphics file that holds the background pattern that you want to use.

4.4.2 Working with Image Files

All artwork and photographs found on the Web are stored in binary files. These files are stored on a Web server along with the HTML files that refer to them. There are many ways to obtain graphics that you can use on your Web pages, including clip art on the Web, digital cameras, scanners, and software for artists (or adventurous amateurs).

File Formats Used for Images Two file formats are used for Web page graphics: the GIF format and the JPEG (JPG) format. The **GIF (Graphics Interchange Format)** format is best for line art, cartoons, and simple images. The **JPEG (Joint Photographic Experts Group)** format is better for photographs and artwork that include many colors or special effects. Figure 4.9 shows a GIF image acquired from a book via a scanner. Be careful with images from books, magazines, and newspapers—they are usually subject to copyright restrictions (see Section 4.10). This file is named `woodcut2.gif`, and its size is 38K.

Figure 4.9:
A 38K GIF Image
Acquired from a
Scanner

THE BADGER-DOG AT WORK.

The scanner originally created a TIFF (Tagged Image File Format) file (another graphics format) that was 100K. Then a software tool was used to convert the TIFF file into a GIF file. The GIF image looks as good as the TIFF image, but it is considerably smaller. Keeping graphics files small is important when you are putting them on the Web. This is because smaller files mean faster Web page downloading. As a rule of thumb, try to use image files that are no larger than 40K. The GIF format is very good for the Web because it can significantly reduce the size of an image file without compromising the quality of the image.

The JPEG file format is better suited for high-resolution photographs and sophisticated artwork that contains many colors (see Figure 4.10). Software tools that convert graphics into the JPEG format typically allow users to control the amount of compression applied to the image. In this way, the user can control the trade-off between file size and image quality. Some images can be greatly compressed without visible detriment, but eventually a large amount of compression causes the quality of the image to degrade. Some amount of degradation might be worth an additional reduction in file size, but eventually the image will become unacceptable.

When large images cannot be reduced effectively via compression techniques, Web page authors have other tricks that they can use. For now, let's look at the HTML element that allows you to add images to Web pages.

Adding an Image The `<IMG>` tag is used to place image files onto a Web page. An `SRC` (source) attribute inside of `IMG` is used to specify the file that contains the image. Suppose that you have a file named `dachsie.jpg`. You can add it to a Web page by using the tag `<IMG SRC="dachsie.jpg">`.

Image tags belong in the Web page `BODY`, and the placement of the tag within the HTML file determines where it appears on the Web page.

The `IMG` tag creates an *inline image* on the Web page. Understanding inline images will help you understand how the image will appear on the page display. An **inline image** is an image that is treated like a single, alphanumeric character like that created when you type keys on a keyboard. If you place an `IMG` tag between two sentences, it will be inserted as if it were another typed character. The main difference is its size. That is, the image that you insert is usually larger than the characters in your Web page display. This forces the Web browser to rework the text placement near the image. Figure 4.11 shows what happens when an inline image is placed in the middle of a paragraph.

Figure 4.10:
A 107K Photograph
in the JPEG Format

Figure 4.11:
An Inline Graphic

The dachshund was originally used to hunt badgers, wild boar, foxes, and rabbits.

```
<IMG SRC="Donutprofile3.gif"
ALT="a dachshund head">
```

The name "dachshund" means "badger dog" in German, where these dogs were first bred. Woodcuts and paintings from the fifteenth century show badgers being hunted by dogs with short legs, long bodies, and hound-like ears.

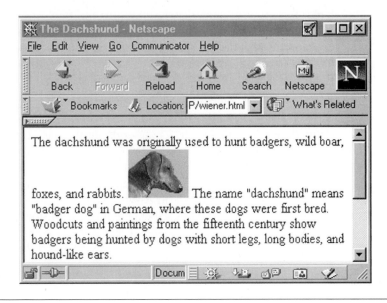

IMG Tags and the ALT Attribute

Some people use a browser named Lynx that does not display graphical elements. **Lynx** is an older text-based browser that is still used in environments in which bandwidth is at a premium or other network limitations apply. If you usually incorporate many visual elements on your Web pages, you should also consider how your page will look in Lynx. Some larger commercial sites support an alternative set of Web pages for Lynx users. (You might have seen a mysterious link on a commercial site that says simply "text only"—that's the welcome mat for Lynx users.)

You might not want to go that far, but you should get into the habit of adding ALT attributes to all of your IMG tags. The **ALT attribute** allows you to specify a line of text that will be displayed to the Lynx user in place of the image. This at least gives the users some idea of what they are missing.

To see how your Web page looks under Lynx, go into your browser's preference (or option) settings and *turn off* all of the graphics. Then, when you view your page, you'll have an idea of how it will appear to users of Lynx. Also, be aware that the ALT attribute is not just for Lynx users. Visually impaired users can now use text-to-voice readers to render Web pages. They depend on ALT attribute values, instead of graphics, to convey important content.

The Web browser needs to make room for the oversized inline graphic, so it increases the vertical space set aside for the text line that contains the graphic. This is a reasonable interpretation of the HTML file, given no additional directives, but it is probably not the best way to combine text and graphics.

Aligning Images A more attractive combination of text and graphics can be obtained by alternating left-justified and right-justified images, with text flowing down and alongside the images. This is done by using the ALIGN attribute in the IMG tag (see Figure 4.12).

When you include an ALIGN attribute in the <IMG> tag, any text near that image will automatically flow around the image, which is almost always what you want it to do. You can also control the vertical alignment of an image relative to its text baseline by using the ALIGN values BOTTOM, TOP, and MIDDLE.

Additional control over text behavior around an image can be achieved by inserting a CLEAR attribute inside of the <BR> tag. When a <BR> tag with CLEAR=LEFT is encountered, the browser immediately interrupts the flow of text and resumes it on the next available line that has no image set against the left margin. When CLEAR=RIGHT is used, text is resumed on the next available line that has no image set against the right margin. To drop the text to the next available line with no images on either margin, use CLEAR=CENTER.

Two other important IMG attributes are HEIGHT and WIDTH. Each image has vertical and horizontal dimensions that should be specified in the IMG tag. If you tell the browser the dimensions to expect, it can work out the page layout and print the text without having to wait for each image to download. If you don't include these dimensions, the page will still display properly, but it will take longer to display. This is because the browser will have to wait for each image to download in order to find out how much space should be set aside for it. A Web page that can display its text while it waits for the images is easier on users, especially those with slow Internet connections.

Figure 4.12:
Using the Align
Attribute to Make
Text Flow around
Images

```
<IMG SRC="Donutprofile3.gif"
  HEIGHT=54 WIDTH=70
  ALIGN=LEFT>
```

The dachshund was originally used to hunt badgers, wild
boar, foxes, and rabbits.

```
<IMG SRC="woodcut2.gif"
  HEIGHT=232 WIDTH=219
  ALIGN=RIGHT>
```

The name "dachshund" means "badger dog" in German, where
these dogs were first bred. Woodcuts and paintings from
the fifteenth century show badgers being hunted by dogs
with short legs, long bodies, and hound-like ears. To
this day, the dachshund's short muscular legs are well
suited for burrowing into tunnels and underground lairs,
although the breed has never been active as a hunting dog
in the United States. As pets, dachshunds are lively,
loyal, and assertive watchdogs.

Image Files and HTML Files

When you develop your Web page locally, keep your image files in the same directory as the HTML files that refer to them. All browsers look for `SRC` attribute files in a location that is *relative to* the HTML file being rendered. If both files are in the same directory, it is enough to specify the name of the image file. However, if you are comfortable working with directory paths, you can use different directories, as long as you specify the correct directory path in the `SRC` attribute. If you are not familiar with directory path notations, don't worry about it. Simply keep all of your files in the same directory.

Scaling Images   Sometimes, an image is not the right size for your Web page. It might be too big, or perhaps you don't think it's big enough. In these cases, you need to **scale** the image, that is, resize it by increasing or decreasing its dimensions on the Web page. It's easy to adjust the amount of space allocated for an image by changing its `HEIGHT` and `WIDTH` attributes. If you want a larger image, increase the attributes' values. If you want a smaller image, decrease them. The woodcut image shown in Figure 4.9 was scaled from its original dimensions, 927 × 876, to a smaller size, 232 × 219, by dividing the original height and width by 4.

When you resize an image, be careful to preserve the original scale (the height:width ratio) so that the resized image is not distorted. Also, keep in mind that shrinking an image by scaling it *does not* reduce its memory or bandwidth requirements. To reduce download times, you must *compress* the image.

Finding an Image's Dimensions

If you have an image file, but you have no idea what its dimensions are, open it up using your Web browser. You will either see the height and width in the title bar of the browser window or be able to see both by viewing Page Info (look under the View menu). Let your browser tell you what you need to know.

Transparent GIFs   There are many tools and special effects that you can use to make your graphics more striking. Many of them do not require artistic talent. One that every Web author should know about is the effect achieved by transparent GIF images. A **transparent GIF** looks as if it was drawn directly on your Web page (see Figure 4.13). To create a transparent GIF, you designate some portion of the image as the background of the image. Then, whenever that image is placed on a Web page, the image's background region behaves as if it were transparent, inheriting the background color (or pattern) of the Web page beneath it.

Figure 4.13:
A Transparent GIF

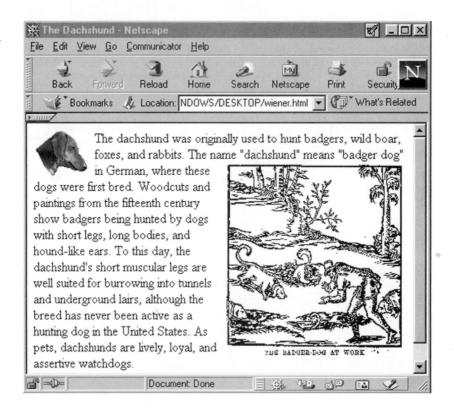

Transparent GIFs work well on images that have clearly defined backgrounds. Line art and cartoons work well. A photograph can be turned into a transparent GIF after some digital tinkering with the right graphics tools. The trick is to make the background of the image one solid color so that it will be obvious which pixels should be replaced with the background color (see Figure 4.14).

Figure 4.14:
Transforming a
Photograph into a
Transparent GIF

There are many good image editing tools available to help you doctor your images . If you want to turn a photograph into a transparent GIF, you will need to edit the background of the photograph in order to make it one uniform color (even if a photograph appears to have a uniform background color, there are almost always a few different colors dispersed throughout that region— you can see them at the pixel level when viewed with an image editor). Pick a color not found elsewhere in the picture. If the background color occurs in places other than the background, those pixels will be replaced by the Web page's background as well. Once the image has been prepared, you can convert it to a transparent GIF. Figure 4.15 shows a Web page service that will help you to convert plain GIF files into transparent GIF files, as long as you can upload the image that you want to convert onto a public Web server (see Section 4.9).

Figure 4.15:
Creating a
Transparent GIF on
the Web

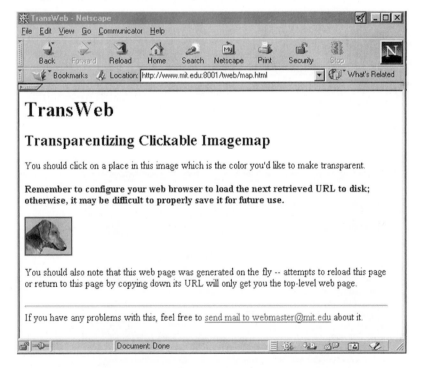

Once you have a transparent GIF, you can experiment with various background colors to find one that works well with the image.

Transparent GIFs are often used for buttons and navigational icons as well as larger pieces of artwork. A few small transparent GIFs can dress up a Web site without overpowering it. Keep them small (in terms of bytes) so that they don't slow down your Web page's downloading. Transparent GIFs can also be used in various ways to create special effects and color-coordinated page layouts.

Images for Web Page Backgrounds Before leaving the topic of images, let's return to the question of how to add a background pattern to your Web page. The mechanics are simple. You need only add a BACKGROUND attribute to your BODY tag and specify the name of a graphics file, just as you do for SRC attribute inside of IMG tags. The browser that is displaying your page will place the background file in the upper left-hand corner of the Web. It will repeat the background display behind your other Web page elements in a tiling pattern from left to right and from top to bottom the number of times needed to fill the display window (see Figure 4.16).

Some files work better as tiles than others for patterned backgrounds. Experiment with backgrounds of your own design. Keep the files small (byte-wise) so that you don't slow down your page's downloading. If you cannot resist using a large file for your back-

Figure 4.16:
Web Page Tiled
Pattern Background

```
<BODY BACKGROUND="bk.jpg">

<H1 ALIGN=CENTER>The Dachshund</H1>

<B><FONT SIZE=+1>

The name "dachshund" means "badger dog" in German, where
these dogs were first bred. Woodcuts and paintings from
the fifteenth century show badgers being hunted by dogs
with short legs, long bodies, and hound-like ears.

<P>

To this day, the dachshund's short muscular legs are well
suited for burrowing into tunnels and underground lairs,
although the breed has never been active as a hunting dog
in the United States. As pets, dachshunds are lively,
loyal, and assertive watchdogs.

</FONT></B>

</BODY>
```

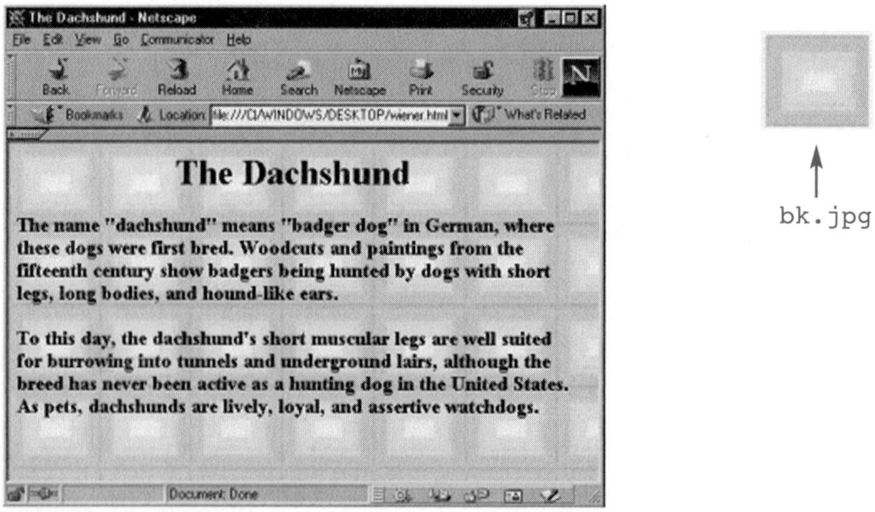

bk.jpg

ground pattern, you can add both a `BGCOLOR` attribute and a `BACKGROUND` attribute to your `BODY` element. The background color will appear first while your background file is downloading. This will give a finished-looking page for visitors to view while the background is loading.

A common design mistake that many beginners make is to go overboard with background patterns. Don't use a background pattern that distracts from the content of the page or that makes it difficult to read the text on a page. Background patterns should be subtle and, well, in the background.

Large bold headings can stand out against background patterns, but you might need to beef up any regular text that is on top of the background. Boldface fonts and oversized fonts are often needed to keep text readable against a background pattern. Also, check your color combinations so that the text contrasts well against the background. Dark text on a dark background pattern will drive away visitors.

Restraint, Restraint, Restraint

If you are new to computer graphics and are playing around with image editors and paint programs for the first time, it is tempting to pack too many visual elements onto your Web pages. It's fun to play with all of the new tools, and you naturally want to show off your new toys. The result is often a confusing hodgepodge of too many things that don't work well together. Here are some tips to follow for good Web page design.

- Design your Web page with restraint. Don't allow images, backgrounds, and special effects to fight each other.
- If you want to show off many graphics, spread your goodies over many pages. Pick one graphical theme for each page and stick to it.
- If you have a background pattern, avoid putting images on top of that background.
- If you want to include many pictures on your page, use a solid color for your background and forgo a background pattern.

Print pages look jumbled if they contain too many different fonts. Similarly, Web pages look confused if their visual elements are not carefully coordinated.

One of the better ways to add a background to a Web page is to run a border down the left side of the page that does not repeat anywhere else on the page. The spiral notebook effect in Figure 4.17 is the work of a background pattern that is 999 pixels wide and 18 pixels high. The pattern was tiled as for any Web page background. However, the image is quite wide, so you need a very large monitor to see it repeat near the right-hand side of a page display. As long as the background is displayed within a normal-sized display window, you'll see only the tiles repeating along the vertical dimension, which produces the spiral binding pattern.

Much of the fun associated with Web page design happens behind the scenes with software designed to help you produce digital images that have cool effects. Photographs can be retouched to remove imperfections, and text can be twisted and tweaked ad infinitum. In addition, massive libraries of clip art are available on the Web (at no cost!) if you absolutely must have, for example, a penguin dancing on a soccer ball. In fact, the Web offers all sorts of resource and tool archives for Web page designers that go far beyond the realm of clip art.

Figure 4.17:
A Wide Background Pattern That Results in a Border for a Web Page

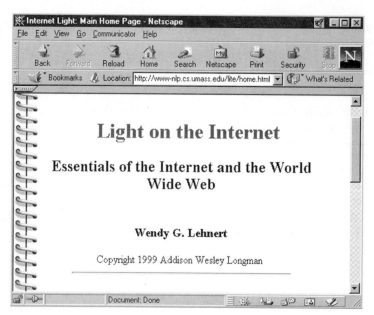

Web Page Construction Checklist #3

1. Explain how to change the background color of a Web page.
2. When should you use the JPEG file format? The GIF format?
3. What HTML element is used to insert inline graphics on a Web page?
4. How does a transparent GIF image differ from a nontransparent GIF?
5. What HTML tag and tag attribute are used to set a Web page background pattern?

4.5 THREE TYPES OF HYPERLINKS

Using only a few formatting commands, you can create a simple Web page of text. It won't be hypertext, however, until you add some hyperlinks. There are three types of HTML links (URLs), each used for a different type of situation:

- **Absolute URL**: Connects two Web servers.
- **Relative URL**: Connects one page to another page in the same Web site.
- **Named anchor**: Connects two locations on the same Web page.

If you create a Web site of any complexity, you will need all three types of links. They are not difficult to create, so there is no reason to be stingy with them. All have two components:

- Link label (the visible link on a Web page—the label can be a piece of text or an image)
- Link destination (the target destination)

Once you understand these two components, you'll be able to add any links that you need to your Web pages.

4.5.1 Absolute URLs

Suppose that you want to add a link to a page that is written by a different author and located on a different Web server. This is an **absolute URL**. It requires not only the URL of the original page but also that of the other page. To set up an absolute URL, you mark a label that will operate as the link on your Web page. The label could be a segment of text embedded in a paragraph, an item in a bulleted list, or, if you want to create a clickable image, an **IMG** element.

For example, suppose that you are creating a Web page about tree houses and you want to link to a page that contains tree house construction plans that has the following URL:

```
http://www.treehouse.com/construct/plans.html
```

This URL is the destination for the link.

A link is created by using a pair of *anchor tags (A-tag)*, **<A>** and **</A>**. The link label goes between these two tags (see Figure 4.18). This is one HTML tag pair whose closing tag (**</A>**) you don't want to forget. If you omit it, your link label will include any text and images that follow the **<A>** tag until the next **</A>** tag: if there is no **</A>** tag, the link label will extend throughout the remainder of your Web page. The destination for your link is added to the A-tag as the value of a *hypertext reference* (**HREF**) attribute inside of the A-tag.

```
<HTML>

<HEAD>

<TITLE> How to Build a Tree House </TITLE>

</HEAD>

<BODY>

<H1 ALIGN=CENTER> How to Build a Tree House </H1>

<P>

If you want to build a tree house,you need a tree, some good
lumber, and a few tools.

A <A HREF="http://www.treehouse.com/construct/plans.html">
construction plan</A> is also a good idea, but some people
think they can wing it.

<P> Make sure the tree is large enough to support the extra
weight. Sometimes a stand of two or three trees works nicely.
If you distribute the weight over two or three trees, smaller
trees can be considered.

</BODY>

</HTML>
```

The text label associated with the new hyperlink will appear on your pages as boldfaced or underscored or colored, depending on the Web browser that displays the page. Figure 4.18 shows the result.

Figure 4.18:
A Web Page with
an Absolute URL

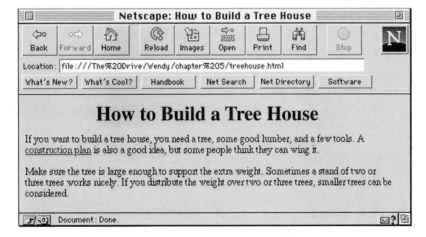

That's all there is to it. If the URL is current, and you insert it into your HTML file without typos, it should be operational. ***Always check each link that you add to a Web page to be sure that it works.*** Visitors get frustrated by nonworking links, so keep your Web page in good operating condition. To maintain your Web page properly, periodically check it to verify that all links still work. It is not enough to know that a link was working when you created it. A link that works today might not work tomorrow, if the page's author renames some files or directories. Ongoing maintenance is needed to ensure an operational Web page next week, next month, and next year. This is one of the hidden costs associated with posting pages on the Web. It's fun to create new Web pages, but most people find that maintaining them is tedious.

4.5.2 Relative URLs

When you have multiple Web pages in the same directory on your Web server, you can insert links to your own pages without specifying the full URL (although the full URL will also work). You instead can use a shortcut address that consists of only the file's name and its location *relative to the current directory*. This is a **relative URL**.

The simplest relative URL connects two pages that are in the same subdirectory. Here's what an example A-tag would look like:

```
<A HREF="booklist.html"> .... </A>
```

Relative URLs work only when the destination is on the same Web server as the page that contains the link. If you see a relative URL on someone else's Web page, you cannot simply copy that link and expect it to work on your Web page. You must convert the relative URL to an absolute URL in order to make it operational on your own Web page.

If your Web pages are stored in a different directory, you will to need to include a directory path to the filename in the relative URL. If you are familiar with directory paths, you know what to do. If you are not, avoid the added complication of trying to use them by keeping all of your Web pages in the same directory.

Use Relative URLs Whenever You Can

When you create a link to another Web page on your own site, you can use either a relative URL or an absolute URL. It's best to choose relative URLs. Doing this will make your Web pages *portable* if you need to move them from your current Web server to a different Web server. When a Web page is **portable**, you can relocate the page on a new Web server and all of its links will still be operational. People do switch Web servers for various reasons. When you move your Web pages, you want to install them on the new server with a minimal amount of work and adjustment. If your internal links are all absolute URLs, you will have to edit them to replace the old domain name with the new domain name. If the links are all relative URLs, they will work as-is on the new Web server (unless you change your directory structure).

You can't know when you might need to move your Web site to a new server, so plan for an uncertain future and opt for relative URLs whenever possible.

4.5.3 Named Anchors

The third type of hyperlink is a **named anchor**. This link points to another location in the same document. Setting up a named anchor takes a little more work than setting up absolute and relative URLs. This is because you must mark the destination location in the current document so that the Web browsers can find it. This is done with a **NAME** attribute inside of an A-tag.

Here's how it would work if the previous tree house example were longer and contained different sections in which various subtopics were discussed in some detail. Suppose that you want your page to include a bulleted list at the beginning that will be a clickable table of contents. You can do this by making each item on the list a named anchor that points to some other section in the same document. The HTML source code would look like this.

```
<HTML>
<HEAD>
<TITLE> How to Build a Tree House </TITLE>
</HEAD>
<BODY>
<H1 ALIGN=CENTER> How to Build a Tree House </H1>
<P> If you want to build a tree house,
you need:
<P>
<UL>
<LI> <A HREF="#tree">a tree</A><BR>
<LI> <A HREF="#lumber">some good lumber</A><BR>
<LI> <A HREF="#tools">a few tools</A><BR>
</UL>
<P> A construction plan is also a good idea, but some people
think they can wing it.
<H3><A NAME="tree">A Tree</A></H3>
<P> Make sure the tree is large enough to support the extra
weight. Sometimes a stand of two or three trees works nicely.
If you distribute the weight over two or three trees, smaller
trees can be considered.
   .
   .
   .
<H3><A NAME="lumber">Some Good Lumber</A></H3>
   .
   .
   .
<H3><A NAME="tools">A Few Tools</A></H3>
   .
   .
   .
</BODY>
</HTML>
```

Figure 4.19 shows the result.

Figure 4.19:
A Clickable Table of Contents Created by Using Named Anchors

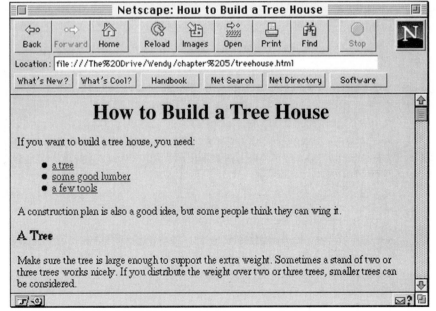

A named anchor uses the same HREF attribute, just like absolute and relative URLs, but instead of specifying a URL or a filename as the attribute, you specify a link name. To help Web browsers understand that this HREF value represents a named anchor, you must insert a pound (#) character at the beginning of the link name (as shown above). Then you need to ensure that each named anchor is anchored to a marked location somewhere in the current document. These anchors are also marked with A-tag pairs, but the anchors contain a NAME attribute instead of an HREF attribute (see Figure 4.19).

Named anchors help visitors move through a page's text in a nonlinear fashion. If you create a clickable table of contents, you should insert additional named anchors at the end of each "chapter" that will take visitors back to the table of contents; these links are often labeled "Back to Top." Good Web page design includes anticipating all of the directions that a visitor might want to go and making getting there as easy as possible.

4.5.4 Testing Your Hyperlinks

After you update your Web page, always check the new version to ensure that it properly displays and that links work. Watch out for the following scenario.

1. You view one of your Web pages and find a problem with one of the links.
2. You replace the faulty link with an updated link and save the modified file.
3. You view the new Web page to check it, but the problem is still there.

To avoid this, be sure that you're viewing the newly updated HTML file. If the Web page is being retrieved from a disk cache, you're seeing the original file instead of the updated one. Before concluding that your update isn't working, click the Reload or Refresh button to see the new file.

Web Page Construction Checklist #4

1. Explain the difference between an absolute URL and a relative URL.
2. Explain why using relative URLs is better than using absolute URLs.
3. Add an absolute URL to a Web page, and then test it.
4. Add a relative URL to a Web page, and then test it (you'll need a second Web page for this).
5. Create a named anchor, and then create a second named anchor that links to the first one.

4.6 PAGE LAYOUTS WITH TABLES

If your Web pages are mostly text and largely utilitarian, you can skip this section. However, if you want your Web pages to grab attention and show off your content in style, you'll want to use HTML's *TABLE element* to control the layout of your graphical elements.

Tables have a lot to offer; for example, you can do the following:

- Change your background colors for different areas of the same page.
- Add margins around your text so that there is more room between the text and the edge of the browser's display window.
- Create an image that has clickable regions (as in a graphical navigation menu).
- Create a two-column text display to make a Web page look more like a newsletter.

- Override a busy background pattern with regions of solid colors in order to make text segments easier to read.
- Add a three-dimensional frame around a picture to give your Web page a look of depth.
- Center an image on a Web page no matter how the browser window is resized.
- Display a table of numbers.

Tables are powerful tools because they can adjust to any browser window and give the Web page author a lot of control over the layout of different visual elements.

Creating Tables the Easy Way

Tables are simple enough to create, in theory. In practice, it's easy to mess them up. A large, complicated table involves a lot of tags and tag attributes. If you are doing all of the HTML manually, check your progress with a browser often so that you can isolate errors sooner rather than later.

To save yourself a lot of time and trouble, use a good HTML editor when you are working with tables. Although not necessary, it makes table creation much easier.

All tables contain *rows and columns*. The tag structure for tables in HTML requires a distinct row element for each row of the table. Within each row are placed distinct column elements for each column. The simplest possible table is a table that has one row and one column. If you have ever studied arrays or matrices in a mathematics class, an HTML table may look to you like an array. The basic idea is the same, but with tables, the rows and columns are not indexed, so you can't refer to them with subscripts. In HTML, each table element contains a collection of nested elements that define the structure of the table (see Figure 4.20).

Figure 4.20:
A Table with One Row and One Column

```
<TABLE>
  <TR>
    <TD>
      <IMG SRC="donut.jpg" ALT="a dachshund">
    </TD>
  </TR>
</TABLE>
```

The table in Figure 4.20 contains one table row, specified by the `<TR>` and `</TR>` tag pair. Within that row is one table data element (sometimes called a *cell*) specified by the `<TD>` and `</TD>` tag pair. The table data element corresponds to one column inside of the row. An image is inserted inside of the table data element. This is a very simple table that contains a single graphic. Although the nesting of table data elements inside of table row elements might seem cumbersome, it does give you a lot of flexibility. In HTML, different rows inside of a table do not have to contain the same number of columns. Examples of this very useful feature are given later in the chapter.

4.6.1 Creating Borders by Using Tables

If you insert the table in Figure 4.20 on a sample Web page, it won't appear to add anything to the image display. You can see the table better if you add a `BORDER` attribute to the `TABLE` tag. Try adding `BORDER=5` ; the result is a JPEG image framed by the containing table, as shown in Figure 4.21.

Figure 4.21:
A Table Border
Creating a Picture
Frame Effect

HTML tables are powerful because you can put anything inside of a table's data element, even another table. Figure 4.22 shows how to use tables to display and emphasize blocks of text. It also shows how a background pattern can run behind multiple tables, thereby giving the page a more interesting look without sacrificing the legibility of the text.

Figure 4.22:
Making Tables
Distinctive by Using
Borders

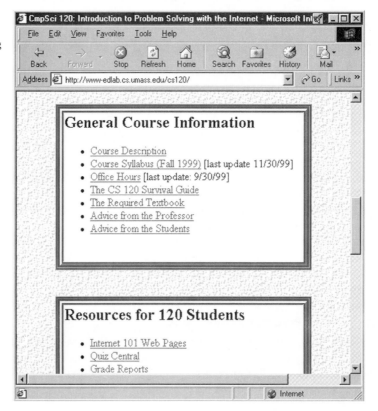

Adding attributes to your tables makes them more powerful. For example, you can control how much of the display window the table should occupy by setting WIDTH and HEIGHT attributes inside of the TABLE tag. You can give these attributes constant values if you want the dimensions to be a fixed number of pixels, or you can specify a percentage of the total width or height of the window. If you use percentage values, the table will dynamically adjust itself whenever the browser window is resized. Figure 4.23 shows the HTML for a table that will always resize itself to fill (almost) all of the available space. This was accomplished by setting the WIDTH and HEIGHT attributes to 100%.

Figure 4.23:
Centering an Image in Any Browser Window

```
<BODY BGCOLOR="#CCCCFF">
<TABLE BORDER=5 WIDTH=100% HEIGHT=100% BGCOLOR="#000000">
  <TR>
    <TD ALIGN=CENTER>
      <IMG SRC="donut.jpg" WIDTH=424 HEIGHT=280 ALT=
      "a dachshund">
    </TD>
  </TR>
</TABLE>
```

Next, a background color (#000000 = black) was assigned to the table by using a BGCOLOR attribute. Finally, the ALIGN attribute was set to the value CENTER inside of the TD tag. The resulting display is shown in Figure 4.24.

A border and a contrasting table background in Figure 4.24 make the table element more visible. If you remove the BORDER and BGCOLOR attributes in the TABLE tag, you will see only the graphic, perfectly centered in the browser's window on a colored background. The image will remain centered even when you resize the window.

Figure 4.24:
Applying a Background to a Table

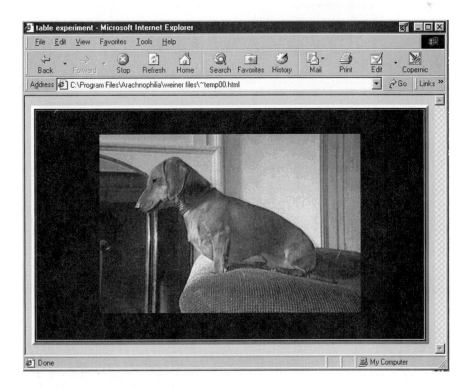

4.6.2 Creating Margins by Using Tables

Suppose that you want to run a border down the left side of your Web page (see Figure 4.17). It's easy enough to create an image file that can be tiled into a border background. However, if you do only that, you might see text running into your border (see Figure 4.25). Borders and text should be separated.

You can keep the visual elements on your page separate from a border by creating a table that has an empty column that runs the entire length of the page (see Figure 4.26).

Figure 4.25:
Borders and Text Running Together

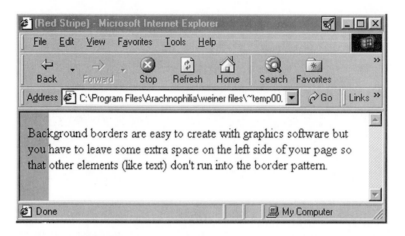

Figure 4.26:
An Empty Table Column Acting as a Margin Setting

```
<BODY BACKGROUND=redbar.gif>
<TABLE HEIGHT=100%>
  <TR>
<!--column #1-->
    <TD WIDTH=10>
      <!--this TD element should be left empty-->
    </TD>
<!--column #2-->
    <TD>
      <!--all other visible elements go inside this TD
          element-->
Background borders are easy to create with graphics
software but you have to leave some extra space on the
left side of your page so that other elements (like text)
don't run into the border pattern.
    </TD>
  </TR>
</TABLE>
```

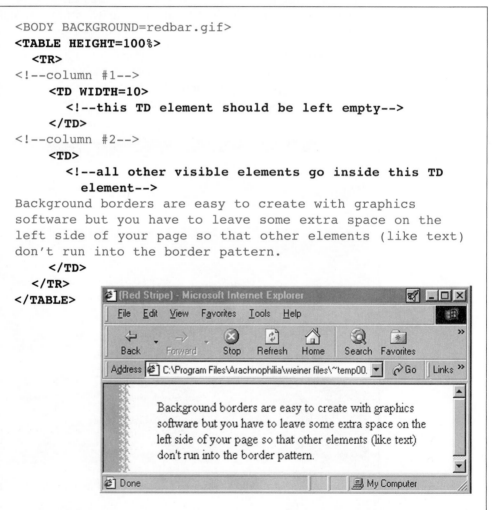

You reserve one column for the border pattern and one for all of the other visual elements of the Web page. In this way, you ensure that the two regions stay separated from each other (see Figure 4.26). If the border is to be a solid bar, you don't need a background graphic. You can simply create a table column with a fixed pixel width and a solid background color.

Some pages work nicely in a newsletter format with two columns of text. You can use a table to achieve this look, but you won't be able to "chain" the text across the columns (that is, text in the left column won't flow into the right column). To do this, create a two-column table and fill the columns with formatted text, as if each column were a separate Web page. Figure 4.27 shows a table that contains one row and two columns. Each column has a `WIDTH` attribute set to 40%. Additional whitespace has been placed between and around the columns by including a `CELLPADDING` attribute inside the `TABLE` tag and setting its value to 20 pixels.

Figure 4.27:
A Two-Column Table with Cell Padding

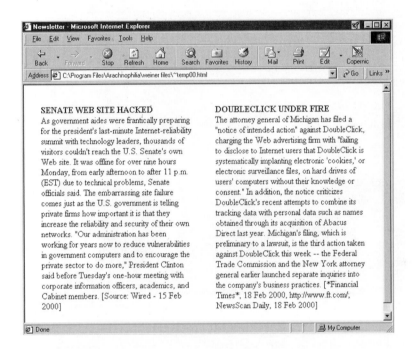

Although tables can be very effective with text, think carefully before you put a lot of text into a multicolumn format. Lynx does not support tables. In Lynx, the text will be visible, but all of the whitespace in each row will be compressed and the remaining text will be left-justified. As a result, a Web page like that shown in Figure 4.27 will be impossible to read. If your Web site is primarily text, keep it accessible to Lynx users. Either avoid tables altogether, or offer an alternative set of pages designed for Lynx.

4.6.3 Organizing Graphical Elements in Tables

As we've seen, tables are a powerful device for Web page layouts. Table cells can contain text, graphics, hyperlinks, and each cell can also have its own background pattern or background color. In this section, we will look at ways to modify the size of table cells so different cells can be different sizes. When a table's displays visual elements cells occupy differently sized regions, the predictable boundaries based on a fixed number of rows and columns are less apparent, and our Web page takes on a more fluid look.

Arranging Images Although tables can be used to break text into segments, they can also be used to format images in a picture gallery. If all of your images are the same size, a uniform table with a fixed number of rows and columns is all that you need. However, if you have images of different sizes you might need a table that has a different number of columns in each row or perhaps a different number of rows in each column. Figure 4.28 shows a layout of two rows, with one TD element in the first row and three TD elements in the second row. To make the TD element in the first row span all three columns, add a COLSPAN attribute to the TD tag and give it a value of 3.

To extend a column across multiple rows, you can use a ROWSPAN attribute to a TD tag. Figure 4.29 shows a table layout with nine rows, nine columns, and COLSPAN and ROWSPAN attributes. Each rectangle is colored with a BGCOLOR attribute. COLSPAN and ROWSPAN are often used together to create Web page layouts.

Figure 4.28:
A Table Layout That Uses the COLSPAN Attribute

Figure 4.29:
A Table Layout That Uses Both COLSPAN and ROWSPAN Attributes

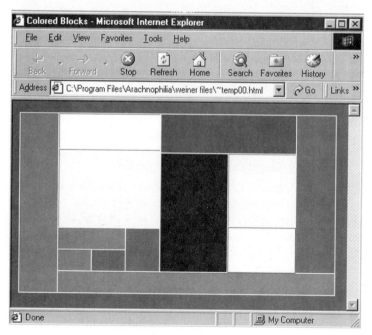

Creating a Navigation Bar Creating a graphical navigation bar or menu is best managed by using some additional software, such as Microsoft Paint (see Figure 4.30). A special-purpose image splitting utility is needed to divide the image into rectangular sections that are then reassembled as a table. The example shown in Figure 4.33 was created by using Paint and a freeware utility called **Splitz**.

Once you've created a graphical image to use as a navigation bar, you input that file into a tool that will divide the image into rectangular subsections that can then be reassembled back into the original image, but with different parts of the image appearing in separate cells of an HTML table. Figure 4.31 shows Splitz at work on the navigation bar created in Figure 4.30. The Splitz user specifies where the vertical and horizontal cuts should be made: In this case, it makes sense to chop up the image along the vertical boundaries separating the menu items.

Once the cuts have been made, Splitz generates separate image files for each subsection of the original image (in this example, five image files) and then creates the HTML code for a table. This code will reconstruct the original image (see Figure 4.32).

Figure 4.30:
Using Paint and Splitz to Create a Navigation Bar

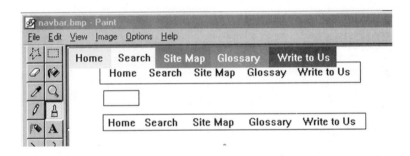

Figure 4.31:
Dividing an Image into Subsections

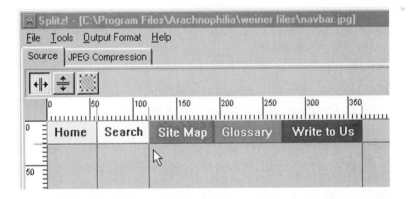

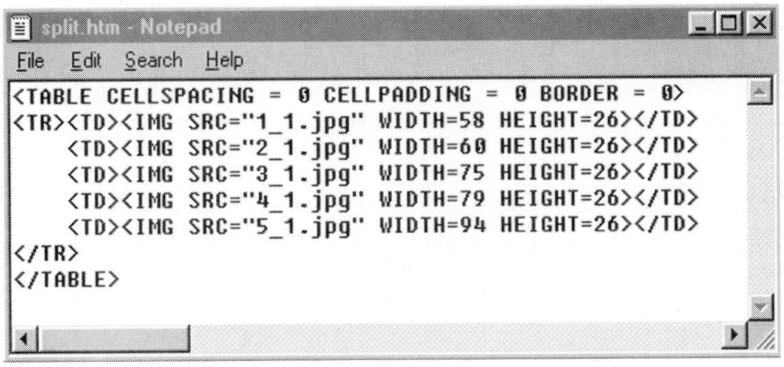

Figure 4.32:
Reassembling the Original Image in an HTML Table

```
<TABLE CELLSPACING = 0 CELLPADDING = 0 BORDER = 0>
<TR><TD><IMG SRC="1_1.jpg" WIDTH=58 HEIGHT=26></TD>
    <TD><IMG SRC="2_1.jpg" WIDTH=60 HEIGHT=26></TD>
    <TD><IMG SRC="3_1.jpg" WIDTH=75 HEIGHT=26></TD>
    <TD><IMG SRC="4_1.jpg" WIDTH=79 HEIGHT=26></TD>
    <TD><IMG SRC="5_1.jpg" WIDTH=94 HEIGHT=26></TD>
</TR>
</TABLE>
```

Although the table in Figure 4.32 looks like the original navigation bar, now that it has been recast as a table, you can associate different links with each table data element. Each of the five images inside of this table can now become an anchor for a link (see Figure 4.33).

One last action removes the borders around the image elements in the navigation bar so that the final navigation bar looks exactly like the original created with Paint. If you place a BORDER attribute with a setting value of 0 inside of each IMG tag in Figure 4.32, the highlighting shown in Figure 4.33 will go away.

Figure 4.33:
The Final
Navigation Bar

Web Page Construction Checklist #5

1. Use a table to add a three-dimensional frame around an image.

2. Create a 3 × 4 table—three rows and four columns—and type the name of a city inside of each table cell.

3. Add background colors to the 3 × 4 table so that each row has its own color.

4. Nest the 3 × 4 table inside of another table so that the grid is always centered after the window is resized.

5. Replace the first column of the 3 × 4 table with a solid vertical bar by using ROWSPAN.

4.7 | NAVIGATION MAPS WITH FRAMES

When you build a large Web site that has many pages, you need to think carefully about navigational features. Visitors who are not familiar with your site will need signs and guideposts. Navigation bars (see Section 4.6.3) and navigation menus are useful for large Web sites, but to provide maximal ease of use to your visitors, they need to appear on each Web page. You'll make life easier on your visitors if you show them *the same* navigational options on each page. In effect, you want one part of each Web page to remain constant across your entire site. You can accomplish this by duplicating the same navigational device (for example, a menu or a map) on each page. However, this is tedious and, more important, a nonoptimal use of bandwidth. A much better solution is to use HTML *frames.*

A frame allows you to partition a Web page into multiple segments so that you can display a different HTML file within each segment. Think of each frame as a small, independent browser window. By using frames, you can set up links that alter the content of one frame without disturbing the contents of the other frames.

You have probably seen frames in action at search engine sites, Web portal sites, and other large commercial sites. Some sites run, at the top of each Web page, a horizontal frame that contains a navigational bar. Other sites run a vertical frame segment along the left side of each Web page for the same purpose. Some sites use both. Windows are resized from the lower right-hand corner, so it makes sense to place navigational tools in the upper left-hand corner where they will always be visible (or at least partially visible) no matter how the browser window is resized.

Frames are not difficult to set up, but you must design frame pages carefully so that they can be viewed without excessive scrolling by the visitor. A vertical frame with a long list of navigational choices might require some scrolling, so visitors will be able to figure out that additional elements are available. However, avoid page displays that require horizontal scrolling (people are more accustomed to layouts that scroll vertically). When you create a frame for a Web page, you can specify a *scrolling frame* or a *nonscrolling frame*. We will see how in the next section.

4.7.1 Creating a Frame

To create a frame, insert a `FRAMESET` tag immediately after the `HEAD` element on your Web page. Whenever you include a `FRAMESET` element inside the HEAD, you do not need a `BODY` element. All of the visible content will be stored in other HTML files referenced by the FRAMESET. A Web page that contains frames does not contain any visible content of its own—it can only display content found in other HTML files. `FRAMESET` divides the page display by using a `COLS` attribute, a `ROWS` attribute, or both. Each attribute takes as its value a set of percentage values separated by commas. For example,

```
<FRAMESET COLS="20%, 80%" ROWS="60%, 40%">
```

divides the Web page into four frames (see Figure 4.34). You can have as many rows and columns as you want, but most layouts require only two rows (for a horizontal navigation bar) or two columns (for a vertical navigation menu). More complicated layouts can be achieved by *nesting* frames.

Figure 4.34:
A Web Page with
Four Frames

Figure 4.35:
A Web Page with a
Scrollable Frame

```
<FRAMESET COLS="70%, 30%">

<FRAME SRC="fig21c.html" SCROLLING="no">

<FRAME SRC="fig21a.html">

</FRAMESET>
```

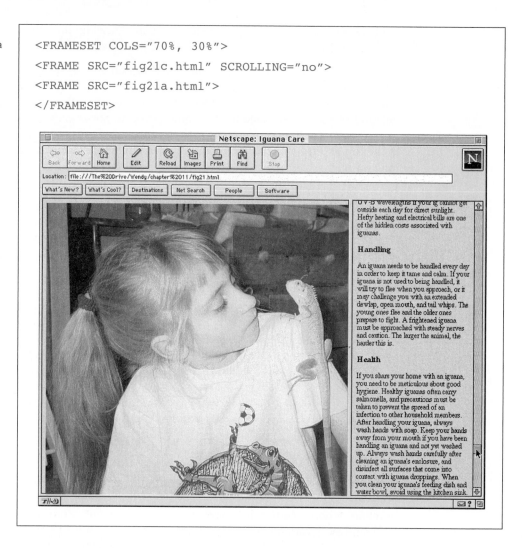

To fill each frame with visible content, use a **FRAME** tag with an **SRC** attribute. If you want the frame to be fixed, set the **SCROLLING** attribute to no. The following construction produces the Web page shown in Figure 4.35.

Some browsers, such as Lynx, don't support frames, and some people don't like frames even if their browsers do support them. Frames make it difficult for other Web page authors to create their own links to your Web pages, so if you want to encourage pointers to your site, think twice about using frames. Sites with a lot of dynamic information that changes every day (for example, a search engine) are better suited for frames than are sites with relatively stable information. It is easier and safer for a Web site author to edit one frame that requires frequent updates than it is to dive into a large complicated Web page in order to update different parts of that page as needed. Frames allow an author to break a Web page display up into separate modules. Then some modules can be updated regularly while others are relatively constant. Modular designs are especially valuable when a large site is maintained by more than one person: different people can concentrate on their own separate modules and not step on each others' toes when modules require updates or revisions.

4.8 A WEB SITE CONSTRUCTION CHECKLIST

Now that you've been exposed to some of the details of HTML, step back and consider the big picture. A good Web page author must try to anticipate the needs and interests of a page's visitors as much as possible. It is easy to forget this when you're first learning HTML and are preoccupied with the practical aspects of Web page construction. Read this section now to familiarize yourself with the big picture issues. Then review it as you gain experience and begin to feel at home with Web page design.

4.8.1 The Three C's of Web Page Design

While developing your Web pages, always remember the three C's of Web page design:

- Quality *content*
- Reader *convenience*
- Artistic *composition*

Most important, be sure that you have quality content. Check your facts, cite sources when appropriate, and produce a credible document. Next, consider potential visitors. Construct your Web pages with their convenience in mind. Make it easy for them to find things, move around, and view the page as you intend it to be viewed. And keep download times to a minimum. Then, and only then, should you concentrate on artistic composition. The look and feel of your Web page will be appreciated only if the first two concerns are adequately met. Beginning Web page authors often are so enamored with the fun of digital graphics that they forget about content and convenience. It's fine to have fun, but be sure that the cosmetics aren't getting more of your attention than the content.

The following sections review some of the important points to keep in mind when designing Web pages.

4.8.2 Avoid Common Mistakes

If you spend much time on the Web, you've probably seen pages that are exemplary, as well as some that are frustrating or disappointing in some way. When you create your own pages, try to avoid the mistakes that others have made while building on the styles and organizational layouts of pages that you admire.

Hypertext should be readable as normal text and subject to all of the usual rules of good writing. In addition, links should be self-explanatory so that visitors can quickly decide which to visit.

Keep the text as concise as possible to minimize scrolling. Sometimes, it is a good idea to limit each topic to a short page that can be viewed in its entirety without any scrolling. A richly linked collection of many short pages loses the linear organization of a traditional text, but it is convenient for someone who is browsing. Your visitors control the content of a hypertext document by choosing to traverse some links but not others. An effective Web page author will create pages that read well no matter which pathways are followed.

Web page authors have less control over their creations than do authors of traditional text because visitors can move through a Web page in many ways. Well-written pages will encourage this and ensure that each pathway through a Web site remains coherent.

4.8.3 Check Pages before Installing Them

All Web pages should be written, viewed, and tested before being installed on a Web server. You can develop your Web pages on any convenient computer platform (for example, a home personal computer). After you've uploaded your pages to a Web server, check them one last time. Don't experiment with Web page development on a public server; keep your Web page experiments to yourself.

If you're serious about designing robust Web pages that will look the way that you want them to, you must install more than one Web browser on the machine on which you develop the pages. Viewing your pages with different browsers will give you a good idea about the features that are industry standards and the features that are browser-specific. If half of the population is using MSIE and you're checking your pages with Navigator only, your pages might look horrible to half of the people who access them.

A Web author's life would be easier if everyone used the same browser. A professional Web page designer checks each page on perhaps half a dozen different browsers to ensure that the page will display properly in each case. The relatively large number of browsers available to Web users creates a lot of work for serious Web page designers. You should, at least, use the two most currently popular browsers (Navigator and MSIE) to check your pages before posting them.

Remember, too, that there will always be a sizable percentage of the Internet population using a text-based browser, so it is also important to check your pages using Lynx on a UNIX platform.

4.8.4 Use Effective Web Page Titles

Keep your Web page titles short but accurate and descriptive. Search engines treat titles with more weight than they do other text elements. By selecting your titles carefully, you can enhance the visibility of your work to Web search engines and ensure that your titles appear prominently in a list of search engine hits. Web page titles also appear in bookmark files when someone saves a bookmark for your page. So, pick a title that will identify it easily in a list of bookmarks.

4.8.5 Keep Download Times Short

Before adding graphics to a Web page, always think about the download times that they involve. Visitors accessing the site through a modem might be downloading your page at a rate of only 1K to 2K per second. When conditions are unfavorable, that rate can drop to as low as 100 Bps. If you're working on an Ethernet or other fast connection to the Internet, be sure to remember all the people who connect with modems over telephone lines. People using telephone lines can't see Web pages as quickly as you can, and slow Web pages don't win friends. Avoid large graphics at the top of your main page; visitors will be forced to wait while that image downloads.

4.8.6 Make Your Pages Portable

For your own convenience, always create links with *portability* in mind. For example, if you're developing pages on a Mac, the Mac, which is case-insensitive, will forgive you for typing a filename in lowercase when you really meant uppercase. However, if you move your Web pages to a UNIX host, where case sensitivity rules, those filenames will generate unknown file errors. Always enter filenames with care, and don't let a platform-specific convenience lull you into a false sense of security. You can save yourself a lot of aggravation by simply avoiding all uppercase characters in your directory names and filenames.

If you create subdirectories of Web pages, plan to use the same directory structure on your Web page server, with the same directory names and filenames. Remember, relative URLs are always better than absolute URLs for portability purposes, so never use an absolute URL unless you're connecting to an external host. For your own pages, use relative URLs and keep your directory structure stable if you're storing Web pages in multiple file directories.

4.8.7 Choose between State-of-the-Art or Maximal Access

If you're determined to learn as much about Web design as you can, you'll inevitably be tempted to use sophisticated graphics, audio, and maybe even video clips. Remember that the most sophisticated Web page displays are also the most computationally intensive. Anyone operating an older computer with limited memory and a slow telephone line is going to give up on a page designed for state-of-the-art machines. If you create computationally expensive pages, don't expect everyone to see them.

4.9   INSTALLING WEB PAGES ON A WEB SERVER

Once your Web pages are ready for public access, you are ready to install them on a Web server. This often causes beginners some difficulties. There are many ways to install (sometimes called *publish*) a Web page on a Web server, but all require some crucial information that is specific to your particular Web server and your personal computer account on that server. This section describes the general steps needed to upload files to a Web server, but we cannot tell you everything you need to know. You will need to check with your local ISP's customer support resources, your school's help desk, your instructor, or your all-knowing roommate in order to fill in the missing details.

To make your pages visible to people, you must install your HTML files on a Web server. Some commercial sites offer free Web space (usually 10MB) where you can post your pages, for example Yahoo's Geocities, Netscape's NetCenter, and Xoom.com. You need only register at the site and be willing to have a commercial banner ad to appear in the browser window each time that someone visits your site. If you pay for your Web server access by subscribing to a commercial ISP, you can publish Web pages without the ads.

To install your pages on a server, you need to upload (copy) your files onto the server and make sure that they go to the right place on the server. Some people run into trouble because they have the name of their Web server but are not clear about where their Web pages have to go on the server. This typically results in a failure to gain access to the server. Locations for files on Web servers are specified by directory paths. However, there can be more than one directory path. The path you see in a URL may not be the path that you need to use when you upload your files to the server. This can be a cause of much confusion.

Once you've uploaded your pages to the server, you are almost home free. However, there are still some snags that can get you. First, you need to know the URL that will allow you to view your pages with a Web browser. If you don't know that URL, you won't be able to tell people how to get to your site. Second, if your pages are on the server but the general public can't see them you might need to fuss with file protection codes on the Web server. This should never occur on a commercial site, but it can in educational environments where the computer administrators might not be bending over backwards to make your online activities as easy as possible (what did you expect for $20 a semester?).

4.9.1 Six Steps to Publish a Web Page

Here is a summary of the six steps to publish a Web page.

1. Acquire access to a Web server.

   This must be done before you can do anything else. You need to know your userid and password for your personal account on the Web server.

2. Find out the DNS address of your Web server.

   You might be able to find your Web server's DNS address in online documentation for your computer account. Look for a *Frequently Asked Questions* document. This address might have either prefix: `ftp://` or `http://`. These represent the two different protocols that Web servers might support. If you can't find the DNS address in online documentation, visit the Help Desk for your computer account: they will be able to tell you the correct host name for your Web server.

   Warning: You probably won't be able to guess the DNS address that you need. It might be the same www-address that appears in URL addresses for the server, or it might be something different. Chances are, it is something different.

3. Find out the pathname that is needed when you upload files to the server.

   This step is very similar to Step 2. You may be able to find this information online, or you may need to ask the Help Desk staff.

   Warning: Don't try to guess at this directory path. It is probably not the same directory path that appears in the URL for your home page.

4. Upload your Web files to the Web server.

   Do this using an FTP client or a Web page construction tool such as Navigator's Composer. As long as you have the correct information from Steps 2 and 3, you should be able to complete this step. This step is discussed in more detail in Section 4.9.2.

5. Find out the URL to use to view your home page.

   While working on Steps 2 and 3, ask about this URL. Anyone who knows the answer to the first two questions should be able to answer this one.

6. Fix any file protection codes that need fixing (with luck you won't need to do this).

   This step applies only if you've successfully completed Steps 1 through 5 and you still cannot view your home page on the Web server. If you visit your page and the browser displays an error message that says you are not authorized to view the page (it may say something about access permission), then you need to adjust some settings on the Web server that control which files can be viewed by the public and which cannot. If you visit your page and the browser returns a 404-Not Found error message, then your Web page has not been installed correctly. To fix this problem, you'll need to repeat one of the earlier steps.

4.9.2 Uploading Your Pages

If you are using an HTML construction kit, check to see whether it has a publishing feature (conduct a search with the keyword "publish" in the online documentation). If it has one, you will be able to upload your pages using that. If you are not using a construction kit, you can upload files with either Netscape Communicator or Internet Explorer. You can also upload files with an FTP client. In this section, the process of uploading your pages is illustrated by using Netscape Communicator's Composer (a simple HTML construction kit); other software will operate similarly.

The Web page construction tool in Communicator is called the Composer, which is launched from the Communicator menu. Even if you created your Web pages without using Composer, you can use Composer to upload them to a Web server. Follow these steps:

1. From the File menu, select Open Page and then use the directory dialog box to locate an HTML file that you are ready to upload.

2. From the File menu, select Publish. Figure 4.36 shows the window that pops up at this time.

3. Complete all of the fields in the pop-up window.

If you opened a Web page before you reached this pop-up window, the first two fields in Step 3 will be filled in for you automatically. In the third field, "HTTP or FTP Location to publish to," enter the DNS address (from Step #2) and the directory path (from Step

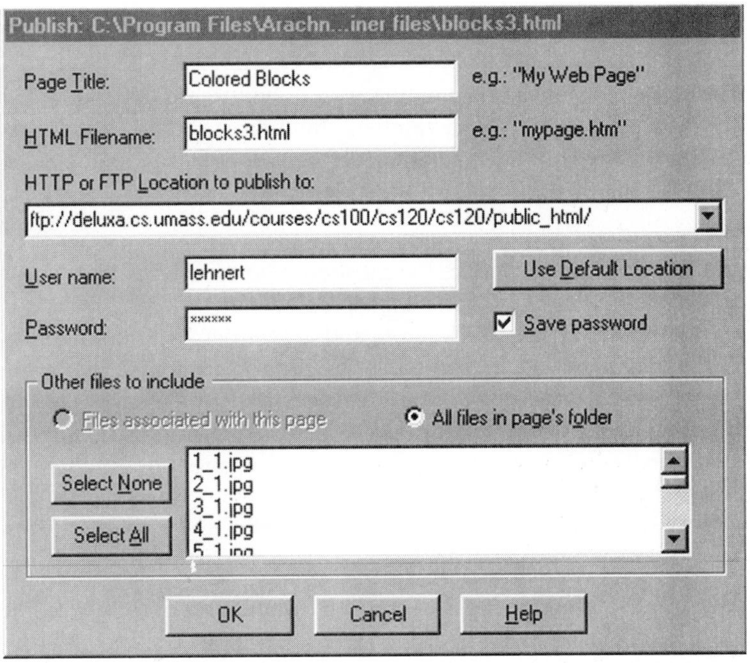

Figure 4.36:
Publishing Web
Pages with
Netscape's
Composer

#3). You will probably need to prefix the DNS address with `ftp://` as shown in Figure 4.36. In some cases, you can use the `http://` prefix. If one doesn't work, try the other. Once you've entered this information, it becomes a default; Composer will fill it in for you automatically next time you need to upload more Web pages. In the next two fields, your userid and password are those for your account on the Web server (from Step #1). Check the "Save password" checkbox so that these entries will be saved for you.

The Composer has a convenient feature that makes it easy to upload groups of related Web pages all at once. If there are other files in the same subdirectory as the current page, you can load all of them along with the open file. Therefore if your whole Web site is in one subdirectory, you can upload the entire site by clicking the radio button "All files in page's folder" and then clicking OK. Alternatively, you might opt for just the files that are referenced by the current page via links on the current page. In any case, it is not necessary to upload one file at a time (which becomes tedious if you have more than one or two HTML files to upload).

File Uploads Cannot Be Undone

If your directory on the Web server already contains a file with the same filename as one of the files that you are uploading, the file being uploaded *will overwrite* the file on the server. You will not see any warnings, and you will not be asked if you want to overwrite the file. It will just happen. Once the original file has been overwritten, you won't be able to recover it if you decide you've made a mistake. Once you upload a file and overwrite an existing file, you can't undo the file upload.

If you have an FTP client, for example WS_FTP for Windows or Fetch for the Mac, then you can upload your files to a Web server by using that client. You will need the same information discussed in the previous Steps 1–3, but you will be able to path your way into the correct Web page directory by clicking each subdirectory along the way. This might seem easier than typing in the complete path as shown in Figure 4.37. However, it also might be slower if any of the intermediate subdirectories contain a thousand or more directory entries (this can happen on some large Web servers that have many user accounts). Either way, you can connect to the server and upload your files.

Text, Binary, or Automated?

Some FTP clients have a setting that you need to check before each upload command. You might need to tell your FTP client the type of file being uploaded: text or binary. Or, your client might offer an automated setting that, when checked, instructs the client to figure this out based on the file extension. If you have an automated option, take it.

All FTP clients can recognize the most common file types used for Web pages. If you have to select this setting yourself, separate your text files (`.htm` and `.html`) from your binary files (`.jpg` and `.gif`) and move them into different upload groups. If you pick the wrong setting for a file, the file will be transferred to the server and no warning or error message will be seen. However, the resulting file will probably be mangled and unusable. If any of your file transfers fail to produce healthy copies of your original files, try the transfer again, paying attention to any file type settings that you might need to reset.

If you do end up with an access permission error after you've uploaded your Web pages, contact your system administrator for assistance. You can fix it yourself, but you will need a working knowledge of UNIX protection codes; most people don't want to be bothered with this. Most Web servers available for general use are programmed to save authors from having to make these protection adjustments. With a little luck, you will never have to deal with Step 6.

4.10 COPYRIGHT LAW AND THE WEB

Copyright laws protect the creative and economic interests of writers, musicians, and artists. In a free society, creative works should be freely distributed, although with some restrictions. However, no one should be allowed to steal a creative work, either by taking credit for its creation or by receiving any revenue from its sale or use.

If you've created a work and would like to distribute it over the Internet, you need to learn more about copyright law than this book can teach you. To maximize your legal protection, consult a legal advisor. Before you post anything, be sure that you understand the consequences of placing your work online. For example, if you intend to publish a written work, you should know that some print publishers won't publish a work if it has been distributed digitally. Once you've made something available online, you can't take it back.

Chances are, you aren't worried about a work of your own creation. Rather, you want to know what you can and can't do with all of the text and graphics online. Web browsers have made it easy to create personal copies of files no matter where they are located. However, you need to know the restrictions that apply to the legal use of those files, specifically the answers to the following most commonly asked questions.

- Can I incorporate files found elsewhere into my own Web pages?
- Can I alter files and make those altered files available online?
- Can I excerpt material and distribute that excerpt online?
- Can I print copies of online materials?
- Can I store on my personal computer files that I find elsewhere?
- Do I have a right to download a Web page and mail a print copy of it to a friend?

Popular software makes doing all of these things so easy that you might have assumed that to do so is legal. However, are these actions legal? Later sections answer each of these questions in detail. First, however, the next section discusses the general concept of copyright.

4.10.1 Copyright Basics

The foundation for copyright and patent law is in the U.S. Constitution (Article I, Section 8, Clause 8):

> The Congress shall have Power . . . To promote the Progress of Science and useful Arts, by securing for limited Times to Authors and Inventors the exclusive Right to their respective Writing and Discoveries.

A copyright confers certain rights and privileges to its owner. Copyrights are normally granted to the author of a written work or to an artist, musician, or other person who creates some intellectual product. These rights can be transferred to another individual or company via a written contract. For example, the author of a book typically transfers his or her copyright to a book publisher in exchange for a publishing contract. Sometimes, copyright privileges are automatically granted to an individual's employer when a work has been generated as part of the person's job.

A copyright protects not only the creator's economic interests but also the integrity of a work. It does so by authenticating its originality. No one can copyright a work that has prior copyright protection. However, someone might challenge the validity of an original copyright if that person can prove that a work was stolen, plagiarized, or adopted from an existing work and modified in minor ways (an argument most often applied to musical creations). Authors normally want to gain widespread readership, but they also want recognition for their work, as well as compensation for the sale of books, magazine articles, and other print distributions of the work.

Copyright laws convey to the copyright owner certain **intellectual property rights**—a broader category of legal protections that include the protection of patents and of trademarks. A copyright normally protects a written document, whereas a patent protects an artifact (invention). Copyrights are automatically associated with all written documents that contain original material, whereas obtaining a patent requires a complicated legal procedure.

The following subsections discuss common questions about copyrights.

Can I Go to Jail for Violating a Copyright?   Yes, but such punishment is unusual. Most copyright violations are treated as civil offenses rather than criminal offenses. In a civil court, you can be sued for damages but can't be sent to jail. Some *criminal* copyright penalties include both large fines and jail terms, but only the federal government can instigate a criminal copyright action. The next time that you play a rented videotape, read the FBI warning at the beginning of the tape for a description of criminal copyright violations.

If I Don't Make Money from a Copyright Violation, Can I Still Be Sued for Damages?   Yes. If you distribute a document online, you might undermine the potential for a profitable print distribution, which could be assessed in terms of lost income to the copyright owner. The fact that you didn't profit yourself is irrelevant.

4.10.2 What Is Protected

The following subsections cover briefly what is protected by copyright laws.

Does an Author Renounce Copyright Privileges When a Work Appears Online? No. An author can relinquish copyright privileges only by putting a work in the public domain or transferring copyright privileges to another party. For a work to be placed in the public domain, the author must include a statement that says, in effect, "I grant this to the public domain." An author can transfer copyright privileges to a third party only by contract. Copyright privileges are not surrendered in the absence of such a contract.

Are All Web Pages in the Public Domain? No. Web pages are all copyrighted and subject to copyright restrictions, unless the Web page author expressly places them in the public domain.

Are All Older Written Works in the Public Domain? How Can I Tell Whether Something Is in the Public Domain? An author is allowed to maintain copyrights on his or her works for his or her lifetime. After the death of an author, the author's heirs or publisher may renew the copyrights for another 70 years. If an author has been dead for 70 years, any materials by that author are considered to be in the public domain.

If something is in the public domain, it might be distributed freely in both electronic and print form. However, it is dangerous to assume that a work is in the public domain simply because it is popular or ubiquitous. For example, the song "Happy Birthday" is not in the public domain.

Does an Author Have to Mark a Document with a Copyright Notice For It to Be Protected? No. An explicit copyright declaration used to be required in the United States. Then the law was changed so that works created after April 1, 1989 are copyrighted and protected regardless of whether they contain a copyright notice. If you see a document that has no copyright notice, you should always assume that copyright protections apply.

Can an Author License Specific Rights to the General Public by Including a Statement Describing the Rights and Privileges Being Granted? Yes. For example, a Web page might include a statement like the following:

> Permission is granted to freely copy (unmodified) this document in electronic form or in print as long as you're not selling it. On the WWW, however, you must link here rather than put it on your own page.

Such a statement effectively allows anyone to reproduce and post an exact copy of the document online in almost any fashion. However, mirrored Web pages are explicitly prohibited.

Another commonly encountered copyright provision reads as follows:

> This work may be redistributed freely, in whole or in part, but cannot be sold or used for profit or as part of a product or service that is sold for profit.

If no such statement is included, you must assume that no such privileges apply. When a copyright provision allows for redistribution without permission, you still must identify the author, source, and publisher (if there is one) in all distributions of the original work.

4.10.3 Personal Use of Online Materials

The following subsections cover briefly what constitutes allowable personal use of online materials.

Can I Print Copies of Online Materials?   If you print one copy for your own personal use, there is no problem. If you want to print copies for friends and the material does not contain an explicit statement about allowable distributions, you should obtain permission from the author or whoever owns the copyright.

Can I Store on My Own Personal Computer Any Files That I Find Elsewhere?   Yes, provided that you don't distribute those files to others or make them publicly available. Keep in mind that the author of the work no longer controls the copy. If you want to reference the file or quote from it later, you should locate a current version, in case the author has changed it.

Can I Download a Web Page and Mail a Print Copy of It to a Friend? This is duplication and distribution. If the Web page doesn't explicitly grant you permission to distribute it freely, you need permission from the author. In the case of a Web page, it is easier to send your friend the URL in an e-mail message. This is the correct way to share Web pages without violating the rights of Web page authors.

4.10.4 Publishing on the Web

The following subsections briefly cover questions concerning what you are allowed to do on your Web pages regarding copyright works.

If a Photograph or Cartoon Has Been Published in a Newspaper or Magazine, Can I Scan It and Put It Online?   No, not unless you track down the owner of the copyright and secure written permission to do so. The copyright owner might be the photographer or artist, a wire service (in the case of a photograph), or the publication in which the work appeared.

Photographs and drawings are protected by default copyright restrictions, like written text is. For example, Playboy Enterprises sued the Event Horizons BBS for distributing unauthorized digital copies of Playboy photographs. It received $500,000 in a settlement. Photographs and artwork often have greater revenue potential than do text documents and must therefore be handled with extreme caution.

Can I Incorporate Files Found Elsewhere on My Own Web Pages? Yes, as long as you observe some restrictions. Most important, you must not make a copy of someone else's Web page and then create a link to that copy. To reference another Web page, create a pointer to the original page. In that way, the author of the page retains control over the material. If the author wants to update, correct, or modify it in any way, you will automatically benefit from those efforts. If the author removes a page from public distribution, your pointer will become obsolete, but removing the page is the author's prerogative.

If you find some graphics on someone else's Web page and want to incorporate them into one of your own Web pages, similar restrictions apply. Because graphics files are commonly copied and redistributed across the Web without proper copyright permissions, there is an excellent chance that any graphic that you find on someone else's Web page has already been pirated and is being used illegally. This is especially true of professional photographs. A responsible Web page author will attempt to locate the rightful owner of any image and secure permission to use it. The owner of the image might want to control the context surrounding the image (for example, any captions under the image) and might therefore refuse permission or reserve the right to withdraw permission, depending on the use of the image. No fair use guidelines apply to images (see Section 4.10.5 for more information about fair use guidelines).

It may occur to you that you can add a graphical image from someone else's Web site by simply referencing the address of the image on the other site's Web server. This practice is known as "deep linking" and it has led to a number of lawsuits. The legal status of deep linking looks unfavorable—one judge has ruled it a "contributory infringement." In any case, the practice is highly controversial and should be avoided.

Some Web page authors ask that you reference their pages at some "top-level" entry point. They don't want you to set up a link to a secondary page if that page wasn't designed to be a self-contained, stand-alone page. When an author explicitly makes such a request, you should respect it. There are also practical reasons for linking to top-level entry points for large Web sites. Webmasters who maintain large Web sites occasionally rearrange its pages and rename its files. If you reference a secondary page directly, your link might become obsolete when the Webmaster reorganizes the files for that site. If you reference the main entry to a Web site and identify the links needed to get to a secondary page, your citation is more likely to require fewer updates.

Keeping Web page pointers current and operational is one of the overhead costs associated with Web page design and maintenance. Anything that you can do to avoid obsolete pointers will be greatly appreciated by your visitors.

Can I Alter Files and Make Those Altered Files Available Online? When you alter a document that isn't yours, you must be extremely careful to acknowledge the extent of your alterations and the source of the original document. Some authors suggest that the altered file be identified as a "heavily edited modification of an original source document by so-and-so, which can be found at such-and-such a location."

If you alter someone else's file and present it as your own, you might or might not be violating copyright laws, depending on how much original material survives verbatim. However, you are probably guilty of plagiarism. Recall that plagiarism occurs when you adopt the substance of someone else's work, rewrite it in your own words, and fail to give proper credit to the original source. If you present the substance of someone else's words, be sure to identify and acknowledge the original source. In an academic environment, plagiarism is a form of academic dishonesty and grounds for serious disciplinary action.

An Exception to the Rule There is one notable exception to this general document modification scenario. If you download the HTML version of a Web page because you like the format of the page, you may retain all of the HTML commands and substitute your own content into the HTML framework, without permission or acknowledgments. The "look and feel" of a computer screen is not protected by copyright or patent and can be freely duplicated without permission. As long as you substitute your own content, you're not violating any copyright restrictions and you're not plagiarizing any material. Indeed, this is an easy way to create a sophisticated Web page, as well as an honorable way to learn HTML.

Copyright Violations Are So Common on the Internet That No One Can Keep Track of Them. What Difference Will It Make If I Add One More Violation? Even if you aren't sued for a copyright infringement, your actions can affect other people and might result in a loss of online resources. For example, there used to be a Dave Barry mailing list on which columns by humorist Dave Barry were posted each morning. Mr. Barry's publisher asked everyone to respect the copyright of those columns by not redistributing the columns. The Dave Barry mailing list worked for a while, until someone chose to ignore the restriction and one of the columns showed up on another mailing list. Upon finding out that the copyright restriction had been violated, the publisher shut down the mailing list. The publisher didn't sue the individual responsible for the copyright violation, but shutting down the mailing list denied thousands of people the enjoyment of reading Dave Barry online. The actions of one thoughtless individual affected thousands of other people. Old Dave Barry columns can be found online in some Web archives, but no one can any longer read new Dave Barry columns via e-mail.

4.10.5 Fair Use Guidelines

The following subsections cover briefly what is covered by fair use guidelines.

Can I Freely Distribute an Excerpt from a Larger Document Provided That I Identify It and Acknowledge the Source?   This is normally okay as long as you conform to the doctrine of fair use. The **doctrine of fair use** allows writers and scholars to refer to other works by quoting excerpts from those works. This is typically done to argue a point, to present evidence, or for the sake of illustration.

What Does the Doctrine of Fair Use Require?   To quote from a copyrighted work, you must follow certain rules of thumb. Note, however, that you might see various differing guidelines for fair use. This is because there are no absolute legal guidelines, only conventions. Widely accepted conventions are safe to use, but be prepared to be flexible if people object to your use of their materials. In this spirit, following are some rules of thumb that you can use when you are working with published text.

- You may quote 300 words from a book or 150 words from a magazine or newspaper article as long as you observe the following guidelines:

  The excerpt is not a complete unit in the larger work (for example, a complete poem, a complete article, or a complete list of rules from a manual).

  The excerpt comprises less than 20% of the original work.

  The excerpt is integrated into your own writing and does not stand alone as a self-contained section or chapter opening.

  You give full credit to the author, source, and publisher.

- If you excerpt a series of quotations from a single work, the total sum of those word counts should not exceed 300 words from a book or 150 words from a magazine or newspaper article.

- If you want to quote a personal e-mail message, a Web page, or an unpublished document, you first must obtain permission from the author to do so.

When fair use guidelines do not apply, copyright permission must be secured for exact quotations from the works of others. Note that *ideas* cannot be copyrighted; it is the specific arrangement of words used to express an idea that is the object of copyright protections. You are always free to summarize or restate the content of any work in your own writings. However, a summation of someone else's work without proper acknowledgment is plagiarism. Always acknowledge a source if you are drawing detailed information from that source.

If an explicit statement prohibits the distribution of an excerpt that normally would be justified under the fair use doctrine, the doctrine can't be applied. For example, suppose that the following prohibition appears in an online document:

> No part of this electronic publication might be reproduced or retransmitted without the prior written permission of the publisher.

In this case, no excerpts can be reproduced without prior consent.

Alternatively, suppose that someone distributes a document that contains the notation "Do Not Quote." If you see that annotation, you can't distribute any excerpts. Explicit restrictions always override default conventions.

I'm Teaching a Class and Want to Distribute Print Copies of an Online Document to My Students. Is This Protected by the Fair Use Doctrine?   The fair use doctrine is commonly invoked by teachers and professors who distribute copies of journal, newspaper, and magazine articles to students in classes as a part of their educational practice. The fact that these activities are nonprofit is commonly thought to protect them under the fair use doctrine. However, some recent court cases associated with the creation of "course packs" by commercial copying services suggest that the application of the fair use doctrine is far from straightforward in these situations.

If you're a teacher, you should investigate these controversies and find out what practices have been adopted by your school. For a timely discussion of this issue, see **"University Copy Centers: Do They Pass The Fair Use Test?"**. If an online document explicitly states that redistribution is permitted, there is no problem with doing so. The question is more problematic for documents that grant no explicit permission, in which case obtaining permission from the author or publisher (who might ask for a royalty) is always prudent.

Can I Excerpt Material and Distribute Those Excerpts Online? Yes, if you adhere to fair use guidelines. To use more material than can be justified under fair use, you should obtain permission from the author or whoever owns the copyright.

4.10.6 Copyright Law in a Digital Era

When you consider the rights and restrictions that apply to online text, think about how easily a text document can be distributed in digital form. If someone posts a document to a mailing list, it might be accessible through an archive for years to come. Copies of it might be mirrored at countless Web sites and redistributed repeatedly via e-mail. If the original author wants to correct an error in the original document or revise it with important updates, recalling all of the copies of the original version will be impossible. The author no longer controls the document in the same way that a publisher can control print editions of a book.

Everyone benefits when authors retain maximal control over the digital distribution of their documents. This is the only way to minimize the propagation of misinformation or outdated information. In addition, it gives everyone access to the best-quality information online. In the interest of effective online communication, you must be sensitive to the rights of authors, no matter where a document was originally posted or how limited the potential scope of the document might be. With 150 million people online, it's impossible for anyone to predict the digital trajectory of an online document.

The body of law that establishes precedents for copyright law is always challenged when new technologies emerge. Important precedents are being established on the issue of data collections. For example, can the contents of a database be copyrighted? Can someone own the data that describes the human genome? Can someone own the DNA sequences associated with a specific gene? As soon as a technology makes it possible to ask a thorny question about new forms of intellectual property, court cases require judges and juries to attempt to sort out relevant precedents.

For example, in 1991 the U.S. Supreme Court decided that no one can copyright the information contained in a telephone directory's white pages (*Feist* v. *Rural Telephone*). According to the court, no copyright can be granted for a compilation of facts unless the compilation entails some original "selection, coordination, or arrangement" of those facts. Some databases are compiled at great expense and represent an investment that could give a company a clear commercial advantage. Exactly when do the criteria of "selection, coordination, or arrangement" apply? These legal questions are largely untested, but databases are key components of many online resources. Thus it is reasonable to assume that copyright protections apply to subject trees, clearinghouses, and file archives.

In 1993, the Clinton Administration created its Working Group on Intellectual Property Rights as part of the Information Infrastructure Task Force. Its purpose was to resolve concerns about intellectual property and the digital distribution of text, images, video recordings, and audio recordings. A proposal advocating a revision of copyright law was released in 1994, but it has met substantial resistance because it would interfere with free and open communication among the scientists and educators for whom the Internet was originally designed. As in many endeavors, there is tremendous tension between advocates for commercial profit and legislative policies designed to protect the public good.

In October 1998, the On-Line Copyright Infringement Liability Limitation Act was signed into law in an effort to strengthen intellectual property rights on the Web. This new law protects an ISP from liability for copyright infringements on the ISP's Web servers, as long as the ISP has no prior knowledge of the infringement. However, once the matter is brought to its attention (for example, if a copyright owner complains to the ISP), then the ISP must disable online access to the material in question. This means that you must use with care the clip art and the fonts that you place on your Web pages. If you're not authorized to redistribute them, your Web pages could be yanked from their server. It's too early to say what the impact of this new law will be on the Web and the ISPs who must now respond to all copyright infringement complaints. However, clearly we are past the point of "anything goes" with respect to copyright infringement on the Web.

In a digital environment, questions of ownership and control need to be carefully reexamined. When text was restricted to physical print, controlling distribution of that text was relatively easy. The advent of copying machines eroded that control and forced people to rely to a greater extent on voluntary compliance with copyright laws. Now the rapidly growing body of digital text has upset the balance yet again, forcing people to assume even greater responsibility for voluntary compliance with existing laws. During periods of swift technological change, everyone needs to stay abreast of major court decisions, new legislation, and public policy debates. These are the forces that shape new behavioral codes and social responsibilities in our increasingly technological society.

Things to Remember

- An HTML editor saves you time if you need to create many Web pages.
- You can learn HTML by examining the HTML (source) files of pages already on the Web.
- Different Web browsers can display the same Web page differently.
- Keep your image files small (30K–40K) for faster downloads.
- Use graphical elements with restraint.
- Remember that Lynx users can't see graphics or table layouts.
- Check to see that your pages look good in different-sized browser windows.
- Check all hyperlinks on your pages to make sure that they work correctly.
- Do not violate copyright laws when you add materials to your Web site.

Important Concepts

absolute URL—a hyperlink to a Web page on a different Web server.

copyright restriction—a prohibition on the duplication and distribution of intellectual property.

GIF file—an image file in a format especially well suited for line art.

Hypertext Markup Language (HTML)—the markup language used to format Web pages.

HTML tag—a marker within an HTML file that delimits an individual HTML element.

HTML tag attribute—a variable within an HTML element.

HTML source file—the text file downloaded by a Web browser and used to display a Web page.

hyperlink (link)—a clickable element on a Web page.

inline image—an image positioned inside of a text file as if it were a single, oversized character.

JPEG file—an image file in a format especially well suited for photographs.

named anchor—a hyperlink to another location on the current Web page.

relative URL—a hyperlink to a Web page on the same Web server.

Where Can I Learn More?

Learning HTML by Example `http://www.ida.net/users/pbmck/learn/00conten.htm`

HTML 4.0 Reference `http://www.htmlhelp.com/reference/html40/`

Web Monkey `http://hotwired.lycos.com/webmonkey/`

Devs.com HTML Design 1 `http://www.devs.com/zresources/html.html`

Problems and Exercises

1. Which two file extensions signal a Web browser that a file is a Web page file?

2. What four HTML elements should be present in any Web page file?

3. Explain why you should always include `HEIGHT` and `WIDTH` attributes for an image file even if you don't need to scale the original image.

4. Describe in detail a Web page layout that uses a table in which the table's `WIDTH` attribute should take a percentage value. Describe in detail a layout in which that attribute should take a constant (pixel) value?

5. What HTML tag reproduces text exactly as it is typed, preserving all whitespaces and blank lines?

6. When does a Web page not need a `BODY` element?

7. Why do some people dislike frames?

8. Explain the difference between a 404-Not Found error and an access denied error.

9. **[Find It Online]** HTML contains some special characters that are often useful when the character you want to print is ignored (as with whitespace) or interpreted as part of HTML (as with left and right angle brackets). Search some online HTML documentation, and find out how to make a Web page display the following line (exactly, with all of the HTML tags showing) *without* using a `PRE` or `CODE` tag:

   `<HEAD><TITLE>My First Web Page</TITLE></HEAD>`

   Create an HTML file, and check your solution by viewing it with a Web browser. Have you been able to recreate the text exactly as it appears above?

10. **[Hands-On]** What happens if you put an `H1` tag inside of a `HEAD` element? What if you put a `TITLE` tag inside of a `BODY` element? Does it matter if you reverse the order of the `HEAD` and the `BODY` elements in an HTML file? (Try it to see for yourself.)

11. **[Hands-On]** View the following HTML with a Web browser, and describe what you see.

```
This is line number 1.
<P><P><P>
This is line number 2.
<P>
This is line number 3.
<BR><BR><BR>
This is line number 4.
<P>
This is line number 5.
 <P> <P> <P>
This is line number 6.
```

What does this tell you about adding whitespace to your Web pages?

12. **[Hands-On]** Visit a Web page that has images, and download some image files using your browser. Point to the image that you want to keep, click the right mouse button, and click Save Image As from the pop-up menu. If you are using a Mac, hold down the Shift key when you click your mouse in order to see the same pop-up menu.

13. **[Hands-On]** Create a Web page that has images on both sides of the page, with text flowing continuously between the images. Add a sequence of left-justified images with text flowing along the right side of the images and no text or blank lines separating the images along the left side of the page.

14. **[Hands-On]** What happens if you reverse the HEIGHT and WIDTH attributes of an image on a Web page? (Try it to see for yourself.)

15. **[Hands-On]** If you have a graphics tool (the Paint program that comes with Windows will do), create an image file to add a red stripe down the left side of a Web page. Convert your file to a GIF or JPEG format, and add it to a Web page that contains some text. Use a table to create a left margin so that the text does not run into the red stripe.

16. **[Hands-On]** Use a table to create two columns of text on a Web page. Insert a quarter inch of whitespace between the two columns. Make sure that your columns are evenly spaced and will look good if the browser window is resized.

17. **[Hands-On]** Create a Web page that has an image that is perfectly centered against a black background, no matter how the browser window is resized.

18. **[Hands-On]** Create a Web page that has solid bar stripes running down both the left and right sides of the page. Make sure that the borders make appropriate adjustments when the browser window is resized.

19. **[Hands-On]** Reproduce the table layout in Figure 4.29 (you can download images from a copy of **Figure 4.29 on the Web** for this exercise). Nest one table inside of a second table in order to keep the four images grouped in a fixed configuration that stays centered in the browser window, no matter how the window is resized.

20. **[Hands-On]** Upload a Web page file to a Web server using a Web browser or an FTP client. What is the URL for your Web page? Make sure that the page is visible on the Web.

CHAPTER FIVE

Find What You Want–Fast!

CHAPTER**GOALS**

- Find out how to analyze your information needs in order to select appropriate tools for the job.
- Learn how to search subject trees and clearinghouses for useful information and resources.
- Discover how to use successive query refinement when you visit a general search engine.
- Explore how and when to select a new search mode.
- Find out about advanced search features and specialized search engines.
- Understand how intelligent agents and search bots can help you to manage information needs.
- Find out how to assess the credibility of information on the Web.

5.1 | TAKING CHARGE

The Web opened the Internet to the public, generated a great deal of excitement, and created teenage Web surfers. However, for people trying to integrate the Web into their work routines and professional activities, the Web is sometimes more monstrous than magical. High expectations for the Web quickly deflate in the face of disappointment, often supplanted by frustration and disdain. User-friendly software is supposed to be easy to use, so when it fails to deliver, users tend to blame the software. In fact, some effort is needed on the human side of the equation; otherwise, even the most impressive software is likely to disappoint. Computers may be powerful, but they can't read minds.

Anyone who has used a search engine knows the frustration of trying "to drink from a fire hose." It might be mildly amusing to see that the search engine offers 800,000 documents on the Web that seem to relate to your query. However, most people don't have time to look at more than 20 to 30 document summaries and perhaps four or five actual documents. So, the trick to effective Web searching is to make the first ten documents in the search engine's **hit list**, the ones you want to see.

If you expect to get what you want with your first query, you'll almost certainly be disappointed. You need to take time to think about your search; you'll be rewarded accordingly. An initial search that might bring in 800,000 documents can often be reduced to a few dozen excellent documents, and in only a few minutes. This chapter shows you how to analyze your information needs, create queries, and select appropriate search strategies.

Your ability to find what you need—fast—has little to do with mastering advanced search techniques or being privy to insider search engine tips. Rather, the key is *advance preparation*: some familiarity with the available resources and a thoughtful analysis of your information needs. The most popular search engines overhaul their user interfaces—their "look and feel"—at least once a year in an effort to look current and stay competitive. However, the underlying technology that makes them work remains relatively stable. When you first begin to work with search engines, it pays to consult their online documentation, located under the Help or Search Tips link. Once you're more experienced, the shifting interfaces won't confuse you because you'll know that the underlying mechanism hasn't changed. You can stay up to date on search engines by visiting **Search Engine Watch** (see Figure 5.1), which offers timely articles, reviews, and performance evaluations.

Each time you begin a Web search, first decide which of the following three types of question that you have.

- Voyager

    A **Voyager question** is an open-ended, exploratory question. You use it when you're curious about something and simply want to see what's out there on the Web. You might have some general expectations about the subject, but otherwise you're largely ignorant and willing to be educated. This type of question derives its name from the Voyager space probe. (If the topic of interest were the solar system, you would send out the Voyager space probe to collect as much data as possible, just to see what would come back.) Voyager questions tend to cover a lot of ground and require time for exploration.

- Deep Thought

    A **Deep Thought question** is also open-ended but is more focused and goal-oriented than a Voyager question. It might have many possible answers. This type of question derives its name from the *Hitchhiker's Guide to the Galaxy*, by Douglas Adams. In that book, a computer named Deep Thought sets out to learn the meaning of life. This is a good example of an open-ended question with a specific goal. The search for an answer could go on for quite a while because it's difficult for you to know when you have the answer that you seek. Most people quit when they're too tired to continue or, in the case of Deep Thought the computer, after 7.5 million years. Whenever you want to collect multiple hypotheses, opinions, or perspectives on an issue, you ask a Deep Thought question, which is often philosophical, political, or academic in nature.

- Joe Friday

    A **Joe Friday question** is very specific and characterized by the expectation that there will be a simple, straightforward answer. This type of question derives its name from the 1950s television show "Dragnet." In that weekly show, actor Jack Webb played a police detective named Joe Friday—a dry, businesslike soul who was famous for the line, "The facts, ma'am. Just the facts." With a Joe Friday question, you'll know the answer when you see it and there will be no point in looking further. Questions that ask about names, dates, locations, and other verifiable facts are examples of Joe Friday questions. Once you know how to handle them, most Joe Friday questions can be answered on the Net in a minute or two.

As you explore the various search strategies available on the Web, it will become clear that each of these three question types is best handled by a specific type of Internet resource.

Figure 5.1:
Search Engine
Watch Home Page

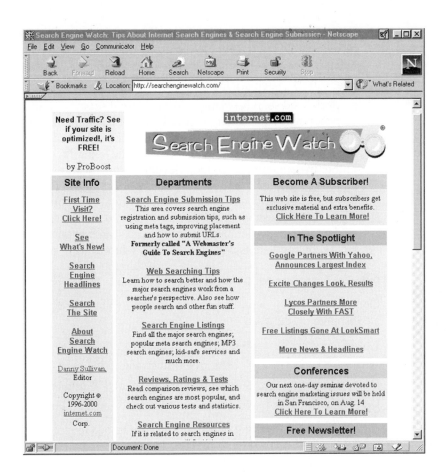

- Voyager and Deep Thought questions require input from multiple documents. Once you've found the right resource, browsing is an integral part of the exploratory process.

- Joe Friday questions require facts. Facts are facts; their context does not require extensive examination.

Four types of Web resources are available to help you to find the answers to questions.

1. Subject tree

   A **subject tree** is a hierarchically organized category of topics with lists of Web sites and online documents relevant to each topic. By navigating the hierarchy, you can find information sources for questions about specific topics. Subject trees are also called **directories** and **topic hierarchies**.

2. Clearinghouse

   A **clearinghouse** is a collection of Web sites and online documents about a specific topic. The topic might be broad, in which case the clearinghouse might be either divided into subtopics or organized hierarchically, like a subject tree. However, a clearinghouse is always more narrow in its focus than a subject tree. A clearinghouse supplies links to the sites or documents.

3. General search engine

   A **general search engine** is a search engine that indexes a large collection of Web pages that users retrieve by entering keyword queries. A general search engine relies on an automated *Web spider* to create a database of documents. They are not restricted to specific topics, and they index more Web resources than do subject trees. It might be difficult, however, to find in a search engine's database the resources that are relevant to a specific question. These databases are very big, and relevant resources can be buried deep in the hit list.

4. Specialized search engine

    A **specialized search engine** is like a general search engine, except that it is limited to Web pages that feature a specific topic. The topic might be broad, as in a clearinghouse, and many specialized search engines use a clearinghouse as a starting point. However, a specialized search engine takes the clearinghouse concept a step further by gathering all of the relevant documents known to the clearinghouse and indexing them for the user; the clearinghouse, as mentioned previously, only supplies links to the documents. It is harder to create a specialized search engine than a general search engine. While a general search engine relies on an automated Web spider to create its database, a specialized search engine relies on a handpicked collection of documents that a person has selected as relevant to the topic.

Different Resources for Different Question Types

Once you know the type of question that you want to ask, you can select an appropriate resource on the Web.

Type of Question	Resource
Voyager	Subject tree or clearinghouse
Deep Thought	Subject tree or specialized search engine
Joe Friday	Subject tree or general search engine

Note that many Joe Friday questions turn out to be Deep Thought questions, once you've dredged up some information. This happens typically with historical events, in which opinions and facts often intertwine. For example, suppose that you thought that there was a straightforward answer to the question "Who invented the telescope?" or "When was the first English dictionary published?" Dig a little deeper, however, and you'll find yourself in Deep Thought territory. When this happens, simply keep going until you're satisfied that you've gathered all of the data that you want.

Not So Fast

With Voyager and Deep Thought questions, don't expect to find all of the information that you need at one site. Depending on the topic, you might need hours, or sometimes days, of careful exploration before you'll be satisfied. With a Joe Friday question, answers come faster. However, don't always stop at the first one that arrives. If you're not confident about the credibility of a source (see Section 5.9), check a second, and maybe even a third, site to make sure that you're getting reliable information.

Note that general search engines are recommended for only one of the three question types: the Joe Friday. This does not mean that they're not useful for the other two types of question. On the contrary, a general search engine can be used to locate clearinghouses or specialized search engines that are on target for Voyager and Deep Thought questions. Some questions must be answered in stages. To learn who invented the telescope, for example, you might start with a general search engine, because you think that you have a Joe Friday question. However, when conflicting answers begin to arrive, you can shift into Deep Thought mode and look for a specialized search engine on inventions or inventors in order to get a fuller picture.

Many questions are best tackled by asking more questions. As you acquire more experience with more Web resources, you will become more systematic about the process of question answering. Each time one question leads you to another question, identify the new question type and go to a resource that's right for that question.

5.2 | MORE ABOUT SUBJECT TREES AND CLEARINGHOUSES

A subject tree is actually a browsing aid. It requires some exploration and yet is designed to get you where you need to go as fast as possible. **Yahoo!** is the Web's oldest, largest, and most popular subject tree. However, other trees include **About** and the **Open Directory Project**. These three are discussed in more detail in the following sections.

5.2.1 Yahoo!

When you browse a subject tree, you start from the *root* of the tree and *branch* out to more-specific topics, at each decision point selecting appropriate options. For example, suppose that you want to send a letter to Elton John and you need his fan mail e-mail address. You can use Yahoo! to conduct a search. On the Yahoo! home page (see Figure 5.2), you need to find a branch of the tree that will head you in the right direction; in this case, that branch is the Entertainment branch:

Entertainment → **Music** → **Artists** → **By Genre** → **Rock and Pop** → **John Elton**

Figure 5.2:
Yahoo!'s Subject Tree

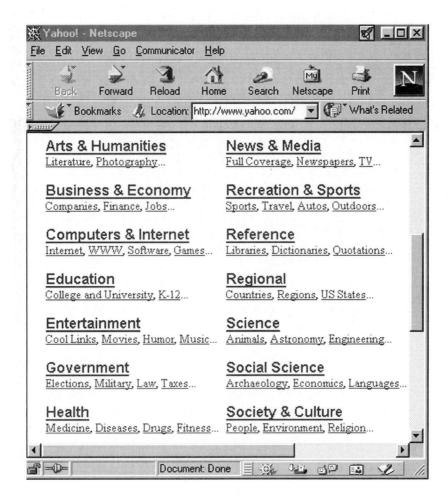

The Elton John page contains a number of fan-related links (*leaves*) that you can explore to find an official or unofficial address to which you can send fan e-mail (see Figure 5.3).

Figure 5.3:
Some "Leaves" on
the Elton John
Branch at Yahoo!

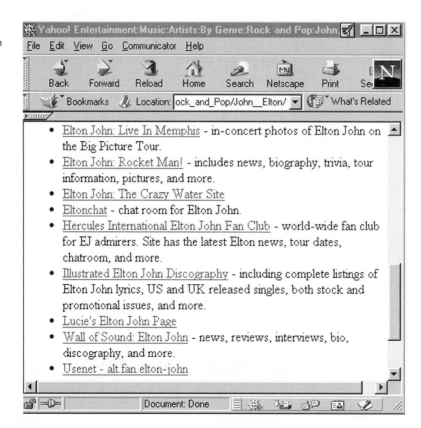

A good subject tree will make getting where you want to go easy. Yahoo!'s subject tree, growing since its inception in 1994, now organizes over 500,000 documents. Note, however, that this is nowhere near as many as those that the largest general search engines handle. Each document is added to Yahoo! by people who check the document for its content and proper position in the tree structure. This keeps the documents well organized; however, it does not mean that every document has been subjected to quality control for content. It is relatively easy to glance at a document to see what it's about. Editorial control requires knowledgeable reviewers and is far more time-consuming.

Although a lot of effort goes into maintaining a subject tree's organization, subject trees are not immune to organizational problems. It is difficult to design a comprehensive hierarchy in a way that seems intuitive to everyone who uses it. Different subject trees use different categories and subtree structures. Although there's no one best hierarchy, some subject trees might be easier to navigate than others.

Another difficulty with subject trees is that it's often impossible to store everything that is relevant to a single topic under a single location in the tree. For example, if you're interested in weaving, should you look under keywords "art," "textiles," or "crafts"? Depending on exactly what you want to know, you might find relevant documents under all of these. This makes it difficult to know when you've exhausted the possibilities in a subject tree. Happily, the larger subject trees are equipped with search engines to help you cover all of the bases. When you use a search engine for a subject tree, you're conducting a site search. A **site search** is a search whose hits are restricted to Web pages within the current Web site.

Subject Trees with Search Engines versus Search Engines with Subject Trees

A subject tree that has a search engine (for example, Yahoo!) allows you to conduct a search that is restricted to the subject tree's subtrees and documents indexed by the subject tree. The main attraction is the subject tree; the search engine is there only to enhance the subject tree. Sometimes a search engine for a subject tree will give you the choice of searching the tree or searching the Web. If you choose to search the Web, you'll leave the subject tree and move to a general search engine.

By contrast, the reverse configuration, a search engine that has a subject tree, is a completely different animal. Examples of this type of configuration are AltaVista, GoTo.com, and Excite. A search engine that has a subject tree returns hits from a large database of documents that includes, but is not restricted to, the documents in its subject tree. In this case, the search engine is the main attraction and the subject tree is an added feature.

A subject tree with a search engine lets you see how many branches might hold documents relevant to your topic. For example, suppose that you want to assemble a long list of different types of clocks. This is a Deep Thought question (it has a focus but it's open-ended). A subject tree is a good place to start. However, you'll definitely want to query the search engine for the subject tree.

Keywords for Site Searches

When you conduct a site search at a subject tree, you're searching for categories in the subject tree as well as for documents. For a Voyager or Deep Thought question, the category hits are more important than the document hits because they show you all of the perspectives that you should consider before you start digging into specific documents.

To yield a good list of category hits, follow these tips:

- Use only one keyword instead of a list of keywords.
- Choose a keyword that is simple and obvious.
- If you can think of different keywords, investigate them one at a time.

Some keywords will open worlds of information, and others will return nothing. You might need to try a few keywords before you find the right one to the tree.

Yahoo! always shows categories and documents. Each Yahoo! **category** is a location in the tree at which you can examine subcategories or jump directly into relevant documents. Documents are always represented by URLs for Web pages (which are not part of the Yahoo! Web site).

When you query Yahoo!'s search engine, the results come back in two parts: category matches and site matches. As an example, go to Yahoo! and enter the query "clocks" (see Figure 5.4).

First shown are category matches. A **category match** shows all of the places in the subject tree where you can examine a branch that has something to do with clocks. In this example, you get back a list of all of the category titles that contain the keyword "clocks." There are 17 different branches on the Yahoo! tree that have something to do with clocks (see Figure 5.5).

After the category matches are the site matches. At Yahoo!, a **site match** is a list of relevant documents found inside of Yahoo!'s subject tree. To avoid confusion about Yahoo!'s

Figure 5.4:
Using Yahoo!'s
Search Engine to
Search for the
Keyword "clocks"

Figure 5.5:
Yahoo!'s
17 Subtrees
About Clocks

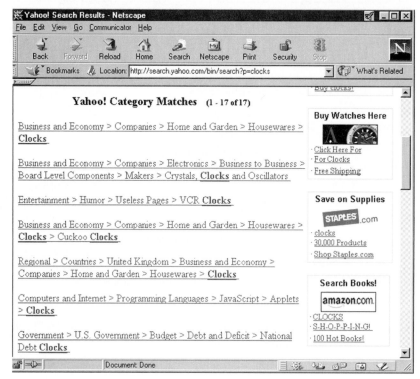

use of the term *site match* and the more general notion of hits returned by a site search, this book refers to Yahoo!'s site matches as *document matches* or *document hits*. This will distinguish them from Yahoo!'s category matches without confounding the idea of a site match with a site hit.

Examine the category matches for the keyword "clocks." Notice that the categories for clocks include one for clocks as housewares, one for businesses that manufacture computer clocks, one devoted to humor about VCR clocks, and one about national debt clocks. Click the housewares/clocks category (see Figure 5.6), and take a closer look. Notice that now there are four subcategories about clocks that might be of interest: Antique@, Cuckoo Clocks(10), Repair(9), and Watches@. Because we are dealing with a subject hierarchy, each of these subcategories corresponds to a branch within the tree structure of the hierarchy, and occupies a fixed position within the larger hierarchy.

Figure 5.6:
Four More
Subcategories

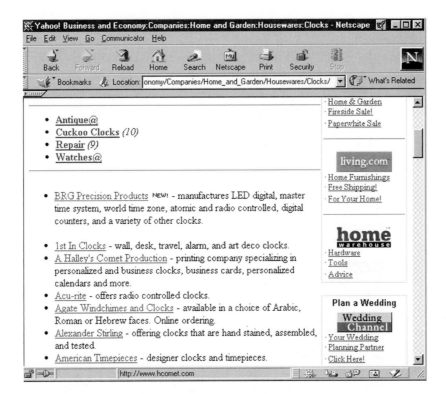

Two of these categories list a number in parentheses, and two are followed by an @ character. Each numbered category is a branch within the current subtree, and the number tells you how many document hits are stored within that particular branch of the tree. The @ character tags cross-listed categories that are found somewhere outside of the current subtree. Those categories are listed here because they are strongly associated with the current category. Both the subtree categories and the cross-listed categories give you opportunities to explore relevant parts of the subject tree. You might not have found the subtree about watches in your initial keyword search for clocks. However, the cross-listing reminds you that watches are a type of clock; you might want to explore that category, also.

Follow-Up on a Site Search in a Subject Tree with Some Browsing

Subject trees are designed to facilitate browsing. Use a site search at a subject tree to find relevant locations within the tree. The resulting category matches are all possible starting points for browsing expeditions. Don't rush into the document hits before you've scoped out all of the category matches. You can miss a lot of information if you narrow your search too quickly.

A large subject tree is a great way to explore open-ended questions because someone else has already figured out what categories relate to a concept and what associations should be made between categories that reside in different parts of the tree. In the clock example, you probably don't need to examine documents as much as you need to explore the category matches to see how many different kinds of clocks you can find.

Although hierarchical organizations are powerful devices for information retrieval, don't let the logic of categories and subcategories lull you into mindlessness. You might still need to think about search strategies for subject trees. Recall the Deep Thought computer in *The Hitchhiker's Guide to the Galaxy*. When asked to explain the meaning of life, Deep Thought worked for 7.5 million years and produced the answer "42." Douglas Adams has many fans, and they have naturally pondered this answer in an effort to understand its deeper meaning. Some have set out to answer such questions as, "What role does the number 42 play in the lives of all dogs?" Subject Tree Exercise #2 asks you to work on that question by using Yahoo!. It is a Deep Thought question (that is, there may not be only one "correct" answer).

Subject Tree Exercise #1: Clocks

Do the following to become familiar with Yahoo!:

1. Search **Yahoo!** and create a list of different types of clocks. Do this search for 15 minutes.
2. How many clocks did you list?
3. Do you think that you've exhausted all that Yahoo! has to offer for this exercise?

Subject Tree Exercise #2: The Role of the Number 42 in the Lives of All Dogs

At this point, it will be instructive to go to the Web and try your hand at this problem before you discuss it further. Visit **Yahoo!** and see if you can find out what role the number 42 plays in the lives of all dogs. Can you find the answer? Take some time to try it before you read any further in this book.

From the question, "What role does the number 42 play in the lives of all dogs?", you might be hard-pressed to find some useful keywords. Specific numbers tend to be bad keywords (many search engines ignore numbers). If you conduct a keyword search at Yahoo! on the keyword "dogs," you'll get 334 category matches and 6,519 documents (site matches). A keyword search on "42" yields 2 category matches (!) and 197 site matches. None of the category matches look promising, and no one wants to wade through long lists of site matches. If you search with the query "dogs 42," you'll find 2 site searches (see Figure 5.7). However, neither looks like it has anything to say about the role of the number 42 in the lives of dogs.

What can you do? You could try to guess at some plausible answers and work backward from those. However, this could take a long time. Maybe you need to think more about the query. Perhaps you were a little too quick to jump on what seemed to be the obvious keywords. Maybe you can think of other keywords that will take you where you want to go by using *associative thinking*.

Associative Thinking

When you think about keywords and categories, sometimes you really have to *think*. Don't just fixate on the immediate question. Ask yourself:

- Who would care about the answer to this question?
- What sort of people might be talking about this topic?
- Are any organizations responsible for posting the information that I want?

Try to associate a query with people or organizations; those connections might be the breakthrough that you need. This type of thinking is called **associative thinking**, and it can be a powerful search strategy.

Figure 5.7:
Yahoo!'s Two Site
Matches for the
Query "dogs 42"

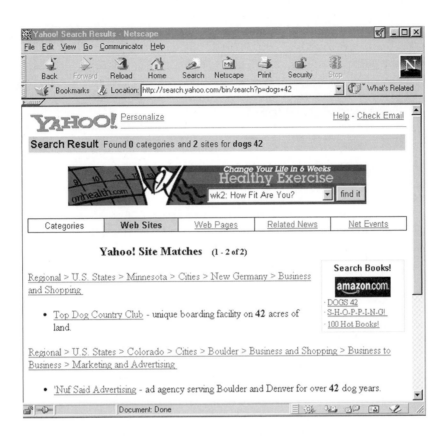

Let's consider the larger context in which this question was originally posed. Where did it come from? What motivated it? If you can answer these additional questions, you'll have some new leads that you can use at Yahoo!. The only people who would ever ask this peculiar question are Douglas Adams fans. So search Yahoo! to learn what is available using the query "Douglas Adams." Yahoo! has a category devoted to Douglas Adams, as well as 35 site hits that mention his name. Once you've made the Douglas Adams connection, you're just a couple of links away from the answer. See if you can find it.

Yahoo!, the largest subject tree on the Web, offers a hierarchy that contains over 500,000 documents and 25,000 categories. On the Web since its beginning, Yahoo! is a major Web portal and has a loyal following. This is a tough act to follow. However, that doesn't mean there aren't other good general subject trees. The following two sections discuss two of these: About and Open Directory Project.

5.2.2 About

If you need solid reliable information on a serious topic, check out **About** (originally called the Mining Company). It is a subject tree that supports over 700 major topic sites, each with its own hierarchical subject tree and each managed by an expert in that subject (see Figure 5.8). About displays category matches and document hits, although the document hits at About are always Web pages written by About **guides**—topic experts who work for About and write overviews about their topics.

About does not index as many Web pages as Yahoo! does. However, all of the pages that it does index have been written or reviewed by an expert in the field who polices Web page content for reliability and accuracy. The About enterprise is very similar to an encyclopedia in its scope and operation. As such, it's a good subject tree for introductory articles and short tutorials. Articles at About can be trusted to contain good solid information.

Figure 5.8:
About: A Subject
Tree Managed by
Experts in 700
Topic Areas

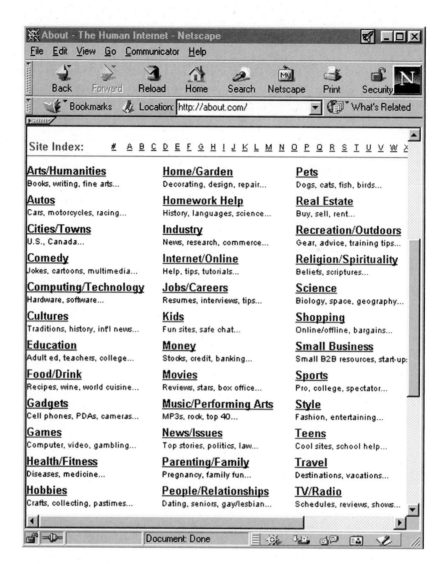

5.2.3 Open Directory Project

Another subject tree with a strong following is run by Lycos.com: the Open Directory Project. Lycos was one of the first search engines with a subject tree. Now, in an aggressive quest to outperform Yahoo!, it's concentrating on its **Open Directory Project**. This subject tree emphasizes practical know-how more than academic expertise, as its home page illustrates (see Figure 5.9), so it might not actually be competing with Yahoo! head-on. The **Open Directory Project** uses a system of category matches and document hits like Yahoo! does, including the @ tag for cross-listed categories.

To expand its Web coverage, the Open Directory Project uses 22,000 volunteers who act as editors in specific content areas—the directory contains over 230,000 categories. Time will tell if a system of volunteers can maintain the quality control that Lycos cultivated in its early years (under the name "Lycos Guides") with paid staffers. In any event, the Open Directory Project is a resource worth bookmarking.

Some of your questions will be general and easily satisfied, whereas others might be more sophisticated and harder to answer. As your information needs shift from casual questions to more demanding questions, you'll need to find new Web resources. This is where clearinghouses come into play.

Figure 5.9:
Open Directory
Project Home Page

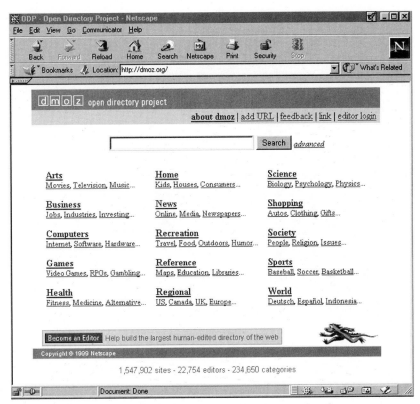

5.2.4 Clearinghouses

Recall that a clearinghouse is a large collection of resources or documents about a topic. On the Internet, some publicly available clearinghouses were created and are maintained by researchers subsidized by federal funding. Others are compiled by commercial interests and might be available only to paid subscribers. A few are compiled by librarians, teachers, or other individuals. Some clearinghouses focus on documents available online, whereas others index documents that are available only in printed form.

Always be on the lookout for clearinghouses that address your interests. Each is organized in its own way and supports its own search tools, so you need to learn about them one by one. Some are slick professional sites, whereas others are minimal lists of plain text and hyperlinks. Figure 5.10 shows the home page for the **Environmental Law Net**, a clearinghouse devoted to environmental laws, regulations, enforcement, and pending court cases.

A relevant clearinghouse is a powerful research tool because it is both comprehensive in scope and maintains high standards for document quality. When you use a good clearinghouse, 90% of the hard work has already been done for you. All you need to do is work your way through the offerings to locate the specific information that you want. Figure 5.11 shows one of the specialized resources available at the Environmental Law Net clearinghouse, a comprehensive list of cases in the state courts of the United States.

There are thousands of online clearinghouses. To conduct some in-depth research, always first check to see if a relevant clearinghouse can help you. Go to any general subject tree for the Web, and conduct a keyword search that includes the word "clearinghouse." For example, **FAST Search** returned over 10,000 documents that contain the word "clearinghouse" in their Web page titles.

Figure 5.10:
The Environmental
Law Net
Clearinghouse
Home Page

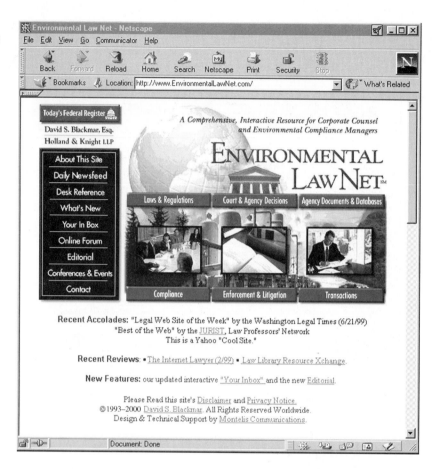

Another good way to find quality clearinghouses is at the **Argus Clearinghouse** (see Figure 5.12). Argus is a *clearinghouse of clearinghouses*, complete with its own search engine and rating system (see Figure 5.13).

You might also find some comprehensive resource pages that haven't been identified with the keyword "clearinghouse." To locate them, think of organizations that might be involved with the topic. Who cares about these issues? Is there a nonprofit group or coalition that might track relevant resources? If you can find such an organization, you might be able to benefit from the work of a professional Internet researcher who has spent a lot more time than you can tracking down relevant resources.

Argus Clearinghouse is a good source for clearinghouses and is unique in its efforts to evaluate available clearinghouses, but many excellent clearinghouses are not listed at Argus. If Argus doesn't have what you want, there are other clearinghouses you can try.

Ready Reference Using the Internet

```
http://www.winsor.edu/library/rref.htm
```

BIOTN (see the alphabetized subject index)

```
http://library.sau.edu/bestinfo/alpha.htm
```

NetGuide

```
http://www.netguide.com/Browse/
```

High-quality clearinghouses can also be found in archive collections of Web site reviews. Many mailing lists review Web sites of all kinds and maintain searchable

Figure 5.11:
A Comprehensive
List of Court Cases
Offered by the
Environmental Law
Net Clearinghouse

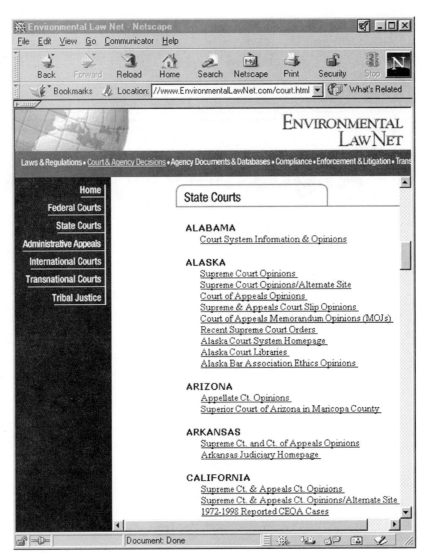

archives on the Web. Some specialize in educational or academic sites, and others focus on popular, often quirky, sites. If you can't find what you want anywhere else, check out the following archives.

Netsurfer Science (all science)

http://www.netsurf.com/nss/search.html

Netsurfer Digest   (all sorts of things)

http://www.netsurf.com/nsd/search.html

Scout Report Signpost (academic/educational)

http://scout.cs.wisc.edu/archives/signpost.html

Always investigate pointers to clearinghouses that might be useful to you. Someone else has already created a comprehensive bookmark file for a particular topic, so you don't have to do it yourself. Clearinghouses are great bookmark entries because they give you fast access to many links via a single URL. If your primary activities on the Web tend to focus in one direction, you might want to set your default home page to an appropriate clearinghouse page so you can hit the ground running each time you get on online.

Figure 5.12:
The Argus
Clearinghouse
Home Page

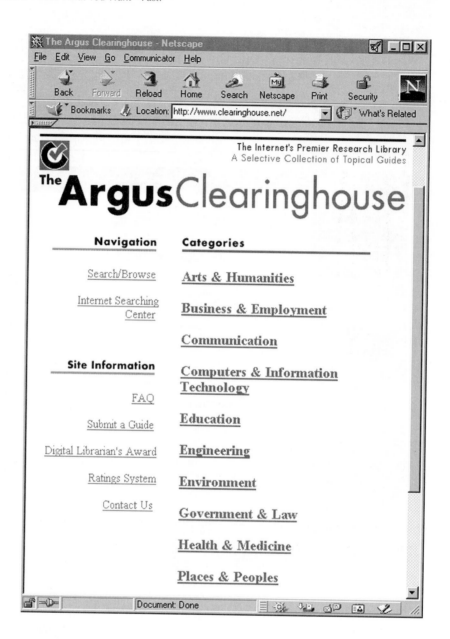

5.3 GENERAL SEARCH ENGINES AND META SEARCH ENGINES

A great deal could be said about search engines. For now, concentrate on purely practical advice. Such engines work hard to be all things to all people, and they sometimes succeed. Even so, sometimes a general search engine is not the best place to start a search.

5.3.1 Some Ground Rules

Before you start, here are some ground rules

Ask Some Key Questions about Any New Search Engine before You Begin a Search
Suppose you're visiting a particular search engine for the first time. Before initiating a search, you should review the information at any link called Search Tips or Help (see Figure 5.14) to learn how the engine operates and what it offers. Here are some of the features that various search engines provide.

Figure 5.13:
A Clearinghouse
Rating Summary

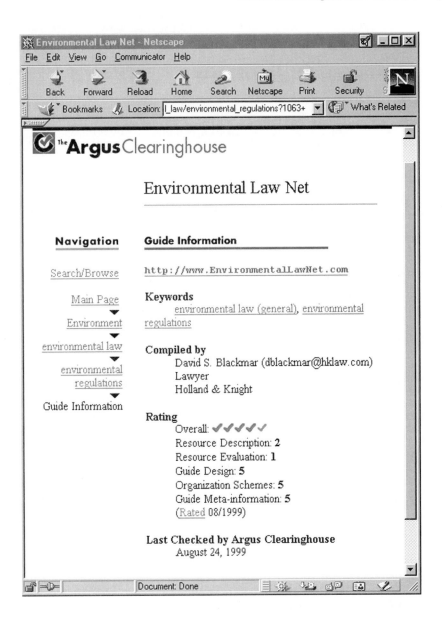

Figure 5.14:
Google's Clickable
Help Page Makes It
Easy to Learn the
Ropes

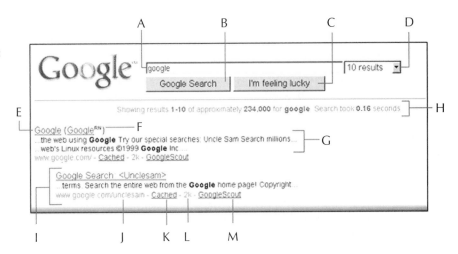

- Return only pages that contain all of the keywords in your query.
- Return pages that contain some but not all of your keywords.
- Automatically look for morphological variations on your keywords. For example, you enter the keyword "book" and the search engine looks for both "book" and "books."
- Look for variations on a word if you enter a keyword with the wildcard (*) character, as in "book*."
- Automatically add synonyms to your query. For example, you enter the keyword "law" and the search engine looks for "legislation."

You need to know what a search engine is doing with your queries; otherwise, you'll be unable to tune your queries effectively.

Never Look beyond the First 20 to 30 Hits for Any Given Query Most search engines are proud to announce how many hits were found, as if you should be impressed to know that the document that you really want might (or might not) be somewhere in a list of, say, 1,200,000 hits. In fact, a good query will display the hits that you most want at the top of the hit list. A bad query is not worth more than a quick glance at the top ten hits. If the top ten hits are off-base, don't waste time looking any further in the hit list. If the top ten hits are pretty good, you might want to look at the next ten or twenty, but no more. If you want to see additional hits, enter a different query.

Experiment with Different Keywords in Different Queries Conducting a keyword search is like learning a musical instrument. The more that you work at it, the better the results. Each search has its own learning curve: some queries are easier to fine tune than others. Start out with a fast query based on the best keywords that you can think of. Examine the hits that come back, and then adjust your original query, broadening it (to bring in more hits) or narrowing it (to bring in fewer hits).

Each new query should benefit from the feedback resulting from the preceding queries through a process of *successive query refinement* (this is described in detail later in the chapter).

Don't Expect the First Query That You Try to Be Your Last No matter how experienced you become with keyword searches, the process will always require adjustment and refinement. Even the experts try one or two preliminary queries before they expect anything very useful to materialize. Don't waste time trying to perfect your first-pass queries; let the search engine's feedback help you out.

5.3.2 Getting Started

Now that you understand the basic process of working with search engines and search queries, it's time to start experimenting with queries. For a Joe Friday query about a mainstream topic (that is, something that many people might want to know about), **AskJeeves** is a good place to start; it's one of the simplest search engines available.

For example, suppose that you want to know who invented the telescope. You type the question that you want answered and then see what is returned. Unlike other search engines, AskJeeves doesn't return hits. Instead, it shows you a set of questions for which it already has answers. Some of these questions will be on target; others will not. However, at least one of them likely is relevant and will give you the information that you want. Figure 5.15 shows how AskJeeves responds to the query, "Who invented the telescope?".

AskJeeves has a database of over 7 million hand-crafted questions and answers. When it analyzes a query, it tries to match the query to one of its question/answer (Q/A) entries. The matching process is not perfect, so AskJeeves takes a few of the best matches it finds and returns each of those for your inspection. For the telescope question, you can see that

Figure 5.15:
AskJeeves's Attempt
to Match Each
Query to a
Question/Answer
Database

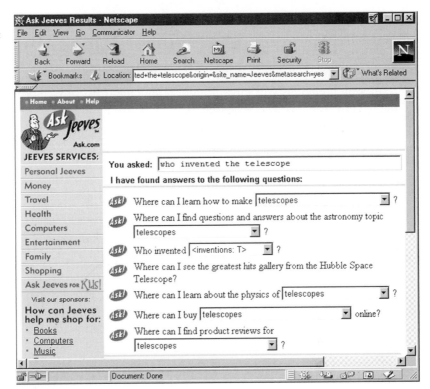

the keyword "telescope" figured heavily in the matching process and took you in some
directions that you don't want to go.

Not All Keywords Are Equal

When you create a query for a search engine, concentrate on using *nouns*. Search
engines don't understand English, even if they encourage users to post a query "in
plain English." They extract some keywords from each query and ignore other words,
for example prepositions and articles. Word proximity is usually taken into considera-
tion, so don't enter your keywords in a random order. If a noun phrase is important,
enter those words in sequence, even if you aren't asking for exact phrase matching. It
is not easy to anticipate all the ways an author might reference your topic, but descriptive nouns may be more reliable indices than descriptive verbs. If you have an important verb in your query, try replacing it with an analogous noun, even if the query
ends up sounding less like real English.

Search Engine Exercise #1: Who Invented the Telescope?

1. In **AskJeeves**, enter the query "Who invented the telescope" (do not include the
   quotes). See if you can find an answer based on Q/A hits that AskJeeves knows how
   to answer.

2. Which hits look promising enough to examine?

3. Do any hits take you to the answer that you desire?

AskJeeves is a wonderful search engine for beginners. It's easy to see whether the questions
returned are relevant to the query and there are no hit lists to ponder and investigate. If

AskJeeves can connect your query to the right answer, you're done. Many questions, however, AskJeeves cannot answer easily. For example, suppose that you need a ranked list of California's 20 largest cities. Although the information seems mainstream, AskJeeves has (at this writing) trouble producing a document that contains this information.

Most search engines will have trouble producing a list of California cities ranked by population. You might be able to find alphabetically ranked lists of cities in California, along with their populations, from which you could derive the list that you want. However, this takes time and you might make a mistake. Sometimes a hit is painfully close but not good enough (you might find a ranked list of the ten largest cities but not the 20 largest). When your queries come up dry, you have two choices:

1. Try different search engines.
2. Try different queries.

Strategies for (1) are discussed next. Those for (2) are discussed in Section 5.4.

Selecting a good search engine for a specific search problem is perhaps one of the most difficult challenges. None cover the entire Web, so experimenting with at least three or four of the better-known ones is a good idea. The document that you need might be available at, for example, AltaVista but not Hotbot. In addition, you can't know whether your document is simply hard to find or not on the Web at all.

Search Engine Exercise #2: Find a Ranked List of California's 20 Largest Cities

Before you read further, try to find a list of California's 20 largest cities. Enter the keywords "California cities populations" at two or three of your favorite search engines and observe what is returned. If you have no favorite search engines (yet), pick from this list:

AltaVista	`http://www.altavista.com/`
FAST Search	`http://www.alltheweb.com/`
Google	`http://www.google.com/`
NorthernLight	`http://www.northernlight.com/`

Meta Search Engines Tapping into multiple search engines is repetitive and tedious, as well as largely mechanical. But there's good news. For every repetitive and mechanical computer activity, someone has probably written software to automate it for you. The automated answer for multiple Web searches is the meta search engine. A **meta search engine** is an engine that sends a query to several different search engines and then returns some number of the top hits found by each. With a meta search engine, you type in your query once, hit Enter, and then sift through the hits that are returned.

The Web Offers Many Good Meta Search Engines

Here are some good meta search engines to bookmark:

DogPile	`http://www.dogpile.com/`
InFind	`http://www.infind.com/`
MetaCrawler	`http://www.metacrawler.com/`
C4	`http://www.c4.com/`
Highway 61	`http://www.highway61.com/`

Many meta search engines are publicly available on the Web. The better ones are careful not to swamp you with too many hits or with duplicate copies of the same hits. A meta search engine collects the top hits from each of the other search engines that it polls and decides how to present them to you. It might attempt to interleave them in a single ranked hit list, or it might let you view them in blocks, one engine at a time. Using a meta search engine leverages your time and reduces your effort, thereby enabling you to streamline your Web searches.

AskJeeves offers the results of a meta search engine in case its database of known questions misses the mark. It lists the top hits for each search engines used; short titles are available on pull-down menus (see Figure 5.16).

Figure 5.16:
AskJeeves Falls
Back on a Meta
Search Engine (Just
in Case)

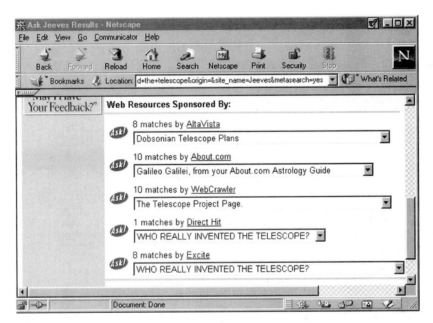

Although the meta search engine at AskJeeves is often helpful, it consults only five other search engines. Thus it might not be as comprehensive as you want. Most meta search engines tap the resources of at least six search engines, and some analyze hits from more than a dozen. Whereas all search engines rank the hits, displaying the best candidate hits first, with a meta search engine, the ranking problem is more challenging. This is because multiple hit lists must be merged and possibly re-ranked in order to create a single hit list. If this **merge-and-rank problem** is not handled well, the advantages of having broader Web page coverage can be lost by an inability to recognize the best hits. Some meta search engines avoid the problem by simply showing you the tops hits from each search engine, making no attempt to merge them in a single hit list. While not an optimal solution, this might be better than your having to look at the results of an ineffective merge-and-rank strategy. Experiment with a few meta search engines to find one or two that you like.

If you give a good query to a good meta search engine, you'll probably find what you're seeking. However, you might have to examine a few documents on the hit list. For example, suppose that you use a meta search engine named **InFind** to track down the list of California cities (see Figure 5.17).

The results are grouped in different ways. For example, hits in one group contain the phrase "California Cities" in their Web page titles. Hits in another are only for documents from California state government agencies. Once you figure out the basis on

Figure 5.17:
Fast Results by
InFind Based on Six
Search Engines

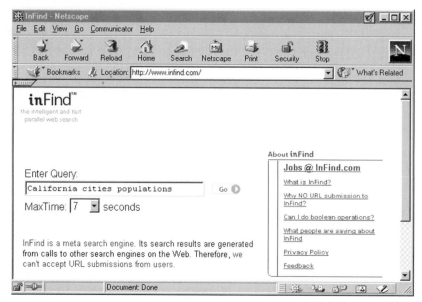

which each group is organized, you might be able to focus on the more likely groups for a closer examination. Although InFind does not offer page descriptions of the Web page titles, these groups can be very informative. In this case, you might expect to find good hits among the state government pages. Some of the choices are shown in Figure 5.18. Can you find the right link?

Meta Search Engine Exercise #1: Find a Ranked List of California's 20 Largest Cities

1. Use **InFind** and the keywords "California cities populations" to try to obtain a ranked list of California's 20 largest cities.
2. Examine the hits that come back to find a list of the top 20 cities.

Your hit list probably won't look exactly like that shown in Figure 6.18. Hit lists, like the Web, shift and change with time.

InFind's hit categories are very useful. However, once you've found one that you like, you might need to visit a number of its hits in order to see which are helpful. Web page titles don't always tell you everything that you need to know. A meta search engine that could merge all of its hits in a single list, with the best hits at the top, would be even better. Can it be done?

Meta Search Engine Exercise #2: Find the ABCDE Rule for Skin Cancer

1. Visit each meta search engine mentioned in this section, and find the five signs of skin cancer (also called the *ABCDE rule* for skin cancer). Don't settle for the similar ABCD rule—make sure to find the ABCDE rule.
2. Which meta search engine was able to deliver this information to you most efficiently? Explain your answer.

One meta search engine, **Copernic 2000**, comes very close to solving the merge-and-rank problem. However, it's not available on the Web. You need to download it and run it on your local machine (not all of the search engines that it polls—only the meta search engine part!).

Figure 5.18:
One of These Links
Is the Right One

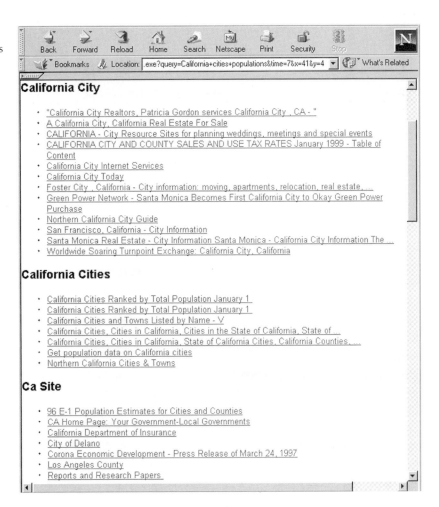

Copernic 2000 works with 16 search engines. It requires a minute or two to collect its results, depending on the speed of your Net connection. However, you can watch its progress with each search engine while you wait (see Figure 5.19).

Once all of the results are in, Copernic merges the results in a single hit list, with a short description for each (see Figure 5.20).

If you've experienced the merge-and-rank problem, you'll appreciate what you see in Figure 5.20. The first two hits, Historical Census Populations, point to the same document. They weren't merged because they are *mirror documents*—the same document is posted on two separate Web servers. This document points to a file that contains a long list of California cities with their populations from the 1990 census. However, the file is formatted for Microsoft Excel™. If you don't have Excel on your computer, and you want to view this file, you'll need to download an Excel viewer. In this file, the city list is ordered alphabetically, so you could to go through it by hand to find the top 20 cities manually. This is not a problem if you use Excel, however, because Excel will reorder the list for you based on the population entries (see Figure 5.21).

However, suppose that you don't have Excel and you don't want to pick through the list by hand to find the top 20 cities. Check to see whether any of the other hits have what you need. The third hit, California's Population, is an elementary school worksheet that lists the ten largest cities in California along with their population figures. This is close. However, you still need ten more cities.

Figure 5.19:
If You Like Progress
Bars, You'll Love
This Window

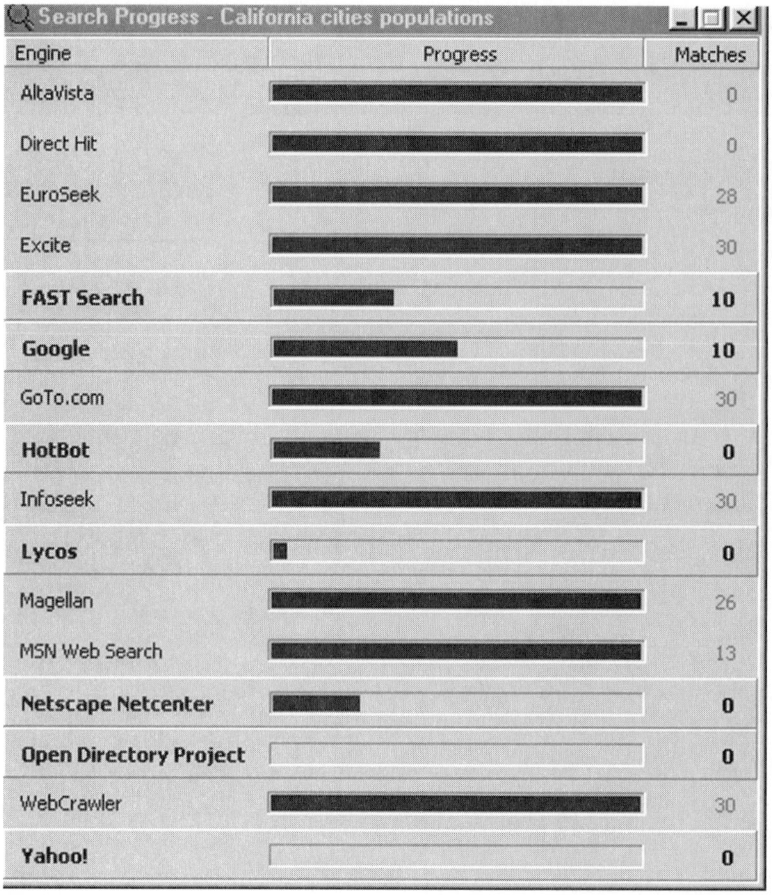

Engine	Progress	Matches
AltaVista		0
Direct Hit		0
EuroSeek		28
Excite		30
FAST Search		**10**
Google		**10**
GoTo.com		30
HotBot		**0**
Infoseek		30
Lycos		**0**
Magellan		26
MSN Web Search		13
Netscape Netcenter		**0**
Open Directory Project		**0**
WebCrawler		30
Yahoo!		**0**

Search Progress - California cities populations

Figure 5.20:
Merged-and-Ranked Hits Produced by Copernic 2000

Title	Address	Score	Engines
Historical Census Populations of Places...	http://www.dof.ca.gov/html/D.../histtext.htm		Excite, FAST Searc...
California State Department of Finance Demographic Research Unit 915 L Street Sacramento, CA 95814 (916) 322-4651 State of...			
Historical Census **Populations** of Places, Tow...	http://goto.com/d/sr;$sessionid$2LOKREIAB...		GoTo.com
California State Department of Finance Demographic Research Unit 915 L Street Sacramento, CA 95814 (916) 322-4651 State of...			
California's Population	http://www.mathstories.../california_pop.htm		Excite, Magellan
Sheet # 76/California's Population Show your work California's population on January 1, 1998 was 33,252,000. Ten Largest **Cities**...			
Reports and Research Papers	http://www.dof.ca.gov/html/D.../repndat.htm		Excite, Magellan, W...
Reports and Research Papers California Demographic Research Unit Reports E-1 City/County Population Estimates with Annual Pe...			
Yahoo! Regional>U.S. States>Californi...	http://sg.yaho.../Departments_and_Programs		HotBot, MSN Web S...
Help - More Yahoos Home > Regional > U.S. States > California > Cities > San Diego > Education > College and University > Publi...			
Relocating to California - Anaheim, Los...	http://relocating.to/relocating-to-california.htm		EuroSeek
Relocating To California? You can save with Cybernet!			
22-0455 COMMUNICATING EFFECTIVEL...	http://www.commandcollege.c.../22-0455.htm		FAST Search
California Law Enforcement Command College 22-0455 COMMUNICATING EFFECTIVELY WITH NON-ENGLISH SPEAKING CUSTOME...			

The next hit, Reports and Research Papers, doesn't sound promising. However, take a look at it because it is ranked immediately under two other documents that come very close to what you want. If you visit this hit, you'll find (not surprisingly) a long list of reports and research papers (see Figure 5.22).

Figure 5.21:
The Top 20 Cities
Shown in an Excel
Document

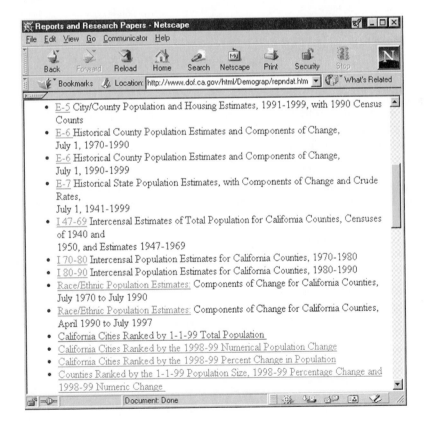

	A	B	C	D
1			**Historical US Census Populations of**	
2			**Places, Towns, and Cities in California,**	
3			**1850-1990**	
4				
5				
6	**Incorporated**	**County**	**Place/Town/City**	**1990**
7				
8	1850	Los Angeles	Los Angeles	3,485,398
9	1850	San Diego	San Diego	1,110,549
10	1850	Santa Clara	San Jose	782,248
11	1850	San Francisco	San Francisco	723,959
12	1897	Los Angeles	Long Beach	429,433
13	1852	Alameda	Oakland	372,242
14	1850	Sacramento	Sacramento	369,365
15	1885	Fresno	Fresno	354,202
16	1886	Orange	Santa Ana	293,742
17	1878	Orange	Anaheim	266,406
18	1883	Riverside	Riverside	226,505
19	1850	San Joaquin	Stockton	210,943
20	1909	Orange	Huntington Beach	181,519
21	1906	Los Angeles	Glendale	180,038
22	1898	Kern	Bakersfield	174,820
23	1956	Alameda	Fremont	173,339
24	1884	Stanislaus	Modesto	164,730
25	1869	San Bernardino	San Bernardino	164,164
26	1956	Orange	Garden Grove	143,050
27	1903	Ventura	Oxnard	142,216

Figure 5.22:
One Link Away
from the Jackpot

Reports and Research Papers - Netscape

File Edit View Go Communicator Help

Back   Forward   Reload   Home   Search   Netscape   Print   Security   Stop

Bookmarks   Location: http://www.dof.ca.gov/html/Demograp/repndat.htm   What's Related

- E-5 City/County Population and Housing Estimates, 1991-1999, with 1990 Census Counts
- E-6 Historical County Population Estimates and Components of Change, July 1, 1970-1990
- E-6 Historical County Population Estimates and Components of Change, July 1, 1990-1999
- E-7 Historical State Population Estimates, with Components of Change and Crude Rates, July 1, 1941-1999
- I 47-69 Intercensal Estimates of Total Population for California Counties, Censuses of 1940 and 1950, and Estimates 1947-1969
- I 70-80 Intercensal Population Estimates for California Counties, 1970-1980
- I 80-90 Intercensal Population Estimates for California Counties, 1980-1990
- Race/Ethnic Population Estimates: Components of Change for California Counties, July 1970 to July 1990
- Race/Ethnic Population Estimates: Components of Change for California Counties, April 1990 to July 1997
- California Cities Ranked by 1-1-99 Total Population
- California Cities Ranked by the 1998-99 Numerical Population Change
- California Cities Ranked by the 1998-99 Percent Change in Population
- Counties Ranked by the 1-1-99 Population Size, 1998-99 Percentage Change and 1998-99 Numeric Change

Document: Done

With a little persistence, you can locate the document that has exactly what you want (see Figure 5.23).

Figure 5.23:
The Jackpot

California Cities Ranked by Total Population January 1, 1999

RANK	CITY	COUNTY	POPULATION
1	LOS ANGELES	LOS ANGELES	3,781,500
2	SAN DIEGO	SAN DIEGO	1,254,300
3	SAN JOSE	SANTA CLARA	909,100
4	SAN FRANCISCO	SAN FRANCISCO	790,500
5	LONG BEACH	LOS ANGELES	452,900
6	FRESNO	FRESNO	415,400
7	OAKLAND	ALAMEDA	399,900
8	SACRAMENTO	SACRAMENTO	396,200
9	SANTA ANA	ORANGE	315,000
10	ANAHEIM	ORANGE	306,300
11	RIVERSIDE	RIVERSIDE	254,300
12	STOCKTON	SAN JOAQUIN	243,700
13	BAKERSFIELD	KERN	230,800
14	FREMONT	ALAMEDA	203,600
15	GLENDALE	LOS ANGELES	199,200
16	HUNTINGTON BEACH	ORANGE	196,700
17	SAN BERNARDINO	SAN BERNARDINO	185,000
18	MODESTO	STANISLAUS	184,600
19	CHULA VISTA	SAN DIEGO	166,900
20	OXNARD	VENTURA	158,300

Searching and Browsing Go Together

The information that you need might be one or two links away from an item on a search engine's hit list. If you see a document that's not exactly on target, check to see whether it contains any links that look promising.

Also, it's important that you stay on track and not get distracted by interesting but irrelevant hyperlinks. Carefully focused browsing just can get you where you need to go when you're hot on the trail of an elusive Web page.

If you had tried Copernic first, you could have found what you needed within 5 minutes. If you do a lot of searching and find yourself struggling with many queries, you might want to experiment with Copernic 2000. It offers a freeware version, which is what we used for this example, as well as two enhanced (but not free) versions that contain additional features. In addition, other meta search engines are available that you can download and evaluate, for example **WebFerret**, another popular choice similar to Copernic.

5.4   SUCCESSIVE QUERY REFINEMENT

Remember, don't expect to get the best hits on the first try. No matter how skilled you become with Internet searches, each new search problem will require some experimentation. Through a process of systematic trial and error, you'll modify and tune your queries to get increasingly better hits. The process of moving from an initial experimental query to a final successful query is called **successive query refinement** (see Figure 5.24).

Figure 5.24:
Successive Query
Refinement

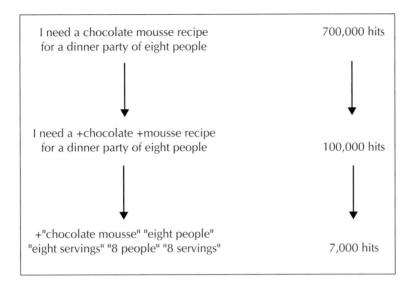

I need a chocolate mousse recipe
for a dinner party of eight people   700,000 hits

I need a +chocolate +mousse recipe
for a dinner party of eight people   100,000 hits

+"chocolate mousse" "eight people"
"eight servings" "8 people" "8 servings"   7,000 hits

With experience, you can become skilled at successive query refinement. However, it helps to know your tools and how to use them.

5.4.1 Fuzzy Queries

The most popular search engines offer a simple query option where you are encouraged to type full sentences or questions that describe your information needs. Such a query is called a **fuzzy query**. A fuzzy query requires only plain English. However, don't confuse fuzzy query processing with human sentence comprehension. Remember, search engines don't understand English (or any other human language). You can enter ungrammatical sentences, incomplete sentence fragments, disjoint phrases, or nonsense words—the search engine won't know the difference. It sees only a collection of keywords.

A fuzzy query is often a good starting point for a search session because it gives you a sense of how large your overall search space will be. A fuzzy query with a large number of keywords will normally return many hits, possibly more than 100,000 if the database is very large. This isn't very helpful, except to indicate that your query is pulling in a large number of documents. If a fuzzy query returns a small number of hits (fewer than 1,000), you know that you're dealing with a relatively small and specialized collection of documents.

The 1,000 Document Limit

Although a search engine might tell you that it has found thousands of hits for your query, no search engine is prepared to deliver more than the top 1,000 hits on the ranked hit list.

You can usually improve the hits at the top of the document by marking keywords in the query as follows:

- *Required keyword*: Mark with a + before the keyword.

  When a keyword has been marked as *required*, the resulting hit list will contain only documents that contain the required keyword.

- *Prohibited keyword:* Mark with an - before the keyword.

  When a keyword has been marked as prohibited, the resulting hit list will contain no documents that contain that keyword.

Most search engines that offer a fuzzy query option let you mark keywords in this way. When a search engine sees these tags, it reduces its hit list by deleting all documents that contain any prohibited keywords, as well as all documents that fail to contain all of the required keywords. As an example, here is a fuzzy query designed to find a recipe:

```
I need a chocolate mousse recipe for a dinner party of eight
people
```

The surviving keywords (those that aren't ignored) are likely to be "chocolate," "mousse," "recipe," "dinner," "party," and "eight." AltaVista returns about 83,325 hits in response to this fuzzy query. By marking keywords as required and prohibited, you could produce a better query:

```
I need a +chocolate +mousse recipe for a dinner party of
eight people
```

AltaVista returns about 20,524 hits for this query. That's still too many. However, revising the query in this way shows that over 75% of the hits from the original query must have been totally irrelevant, so the results of the second query are actually a big improvement.

The query could still return a recipe for a vanilla mousse cake with chocolate frosting. You can eliminate false hits of this sort by using another query feature: exact phrase matching. To do this, enclose important keywords, in this case, "chocolate mousse," within *double quotation marks* (instead of using two separate keywords "chocolate"' and "mousse," which might appear in two different parts of the document), as follows:

```
I need a "chocolate mousse" recipe for a dinner party of
eight people
```

Exact phrase matching means that the entire quoted phrase is treated as a single keyword and that documents that contain that exact phrase will be ranked more highly than documents that don't. Most search engines recognize double-quoted phrases in a query as a signal to perform exact phrase matching. Exact phrase matching can be very useful in fuzzy queries, where both phrases and single words can be marked with + or –.

Search Tips for the Most Popular Search Engines

It takes time to visit each search engine and peruse all of their online documentation. To obtain a quick overview of engine-specific search tips conveniently bundled in one place, go to **FindSpot**, select Search Tools from the main menu, and then click the search engine of your choice (see Figure 5.25). A display will appear that shows important search tips, example queries, and a search box in which you can submit a query to the search engine directly from the FindSpot Web page. This is a great way to get started with a new search engine. Another good place to go for search engine tips and tricks is **The Spider's Apprentice**.

Once you understand how fuzzy queries are handled, you can create queries by starting with an English sentence and then modifying it as needed. For example, the keywords "dinner" and "party" are not likely to get you any closer to chocolate mousse recipes. In fact, including them is probably counterproductive because they might lead to a narrative in which someone goes to a dinner party and eats chocolate mousse. However, you might be able to zero in on recipes by adding a new required keyword, "servings," as follows:

```
+"chocolate mousse" +servings
```

AltaVista returns 1,057 hits for this query. Notice that you did not choose the word "recipe" even though you are looking for recipes. You chose instead a word that you

Figure 5.25:
FindSpot Helping
You Learn How to
Use Search Engines

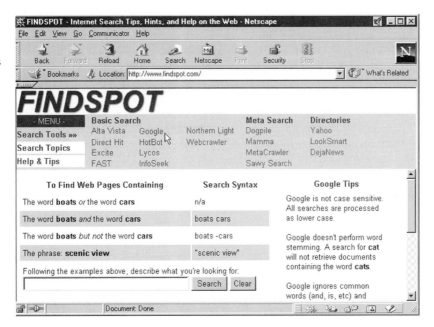

expect to see in a recipe. Successive query refinement can begin with an English sentence, but it often pays to move away from the words in that sentence in order to better anticipate the words that you expect to see in your target documents.

How Numbers Are Handled

Most search engines don't index specific numbers. Instead, they replace numbers with a generic number marker so that numbers will match numbers (just not necessarily the same number). To match a phrase that contains a specific number, check to see whether your search engine includes specific numbers in its document indexes by trying a test query with a required number in it and observing what is returned.

When working with a new query, start with a simple fuzzy query to see how many hits come back. Then narrow your query by marking required and prohibited keywords where possible. Sometimes a quick inspection of highly ranked hits will suggest helpful prohibited keywords that can narrow your query. Continue to refine your query in this way until it results in a manageable number of hits. With good document rankings, you don't need to narrow the query to a very small hit list. A hit list of 1,000 documents with 20 good hits at the top is usually a signal to stop searching. Never judge a search result without a quick look at the top ten hits.

5.4.2 Using Term Counts

HotBot and AltaVista's Simple Search option show you term counts for each word in your query. A **term count** is a statistic that tells you how many times a keyword (term) has been seen throughout the entire document database. This figure is not the same as the number of documents that contain the keyword. Some documents contain the keyword more than once. When a term count is calculated, each instance of the keyword is counted in those cases.

Knowing how often a keyword is used can be helpful. If a query brings in too few hits, you can check term counts to see whether a required keyword was excessively restrictive. Here are two tips to increase or decrease your hit count by using term counts.

1. To increase your hit count, examine your required keywords and remove the required tag from the keyword that has the smallest term count. Required keywords that occur with low frequency are very beneficial when they are on target.

2. To decrease your hit count, add some required or prohibited keywords. Sometimes the inclusion of one additional required keyword will reduce your hits dramatically, even for a fuzzy query.

For example, the following query includes the new required keyphrase, "Julia Child," and produces exactly nine hits on AltaVista, including some that are right on target (see Figure 5.26):

```
+"chocolate mousse" +"Julia Child" +servings
```

Figure 5.26:
A Successful Query Bringing Good Hits to the Top of the Hit List

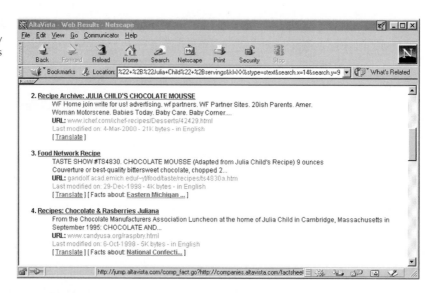

Note that it didn't take a very complicated query to reach these relevant documents. It required only that you refine the query with a highly restrictive required keyphrase (Julia Child). In fact, AltaVista indexes 17,170 documents that contain the keyphrase "Julia Child," 24,196 documents that contain the keyphrase "chocolate mousse," and 339,637 that contain the keyword "servings." So, none of the terms is very restrictive by itself. When combined, however, they result in a very small intersection of documents that contain all three (see Figure 5.27). Always consider keywords in the context of the full query in order to assess their effectiveness in successive query refinement.

Figure 5.27:
An Intersection of Required Keywords

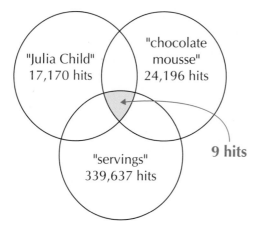

Where Can I Enter a Fuzzy Query

Most search engines offer fuzzy queries as their first search option, often called the Simple Search option. If you are allowed to enter an English sentence or question, that's the fuzzy query, or Simple Search, option (see Figure 5.28). Don't expect to find an input box labeled "fuzzy."

In addition, any search option that allows required (+) keywords and/or prohibited (-) keywords is a fuzzy query option. Most search engines support fuzzy queries although the interface may not make this obvious. For example, to enter a fuzzy query for HotBot, change the default query option "all of the words" to "any of the words."

Figure 5.28:
The Simple Search
Option at AltaVista

5.4.3 Boolean Queries

In general, if you're looking for a very specific type of document, a particular news item that you can date, or an item associated with a specific person (who is not a major news figure), then a *Boolean query* is probably the way to go. A **Boolean query** is a query that consists of keywords, like a fuzzy query, but with **logical operators** (AND, OR, NOT) inserted between the keywords to specify *combinations* of required and prohibited keywords in a logical fashion:

X AND Y	will return only documents that contain both X and Y.
X OR Y	will return only documents that contain either X or Y.
X AND NOT Y	will return only documents that contain X and do not contain Y.

The logical operators AND, OR, and NOT are always recognized by search engines that accept Boolean queries. However, you need to make sure that the search engine is expecting a Boolean query. Before trying a Boolean query, look for a Boolean search mode. (For example, at HotBot, it's in the search mode pull-down menu, and at AltaVista, it's in an advanced search option (see Figure 5.29).

Figure 5.29:
An Advanced
Search Query at
AltaVista

Some search engines have only one input window in which you enter your query; others have two or three. Many such windows come with one or more pull-down menus from which you can set a variety of query preferences, called **query modes** or **search options**. Consult the search engine's online documentation to learn more about these modes or options. At the very least, be sure to scan the entries in all of the pull-down menus, as they will show you the most important preference settings.

Although an unfamiliar interface might make everything look initially strange and confusing, there are only a few standard options that you'll see repeatedly. When you're getting to know a new search engine, watch for the following standard features that an engine might offer.

- If there are two separate query windows, one is probably for fuzzy queries and the other is probably for Boolean queries.
- The first query window that you see is normally the fuzzy query option.
- A window for fuzzy queries will encourage you to use plain English.
- A Boolean query window is often called an Advanced Search option.
- If there's only one query window, check to see whether a pull-down menu controls the query options.
- A pull-down menu might be offered that displays the preferences for your hit lists. You can usually select from two or three levels of detail for each hit.
- You can usually control the number of hits returned per Web page.

Search engines aren't very helpful regarding mistakes in a query. If a query comes back with no hits, you either asked for something that's not in the database or you're in the wrong query mode. If a Boolean query returns an outrageous number of hits, the search engine probably processed it as a fuzzy query. Be aware that a Boolean query in a search window for fuzzy queries will be interpreted as a fuzzy query and all of the Boolean logical operators will be ignored.

Boolean queries are not difficult to master. Nor are they always needed.

When to Try a Boolean Query

The success of a Boolean query depends on how reliably you can predict the presence or absence of specific keywords in your target documents. If you can identify a collection of keywords that you're certain will be present in all of the good hits, a Boolean query can be very effective. If you can identify one or more keywords that will never appear in a good hit (but which might pop up in lot of false hits), you can narrow your query by using the NOT operator.

When Boolean queries fail, it might be due to a logical error in the construction of the query or to some bad assumptions about the keywords being used. You can minimize the risk of logical errors by keeping your Boolean queries relatively simple (or taking a course in formal logic). It is considerably more difficult to make sure that you aren't making a bad assumption about your keywords. If your hit list strikes you as surprising in any way, reconsider your keywords.

 If you know that all of your target documents will contain one keyword or combination of keywords, list them in a Boolean query by using the AND operator—these are the required keywords. The more unusual the required keywords, the better. The AltaVista query in Figure 5.29 shows a query that you hope will find articles that describe the denial-of-service attacks against a number of popular Web sites (including Yahoo! and CNN) in February 2000. The result will be documents that contain the keywords "yahoo" and "CNN," as well as at least one of the three keywords "hacker," "hackers," or "attack." Another restriction limits us to documents created between February 1, 2000 and March 1, 2000. Documents that contain the keywords "denial" and "service" will be ranked more highly in the hit list.

If you can find an unusual keyword that is associated with many false hits (documents you don't want to see), you can filter out those documents by using the AND NOT operator. For example, to find documents about browser cookies while avoiding recipes for edible cookies, you might try a Boolean query with the keyword "cookie" and "recipe":

```
cookies AND NOT recipe
```

5.5 ADVANCED SEARCH OPTIONS

Occasionally, you'll find a question that can benefit from advanced search features. Most search engines offer at least a few advanced features; they'll be under a link named Advanced Search. Hotbot's advanced options are on its home page. However, most search engines take you to a different page for the advanced search options. Each search engine offers a different collection of advanced features, so it's important to read the available documentation before trying out any advanced features for the first time (see Figure 5.30).

Figure 5.30:
Always Read the Online Documentation for Advanced Search Features

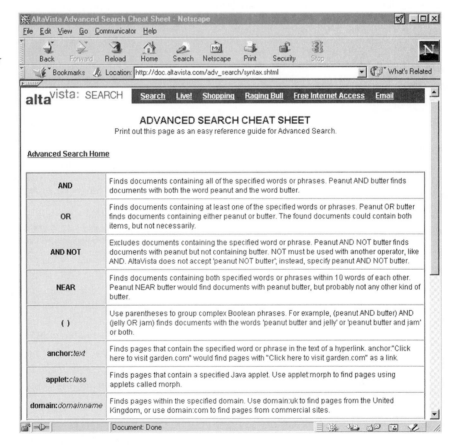

Many search engines let you specify documents dated within a specific time period (a very useful feature if you're looking for current news updates). With AltaVista, you can even control the document ranking criteria. The online documentation for these features is usually well written and easy to understand. Even if you think that you're experienced because you've worked with advanced features at other search engines, take the time to check out the documentation for any new engine with which you aren't familiar. You might find a surprise or two that can have a major impact on your query results.

Some search engines will let you mark keywords with special tags in order to narrow your search in various ways. AltaVista's keyword tags can be very useful if you're trying to narrow a search on a specific topic. For example, a **title:** tag provides for a particular keyword to appear in the title of a Web page (see Figure 5.31). Thus the query

```
title:cookies AND browser AND NOT recipe
```

will return only those documents that contain the keyword "cookies" in the document title.

Figure 5.31:   AltaVista's Keyword Tags

anchor:*text*	Finds pages that contain the specified word or phrase in the text of a hyperlink. anchor:"Click here to visit garden.com" would find pages with "Click here to visit garden.com" as a link.
applet:*class*	Finds pages that contain a specified Java applet. Use applet:morph to find pages using applets called morph.
domain:*domainname*	Finds pages within the specified domain. Use domain:uk to find pages from the United Kingdom, or use domain:com to find pages from commercial sites.
host:*hostname*	Finds pages on a specific computer. The search host:www.shopping.com would find pages on the Shopping.com computer, and host:dilbert.unitedmedia.com would find pages on the computer called dilbert at unitedmedia.com.
image:*filename*	Finds pages with images having a specific filename. Use image:beaches to find pages with images called beaches.
link:*URLtext*	Finds pages with a link to a page with the specified URL text. Use link:www.myway.com to find all pages linking to myway.com.
text:*text*	Finds pages that contain the specified text in any part of the page other than an image tag, link, or URL. The search text:graduation would find all pages with the term graduation in them.
title:*text*	Finds pages that contain the specified word or phrase in the page title (which appears in the title bar of most browsers). The search title:sunset would find pages with sunset in the title.
url:*text*	Finds pages with a specific word or phrase in the URL. Use url:myway.com to find all pages on all servers that have the word myway in the host name, path, or filename--the complete URL, in other words.

If you find a large Web site that you want to search but there's no search engine for a site search, try a **host:** tag to simulate a site search of your own. A host: tag restricts your search to only one Web server. Unfortunately, you can't be sure that every Web page on the site has been indexed by the search engine that you're using, so the **host:** tag is no substitute for a comprehensive site search facility. If you really need a site search facility for a site that doesn't support one, you might be able to create your own client-side site search engine database.

Advanced search features are very effective when you need to zero in on something very specific, such as the answer to a Joe Friday question. With some experience and a little luck, you should be able to pull in shorter hit lists, whose hits are all on target. You might miss some relevant hits, but when you're dealing with a Joe Friday question, you might not mind if a few good ones get away from you.

5.6 SPECIALIZED SEARCH ENGINES

If you can find a comprehensive clearinghouse for a specific topic, you can handle all of your information needs for that topic through the clearinghouse. However, how do you know if a clearinghouse's coverage is comprehensive? Some clearinghouses are not actively maintained and might therefore be missing recently created resources. Others might point to a large number of resources but were never intended to be all-encompassing. How can you know exactly what a clearinghouse does and does not cover? This is a major problem with clearinghouses, no matter how much effort might have gone into them. If you're relying completely on clearinghouses for information on a broad topic, then you have reason to worry about what might be missing.

As an alternative to clearinghouses, specialized search engines focus on a particular topic and therefore offer maximal coverage. The Web offers many specialized search engines. If you find yourself conducting frequent searches on a particular topic, you should look for a specialized search engine in that one area. To find specialized search engines, try a search engine that specializes in this type of search engine. The best one is probably **Invisible Web** (see Figure 5.32).

Figure 5.32:
Invisible Web: A Search Engine for Search Engines

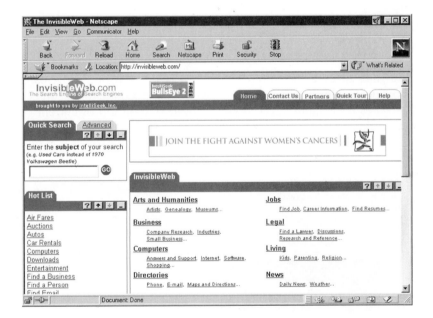

When you conduct a keyword search at Invisible Web, use general rather than specific keywords. You're looking for large searchable sites on a particular topic, so enter a single keyword that best describes your topic. For example, if you enter the keyword "freeware," Invisible Web will find 14 searchable freeware sites (see Figure 5.33).

Many sites that Invisible Web indexes are searchable archives for online publications, public mailing lists, or other large document collections in a specific area. These resources are valuable for Deep Thought questions, when you need to get beyond the introductory articles and dig deep for everything that you can find.

There are other ways to find specialized search engines for topic-specific searches. Visit **CNet's Search.com**, where you'll find another search engine for search engines. Scroll to the bottom of the page, and click the link named Find a Search. You'll reach a page on which you can enter keywords to find searchable resources for specific topics. You may not get as many hits here as at Invisible Web, but you might find some different ones.

Figure 5.33:
Searchable
Freeware Sites
Found by Invisible
Web

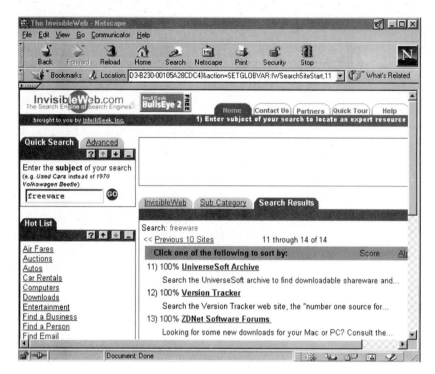

Another place to find both specialized search engines and clearinghouses is **Search Engine Guide**. This site is actually a clearinghouse for resources related to search engines (see Figure 5.34). If you want to stay on top of current developments in the world of search engines, check out its links for newsletters, search engine stories in the news, and the top ten spotlight for the latest and greatest search utilities and services.

Figure 5.34:
A Search Engine
Technology
Clearinghouse

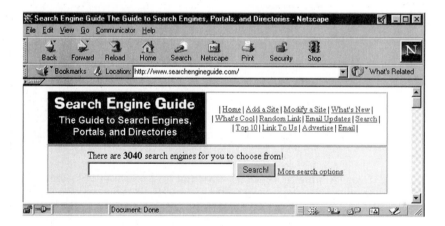

Searchable sites on specialized topics are valuable. However, a searchable site is always limited to a site-specific search. Sometimes, you might want a specialized search engine that can find items at numerous other sites. This is easy to do at Yahoo! and several other Internet portal sites. Recall that Yahoo!'s search engine is restricted to Yahoo!'s subject tree. To look in a specific direction, you can narrow the scope of Yahoo!'s site search by identifying one branch of the subject tree to which you want to restrict your search.

Specialized Searches at Yahoo!

If you've found a useful subtree of Yahoo!'s directory structure, you can conduct keyword searches restricted to that branch. Look for a pull-down menu to the right of Yahoo!'s Search button (see Figure 5.35). Click the "just this category" button before you click the Search button.

Figure 5.35:
Conducting a
Specialized Search
at Yahoo!

This Yahoo! feature makes it easy to conduct incremental searches. For example, you could start at the Yahoo! home page and enter the keyword "software" as a preliminary foray into the subject tree. Yahoo! will return 1,975 category matches, the second one of which is directly under the Computers and Internet subtree: **Computers and Internet > Software**. If you restrict the site search to this branch of Yahoo! and enter the keyword "freeware," you'll find 200 document hits. Had you relied on the subject tree alone, you would have had trouble assembling these 200 hits in any other way because they would have been found in different areas of the subtree. Note that if you drop to the **Computers and Internet > Software > Freeware** subtree, a search on "freeware" produces only eight site matches.

For an incremental search to work, you don't want to go too far out onto any one branch; otherwise, you reduce the number of potential hits. Stay higher in the tree structure, and work with general keywords (as always, with Yahoo!). When you see, for example, 1,975 potential subtrees from which you could choose for your search, look for those near the top of the tree (**Computers and Internet > Software** is only three levels down from Yahoo!'s top level).

Once you become adept at locating topic-specific resources on the Web, you might never want to work with a general search engine again. As the large search engines—and their users—struggle with the inherent difficulties of working with hundreds of millions of documents, specialized search engines could be the way of the future.

5.7 SEARCH BOTS AND INTELLIGENT AGENTS

In recent years, another type of specialized search engine has surfaced in response to commercial interests and e-commerce: the search bot. A **search bot** is a search engine that is highly specialized, covers a number of appropriate sites on different servers, and organizes a database of timely information for users to query and examine. Examples of search bots are all of the comparison shopping sites, at which you can look for the lowest price for a particular retail item. Search bots continually monitor multiple Web sites in order to pull in the most current information in a specific area of interest. They are not limited to formal databases or information that must be formatted in some uniform fashion. Some can consolidate information extracted from free-form text and don't require any special preparations by contributing Web sites. In this respect, the search bots are similar to general search engines. However, specialized search bots preside over somewhat larger categories of information needs. For a searchable clearinghouse of search bots, visit **BotSpot**, which includes shopping bots, stock bots, sports bots, government bots, and software bots (see Figure 5.36).

Figure 5.36:
Finding a Bot at
BotSpot

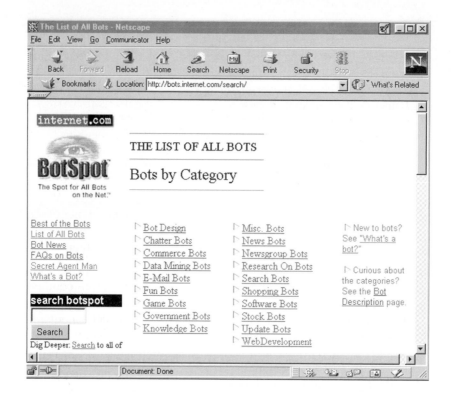

You might already be using the services of server-side search bots if you've customized a Web portal site that reflects your interests. For example, weather bots retrieve weather forecasts for a specific region and stock bots display customized ticker tapes for stock prices. Amazon.com uses a book bot to alert customers about new publications by specific authors, and eBay uses bid bots to inform people of new bids on specific auction items. As the Web continues to grow, it makes sense to turn to specialized search bots for timely, high-quality information.

Most search bots are server-side services. However, some include client-side operations, such as the news bots, which track unfolding news stories. Many client-side meta search engines offer search bot services in order to track prespecified areas of interest (for example, Copernic, **WebFerret**, and **BullsEye 2**). However, these "premium" features are rarely included in freeware or evaluation releases.

An **intelligent agent** is very similar to a search bot. However, an intelligent agent operates autonomously and is finely tuned to the individual needs of a specific user. The two terms are sometimes used interchangeably, but intelligent agents tend to incorporate more-sophisticated techniques and, as such, represent a lively research area in computer science. Some notable intelligent agents are listed at BotSpot under the categories Software Bots and Knowledge Bots.

Search bots and intelligent agents are examples of a fast-moving and exciting area of information retrieval research, one that promises greater productivity in an era of a never-ending information explosion. If you're spending too much time trying to stay on top of everything on the Web, visit BotSpot and look for a search bot to help you cope. You might be surprised to see how many search bots are available to lend a hand (and at no cost!).

5.8 ▮ PULL AND PUSH TECHNOLOGIES

As the Internet becomes more commercialized, content providers are working to find the right balance between pull technology and push technology. **Pull technology** is a distribution technique whereby information is sent to a user on demand. **Push technology** is a distribution technique whereby information is sent to the user without the user's prior permission. A Web browser is an example of a pull technology because you direct the browser to Web locations in order to *pull* requested Web pages to your local host, on demand. E-mail is an example of a push technology because e-mail messages are sent —*pushed*—to you whether or not you want them (this is considered push technology even though you need to launch an e-mail client to see them). When information comes to you automatically and periodically over some indefinite period of time, that's a push delivery mechanism. When information comes to you in response to a specific request and the response has a clear conclusion after which no additional responses are expected, that's a pull delivery mechanism.

With pull technologies, information consumers have more control over the inflow of information. With push technologies, information providers have more control over the distribution of their information. The client/server model accommodates both types of technologies, and Internet users can decide for themselves which they prefer.

Although the term *push technology* sounds vaguely obnoxious, push technologies can operate in unobtrusive ways, much like e-mail. You don't need to bother with it unless you want to, and you can always choose to ignore it. Suppose that you want a local weather forecast each morning. A push technology can have one waiting for you on your computer's desktop at 6:00 A.M. each morning. Maybe you like to track the current prices of six stocks in which you've invested. A push technology can run a little ticker tape on your computer's desktop with only those six stocks on it. Or maybe you've heard about a book that will be published soon and you want to be told as soon as it starts to ship. A push technology can send you an e-mail message announcing its availability.

Push technologies often address ongoing information needs for periodic updates and revisions. One of the most popular applications for push technologies is news tracking. Most people like to stay on top of the news each day. This need traditionally has been filled by newspapers, news magazines, local and national news programs on television, and radio broadcasts. It didn't take long for Web portal sites to discover, however, that users like to customize their Web sites with a selection of news updates taken from different categories. Some people like to see sports scores, and others don't. Different people have different interests, and those differences become apparent when you give people the opportunity to customize personal online news deliveries. Portal customization is big business, and news filters are a big part of that.

If you're a news hound, you've probably gloried in the number of online news sources available to you and then despaired at the amount of time required to take it all in. To address this problem, a new software niche has materialized around the business of customized news delivery. A variety of desktop newsstands are available as freeware for wired news hounds of varying tastes and appetites. For example, **Infogate** (a direct descendent of the original **PointCast** news service) is a freeware download that places a toolbar on your desktop and offers a standard set of features for customized news updates (see Figure 5.37).

Once customized, the toolbar will deliver local weather, selected stock quotes, and news headlines on demand. Users can customize their news preferences from a number of popular sources (see Figure 5.38). The toolbar can be launched, repositioned, saved

Figure 5.37:
EntryPoint Toolbar

Figure 5.38:
Customizing Your
Personal News
Service

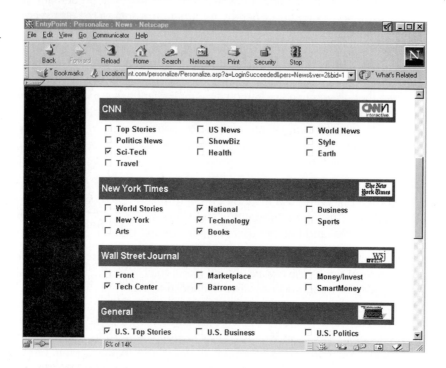

to the task bar, or shut down at any time, thereby making it a polite example of push technology. Even the scrolling news headlines on the toolbar can be halted if the constant parade of text is too distracting.

They can also review current stories by reading headline or lead sentences, as shown in Figure 5.39.

The full text for any available story is only a click away with a Web browser. For most people, EntryPoint's news coverage is welcome and sufficient, offering significant time-saving (once the initial novelty wears off and using the toolbar becomes just another part of the daily routine).

For the really serious news junkie, other applications offer a greater range of publications, content filters, and special features. For example, **newZPrint** is another freeware download that offers dozens of publications, including international newspapers (see Figure 5.40).

newZPrint also offers extensive customization options for each publication, as shown in Figure 5.41.

newZPrint doesn't provide real-time downloads over an open Internet connection, as does EntryPoint, so it's not as nimble as EntryPoint. In all other respects, however, newZPrint is EntryPoint on steroids. It downloads articles on demand and can be programmed to download your selections daily at a fixed time. You can send your daily news to a printer, which will render it in newsletter format (this is very nice if you have time to read during your morning commute). newZPrint even displays articles on your

Figure 5.39:
Scanning Breaking
News as It Happens

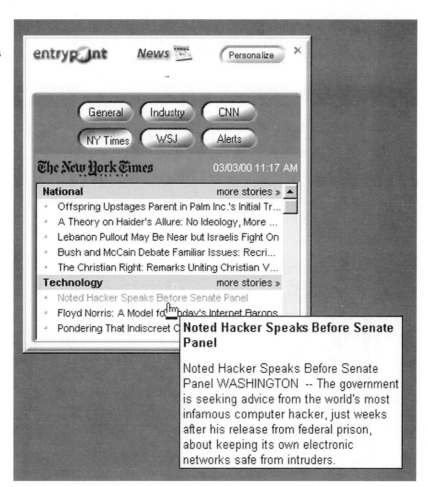

Figure 5.40:
Extensive
Publication Options
with newZPrint

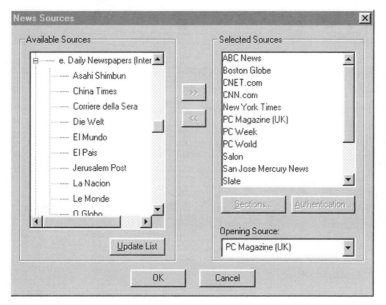

computer in a newspaper-like graphical display (see Figure 5.42) that might be a welcome change from your Web browser if you spend a lot of time on the Web every day.

Figure 5.41:
Tuning Each News
Source

Figure 5.42:
Over the Net and to
the Printer

Given these examples of push technology, you might be thinking that these news services are more like news filters than actual searches. For a search to take place, a specific query must be processed, right? Well, maybe. The line between a filter and a query is a matter of degree. If EntryPoint knows that you're interested in technology articles and not sports, you'll see only technology articles—it will filter out the sports offerings. However, what if EntryPoint could use a set of your keywords and send you articles that contain those keywords, as well as alert you with a sound or a pop-up window whenever a new article that meets your search criteria arrives on its server? This is beginning to feel more like a search. In fact, you have merely applied a *keyword filter* instead of a *general topic filter*. EntryPoint does offer a very primitive keyword filter option that can be used to track articles on a small number of topics (see Figure 5.43). If this feature appeals to you, then investigate the world of search bots for more-sophisticated newsbot services (see Section 5.7).

Figure 5.43:
Keyword Filters for
Breaking News
Stories

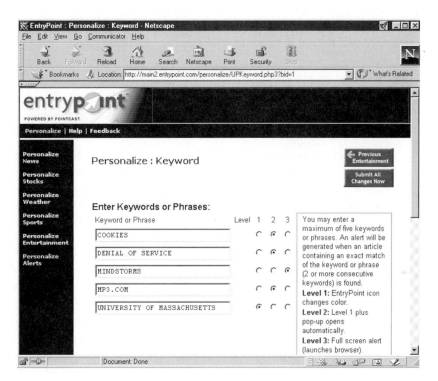

Although these two examples of push technologies are news-oriented, the world of intelligent push technology goes beyond news delivery services. For example, some client-side meta search engines allow you to set up tracking schedules for specific search queries. You can program the engine to process the query as often as you wish, for example once an hour or once a day. The results are then compiled and a summary report generated to inform you of any new results. If you want to stay on top of new developments in a given area, the right query and a tracking facility will help relevant documents find you, so that you don't have to find them.

If the push/pull distinction is beginning to feel a bit muddy, try to keep some simple criteria in mind. The difference has less to do with the underlying technology than the delivery mechanism. Remember, when information comes to you automatically and periodically over some indefinite period of time, that's a push delivery mechanism. When information comes to you in response to a specific request and the response has a clear conclusion after which no additional responses are expected, that's a pull delivery mechanism. Also remember that these concepts make sense only in the context of software. Everything is a pull technology at the level of your computer's on/off button because you must turn on your computer in order for anything to happen. Similarly, you have to launch a software application in order for it to push information at you. At those levels, even push technologies must be pulled. So, start with a computer that's turned on and software that's up and running. That should make it easier to keep the push and pull distinction clean and clear.

5.9 ASSESSING CREDIBILITY ON THE WEB

To use the Internet as a source for legitimate research, you need to develop a critical eye for high-quality information. If you aren't careful with your use of online resources, you might get, and pass on, misinformation—and damage your own credibility in the process. Many information sources on the Web are legitimate and can be trusted. However, many others are unreliable. You must learn to evaluate all online information before you reference it or use it for your own purposes.

Your evaluation should focus on the Web page content. Don't be influenced by a page's look and feel. Beautiful graphics and careful text formatting means that the author cares about the page's attractiveness. However, that doesn't guarantee the information's credibility. If the graphics don't contribute to the information on the page, you might find it helpful to turn them off in order to concentrate on the written content.

The Internet is a **content-neutral medium**. That is, it distributes falsehoods and fantasies as easily as facts and truth. It encourages people to produce pages on anything and everything, and the line between fact and fiction can be twisted in many subtle ways. A delusional author might report wishful thinking or hallucinogenic experiences as fact. If the departure from reality is subtle and believable, assessing credibility with absolute certainty could be impossible. Conspiracy theories thrive on the Internet because conspiracy buffs can easily hook up with one another and find strength in numbers. Always use common sense when assessing information credibility on the Web. If the topic that you're researching involves conspiracy theories or controversial political scandals, everything that you find should be treated with extreme caution.

A good content evaluation can be completed with the help of a *credibility checklist*. Many checklist criteria apply to the evaluation of traditional print documents; others are specific to Web documents. Several useful checklists for Web page assessment are available on the Web. The following sections discuss some of the most common criteria that can be used to assess Web page credibility.

5.9.1 Author Credibility

A page is useless for research purposes if it fails to clearly identify its author, as well as offer additional information about the author either in the current document or via hyperlinks to other documents. The author's institutional affiliation and job title should be available, as well as a telephone number and complete mailing address. Look for a short professional biography on an associated Web page.

An author's e-mail address that ends in `.gov` or `.edu` is evidence of a legitimate institutional affiliation. However, remember that college students and staff members have `.edu` addresses, as well as faculty. The author should make it clear whether he or she is the original author of the material in question. Look for a copyright statement. If there is some doubt about that statement or there is no statement, contact the author to double-check the material's originality. A legitimate author is normally happy to verify authorship.

Try to verify that the author is who he or she claims to be. If someone is identified as a biology professor at Home State University, go to the home page for the university and look for a list of the faculty in the biology department or in a general university directory. Most universities and colleges maintain a faculty/staff directory on the Web. Corporate environments might or might not have online employee directories. However, a telephone call to corporate headquarters will tell you if someone is employed by the company.

Author credibility is normally not a concern if the work has been published by a respected journal or magazine or if you've located a published citation to the work in question in such a journal or magazine. You can double-check anything that someone claims to have published by going to the publication's home page and locating a table of contents that contains the article in question. It is increasingly common for magazines and journals to maintain Web sites, where you can see at least a table of contents, if not an entire article. Checking this will protect you from a fraudulent publication claim.

After you've verified the author's identity, investigate whether the author is qualified to write on the topic. A university professor might not be an expert in an area unrelated to his or her professional specialty. The title "professor" does not automatically confer expertise in all areas, so always do a background check on the author. Look for additional evidence of scholarly activities in that area. The existence of only a single, isolated paper is more questionable than are a dozen papers in the same area. If the author has published other papers in the area but the article in question has not been published, a certain amount of credibility can be assumed from the other publications.

When the author is a writer for a news organization, it's best to verify reported facts independently. If the article mentions a published source for its information, go to that original source document and check it yourself. If no additional sources are cited, look for independent corroborating reports.

5.9.2 Accurate Writing and Documentation

If an article is poorly written and has grammatical errors and misspellings, it might be sloppy with regard to content as well. Serious writing takes time and effort. If you sense that the article was written casually and quickly, it's probably not a good source. In addition, check whether the author references other sources. Are the citations complete? If they are hyperlinks to other online sources, are the links operational and up-to-date? An accurate information source will include correct attributions where needed and disclaimers when information or conclusions are questionable.

If the resource has been published, is the online version identical to the printed version or is it a shorter version? Some magazines post partial versions of their printed articles. The Web site should state clearly whether the article is complete or partial.

5.9.3 Objectivity

If an article's author is affiliated with a commercial entity, try to separate informational content from advertising. This is not always easy. Some pages are carefully designed to make it clear where promotion stops and objective information starts. If no effort has been made to do this and the article is unpublished, you should be concerned about its objectivity.

Scientists working in private industry publish their legitimate research in order to establish credibility within the scientific establishment. Scientific papers are subjected to a process of peer review in order to maintain quality control within the sciences. Evaluating the objectivity of writers outside of the scientific establishment is difficult. However, articles in respected publications are good indicators of objective writing.

Many authors provide information online as a public service. Sometimes authors and their work are supported by or are otherwise affiliated with nonprofit organizations; objectivity can be a problem if these organizations have their own political agendas. If you cite information distributed by an advocacy group, do your own fact checking with independent sources and try to corroborate the information.

5.9.4 Stability of Web Pages

The Web is a dynamic medium, with new information popping up every day. Pages also disappear every day. You can't know whether a page will still be on the Web next year or even next month. This is a problem for people doing scholarly research. However, here are some guidelines that can help you to assess a page's stability.

- Does the page include a date? When was it last revised?
- Is it part of a larger site that has other dated materials?
- Do other Web sites reference the work at this address?
- Is the page part of an institutional resource?

A heavily referenced work might appear at multiple Web sites. If you reference an online source, always reference the *original* URL rather than a copy at a mirror site. The original site usually will be associated with the author or the author's home institution, and it is presumably the most stable site.

No matter how hard you try to select stable Web pages, it's impossible to know how long a Web page will either be available or be available at its current URL. Sometimes, a Web site designer rearranges a Web site, especially if it's growing. This means that old URLs might become obsolete but that the pages are still available, under new URLs. One study found that the lifetime of the average URL is only 75 days. Presumably, this figure is low because a large number of experimental pages created by newcomers to the Web have since ceased to exist, along with Web pages that have moved to new URLs. Regardless, this is a sobering statistic.

5.9.5 Fraudulent Web Pages

Constructing a Web site in another person's name in order to misrepresent that individual is easy. Although it's unlikely that the academic community would do this, bogus Web sites for political candidates were found during both the 1996 and 2000 presidential campaigns. Bogus home pages often are created as parodies of the real thing. If you find material on a page that is blatantly offbeat, contradictory, or surprising in any way, consider the possibility that the page is a maliciously crafted Web page.

Things to Remember

- Use different resources to find different kinds of information.
- Subject trees and clearinghouses are good sources for answers to open-ended questions.
- General search engines are good sources for answers to Joe Friday questions.
- Use successive query refinement to develop effective search engine queries.
- Think carefully about your keywords—look for associative connections to people and organizations.
- Use Boolean queries when you have unusual keywords or combinations of keywords.

Important Concepts

Boolean query—a query format based on logical operators.

clearinghouse—an exhaustive collection of online resources for a specific topic.

intelligent agent—a computer program that searches the Web in order to collect and assemble information from multiple online resources.

query—a list of keywords given to a search engine.

search bot—a computer program that continuously monitors multiple Web sites for information updates.

search engine—a query-driven interface to a document database indexed for keyword retrieval.

subject tree—a hierarchically arranged collection of topic categories and Web page resources.

Where Can I Learn More?

Search Engine Watch `http://searchenginewatch.com/`

Invisible Web—Hidden Searchable Databases `http://websearch.` `about.com/internet/websearch/msubmenu120.htm`

Tool Kit for the Expert Web Searcher `http://www.lita.org/` `committe/toptech/toolkit.htm`

BotSpot `http://www.botspot.com/`

Evaluating Web Resources `http://www2.widener.edu/` `Wolfgram-Memorial-Library/webevaluation/webeval.htm`

A Short Introduction to Information Retrieval
`http://www.birkhauser.com/hypermedia/cyb4.html`

Problems and Exercises

1. Describe and contrast three general types of questions. Why is it useful to categorize your information needs before you conduct a search on the Web? Which question type is best served by general search engines?

2. How does a clearinghouse differ from a subject tree?

3. Organize your list of clocks from Subject Tree Exercise #1 in a hierarchical tree. Don't look at Yahoo!'s hierarchy or try to reconstruct its hierarchy—work out your own. Was it easy to build a tree structure for your list, or did you need to start over a few times? Was this a straightforward exercise or a difficult one? Explain your answers.

4. Explain the difference between a category match and a document match at Yahoo!.

5. Suppose that you've tried several queries at one general search engine and you're not receiving any good hits. What two options do you have at this point?

6. How does a meta search engine differ from a search engine?

7. Describe the merge-and-rank problem of a meta search engine. What can a meta search engine do to avoid dealing with this problem?

8. What will happen if you enter a Boolean query in a fuzzy query input box? If you enter a fuzzy query in the place for Boolean queries?

9. What term tag can you use at AltaVista in order to conduct a search that is limited to one specific Web server? Is this technique equivalent to using a site search facility on the same server (assuming that one is available)? Explain your answer.

10. If an article on the Web has an `.edu` address, is it necessarily more trustworthy than an article at a `.com` address? Explain your answer.

11. What is a content-neutral medium? Can you think of three communications media that are content-neutral?

12. **[Find It Online]** Which accesses a larger database of documents, the search engine at **Yahoo!** or the search engine at **Excite**? Explain your answer. (For the purposes of this question, ignore the fact that Yahoo!'s search pages give you the option of conducting a general search of the Web if you're not satisfied with the hits returned by Yahoo!.)

13. **[Find It Online]** The connection between dogs and the number 42 was discussed at some length in Section 5.2.1. Go to **Yahoo!**, and track down the answer to the question, "What role does the number 42 play in the lives of all dogs?"

14. **[Find It Online]** Visit **FindSpot** (`http://www.findspot.com/`), and read the search tips for AltaVista and Google. Explain how each handles the query

    ```
    dogs —cats collies +basenjis
    ```

    If these two search engines accessed the same document database and indexed those documents in the same way, which engine would return more hits for this query? Explain your answer.

15. **[Find It Online]** Compare and contrast the **Argus Clearinghouse** (`http://www.clearinghouse.net/`) with Invisible Web (`http://invisibleweb.com/`). What do they have in common? How do they differ? Illustrate your points by visiting Argus and conducting a search on the keyword "environment." How many resources does Argus return? Visit Invisible Web, and conduct the same search. How many resources does Invisible Web return? Does it return any of the same resources as Argus?

16. **[Find It Online]** Find the exact date of the denial-of-service attacks on Yahoo! and CNN. The attacks happened sometime between February 1, 2000 and March 1, 2000. First, use the advanced search option at **AltaVista** (`http://www.altavista.com/`). Then do the search again by using an advanced site search at **CNN** (`http://search.cnn.com/`). Which resource made it easier to find the answers? Describe your experience with this exercise at both sites.

17. **[Find It Online]** Suppose that you want to track down all of the Web pages that you can find that reference Wendy Lehnert. To ensure that you don't miss anything, look for all of the possible name variations: Wendy Lehnert, W. Lehnert, Wendy G. Lehnert, W. G. Lehnert, and Wendy Grace Lehnert. Create a Boolean query that will cover all of these variations as simply as possible. (*Hint*: Find a search engine that supports the NEAR logical operator and read the documentation for the use of NEAR. Formulate a Boolean query that uses NEAR for this exercise.) What query did you use?

18. **[Find It Online]** Experiment with Boolean queries to find informational pages about browser cookies. Keep a log of all queries that you try. Don't stop until the top ten hits on your hit list are all general pages about browser cookies; eliminate all false hits associated with recipes, food retailers, and so on. How many queries did you use to find your answers? Which search engine did you use? Did you use any additional advanced search features in addition to a Boolean query? Describe the reasoning that led you to a good hit list. Hand in a copy of your final hit list (use copy-and-paste) with your other answers.

19. [**Find It Online**] Who was the first famous woman mathematician? For what was she famous?

20. [**Find It Online**] Who was the first U.S. president to be born in a hospital?

21. [**Find It Online**] The green iguana is said to have a third eye. Investigate this. How is the third eye used? How does it work? Is it unique to green iguanas?

22. [**Find It Online**] Suppose you hear a song on the radio that you want to track down. You never caught the name of it on the radio, and the only part of the lyrics that you can remember is one line from the refrain ". . . thinking about eternity. . ." Find out the name of the song, the artist who sings it, and the name of a CD that contains the song.

23. [**Find It Online**] Find a searchable Web site (one that has its own site search facility) devoted to the subject of tigers. How did you find it? How hard was it to find the site? List the URL for the site that you found.

24. [**Find It Online**] Sometimes, blonde hair acquires a greenish tint after swimming in chlorinated water. Find out everything that you can about this problem: what causes it, how to fix it, and how to prevent it. Look for different explanations and solutions. For each piece of information that you find, rate its credibility on a scale of 1 to 10. Explain the reasoning behind your ratings.

25. [**Find It Online**] Chapter 5 explained how to add a link to a Web page for an audio clip. If the user clicks the link, the audio clip plays. Find out how to add an audio clip to a Web page so that the music starts playing as soon as the Web page is displayed. What is the solution? How did you find this information?

26. [**Find It Online**] A lot of people know about MP3 files. However, few know about MIDI files. Find out how MIDI files differ from MP3 files. When would it make sense to put a MIDI file instead of an MP3 file on a Web page?

27. [**Find It Online**] Have any U.S. presidents remained unmarried? If so, which ones? How did you find your information?

28. [**Find It Online**] There are three general modes for making digital television work interactively: single mode, simultaneous mode, and pause mode. Describe these three modes, and identify any companies that have developed working technologies along these lines.

29. [**Find It Online**] David Kline estimates that 75% of all corporate wealth is in intellectual property or patents. Who is David Kline? How many U.S. patents were granted to Internet companies in 1995? In 1998? Can business models and processes be patented? Back up your answers with specific sources and details.

30. [**Find It Online**] Can a U.S. public high school legally suspend or otherwise punish one of its students for publishing a satirical or unofficial home page for the school? Assume that the page is produced without the use of school resources. Argue yes or no by citing specific lawsuits concerning censorship by high schools. How did you find your information?

Internet Service Providers

If you have a home computer with a modem, you can sign up with an ISP. Most ISPs offer different service packages and different types of accounts. Most people want to run a graphical Web browser such as Netscape Navigator or Internet Explorer. A SLIP or PPP account supports graphical browsers (as well as other TCP/IP applications such as FTP and Telnet). PPP can automate more of your login procedure than SLIP, but once you are connected, there is no difference between the two types of accounts. Most ISPs offer either SLIP or PPP, but not both. Some ISPs offer "shell" accounts. A shell account is a UNIX account, which is nice if you know UNIX and want to telnet into a UNIX account, but it won't be of any use for Web surfing unless you want to see what the Web looks like through the text-based browser Lynx (something the professional Web-page designers need to do).

You may also hear about POP or IMAP options, which refer to e-mail services (see Chapter 3). POP mail has been an industry standard in recent years and is the most frequently offered e-mail service. IMAP is a newer service that saves mail on the server, whereas POP users save mail on their personal PCs. IMAP is better than POP for people who need to access their mail from different locations. If you need to read mail from the office, from the house, and on the road, try to find an ISP that offers IMAP, but don't be surprised if it is more expensive than a POP option. IMAP requires more disk space and more computing power on the part of the ISP.

As for ISPs themselves, your options will vary, depending on where you live. Heavily populated areas offer more choices than rural areas, but even remote regions of the United States are sometimes covered by more than one ISP. If you can pick and choose, ask the following questions when selecting an ISP:

1. How much do they charge? (Some ISPs are more expensive than others.)
2. Is their modem pool reliable and adequate for the customer base served?
3. How good are their technical support people?
4. Will they let you try their services free for a week?
5. Do they offer any extra services?

We will discuss these questions in some detail so you can better evaluate an ISP on the basis of their answers. The first and fourth questions are the only ones that you can answer without taking a test drive. Happily most ISPs will offer a free evaluation period so you can try them out before you subscribe.

HOW MUCH DO THEY CHARGE?

If you live in an urban area, you should be able to find a service offering unlimited connect time for $20 to $30 per month. You might pay $20 per month as a baseline access charge with no connection-time charges. Or you might pay a baseline charge with additional connection-time charges for each hour after the first 40 hours. The best deals put a ceiling on those connection time charges, so you know you'll never spend more than a fixed amount each month no matter how much time you spend online. Connection-time ceilings may range from $20 to $80 per month, depending on what the market will bear. Most ISPs also charge a one-time set-up fee (usually about $20) to cover the cost of creating a new account.

What do you get for your money? Look for:

- Either a PPP or SLIP account
- An e-mail address with POP or IMAP e-mail service
- Access to 30,000 Usenet newsgroups
- 10MB storage space for a personal Web page, with
- additional Web page space for an extra charge

Keep in mind that you may also have to pay telephone charges whenever you dial into an ISP, so be sure to find a service that can be reached with a local phone call. If you select an ISP that requires a long-distance phone call, your phone bills will probably overwhelm all of your other Internet access expenses.

IS THEIR MODEM POOL RELIABLE AND ADEQUATE FOR THE CUSTOMER BASE SERVED?

The answer to this question determines whether you can connect whenever you want to and then stay connected as long as you want to. Nothing is more frustrating than a busy signal from your ISP when you really need to get online. To find out how often busy signals occur, you have to try a service for a few days and see what happens each time you dial in.

A modem pool is a large bank of modems that your ISP uses to handle hundreds or thousands of incoming phone calls. Along with all the other subscribers, you rely on the modem pool for (1) an available phone line into your ISP account, and (2) a reliable connection that won't disconnect you. If a modem pool isn't large enough for the subscriber population, you may repeatedly get a busy signal when you try to connect. If the hardware in the modem pool isn't of good quality, you may also experience frequent disconnects.

Unfortunately, the adequacy of a modem pool is one of the more unstable aspects of ISP service. An ISP may be doing fine in January but grow dramatically during February—and then in March you start getting busy signals. Successful ISPs sometimes have trouble growing as fast as their customer bases. This is one reason why recommendations for ISPs must be current. *If someone gives you a recommendation for an ISP, be sure that the person is a current customer of that ISP.*

HOW GOOD IS THEIR TECHNICAL SUPPORT STAFF?

Even the most self-sufficient computer user needs high-quality technical support. You may need to report a problem over which you have no control. You may hit a snag with software that isn't working. You may want to request a specific Usenet newsgroup. You shouldn't need to interact with technical support staff on a regular basis, but when you need them, it tends to be important.

Here are some indications that an ISP's technical support is up to speed:

- They distribute their own PC installation package for a graphical Web browser.
- They have a person who works specifically with MAC users.
- They have a 24-hour support line that's available 7 days a week, including holidays.
- They have multiple e-mail addresses for user queries (e.g., billing versus technical support).
- Their staff helps subscribers promptly with any problems during the free trial period.
- They maintain local newsgroups that subscribers can use to discuss questions and problems.

Once again, you need a trial period to assess the situation. ISPs experiencing explosive growth rates often have trouble keeping up with customer-support demand. Services that are excellent one month can be completely unsatisfactory three months later.

WILL THEY LET YOU TRY THEIR SERVICES FREE FOR A WEEK?

Most ISPs will give you a free account for 7 or 10 days. This is important because many questions can't be answered without first-hand experience. Your neighbors may have no problem with busy signals, but they may not be dialing in at the same times you'll want to dial in. A friend may say that the technical support is great, but your friend may have very different needs than you do. Some things you have to check out for yourself.

Any ISP should be able to help you with the necessary software installations so that you can dial up your account and establish a working connection. This is one place where you should be able to get fast and courteous help from technical support staff. If you have trouble getting connected, call for help. It's their job to get you up and running during your free trial period.

If you sign up for a free week, pick a time when you can be online as much as possible. Try to connect frequently to determine whether you get any busy signals. If you get a busy signal on the first try, can you get through on a second or third try? Install some software (e.g., a Web browser) and verify that it works smoothly. Use your newsreader to read messages on the subscribers' newsgroups to learn what people are saying about customer support. If an ISP is failing to perform, you'll see complaints from disgruntled customers. Look for problems that you can take to the technical support staff to find out how quickly, satisfactorily, and courteously they respond. Don't feel embarrassed to ask for help. They are in the business of helping people get underway with Internet access. If they make you feel like you are wasting their time, look for another ISP.

DO THEY OFFER ANY EXTRA SERVICES?

To maintain a competitive edge, some ISPs offer special services. Watch for them and weigh them in making your decision. The following are two specific options that you can ask about.

Most ISPs will offer you space for Web pages that will be accessible by anyone from anywhere. These can be personal or business pages. They may be pages of your own creation or pages that you had a professional Web-page designer create for you. If you expect to set up your own Web site, find out what your ISP can offer you. Many ISPs provide 10 MB of space for web pages as part of their standard service. Additional space should be available for an extra charge.

It is also reasonable to think about what will happen if you need to change ISPs. Chances are that you would like to have e-mail forwarded to your new address, just as the post office forwards mail for you when you change your home address. Most local ISPs will forward your e-mail for a charge, but some services don't forward any e-mail. If you expect to deal with a lot of e-mail that is important to you, ask about forwarding mail when you shop around for an ISP. This is especially important if you ever want to use an ISP for business communications.

CONCLUSION

As you can see, these questions may be difficult to answer without some experience, and even with a trial period, you may find that you haven't been able to do much more than establish a connection. If you have a number of ISPs in your area, and you're not certain that you've picked the best one, don't worry about it too much. The relative merits of the local ISPs could change six months from now anyway, making it impossible for you to be certain that your ISP is the best one available in the long run. Prices, the quality of technical support, and modem pool reliability can all change without warning. ISPs operate in the fast lane and rise or fall accordingly. If you find one whose service seems reasonable to you, be happy and turn your attention to other matters.

When to Talk to Technical Support Staff

Technical support staff are paid to help users of computing facilities work more efficiently and effectively. Increasingly, technical support staffs are also helping people who have questions about the Internet. However, one staff member may be responsible for hundreds of computer users. So it isn't realistic to expect intensive hand-holding, especially on a regular basis. It is also a mistake to assume that the only people who can help you are technical support staff.

If you're a beginner, it is relatively easy to find people who can help you because there are a lot of people who are one jump ahead of you. In fact, someone who is only a little bit more experienced may be more helpful than someone who has moved on to solve more sophisticated problems. If you ask around, you'll probably find someone who is both able and willing to help, if only because most people love it when someone asks them for advice.

The following resources are often available to college students:

- Friends and acquaintances who are experienced with computers
- Other students who use the same type of computer and software
- Any online help files or local discussion groups for beginners

When you subscribe to a commercial ISP, the rules for obtaining technical support are somewhat different. In that case, you have a right to ask for all sorts of help—whenever you need it—and, ideally, the ISP will deliver good technical support as a part of its contract service to you. Then, once you've gotten off the ground, you can peruse online bulletin boards on which fellow subscribers post questions and ask other subscribers for help with problems. Sometimes online discussions can solve your problems and sometimes they can't, but it is always worth a try, especially if you're unable to get a fast response from technical support staff.

In general, a good technical support person is a valuable resource and should be treated accordingly. If you're lucky enough to have good technical support staff available to you, remember that they're handling many problems in addition to yours. Don't take up more of their time than absolutely necessary. Many problems are easily solved, but others require extra effort and patience. Some truly nasty problems defy solution no matter how many people give it their best efforts. But most problems can be solved.

If you've decided to contact a technical support person with a question, take a few minutes to collect some relevant information before doing so. For example, suppose that you keep getting the same error message each time you try to start up a new piece of software. You can save yourself and the technical support person a lot of time if you get ready:

- Copy down what the error message said verbatim.
- Know the name of the software in question, including its version number.
- Know what operating system you're running (e.g., Win98 or MAC OS8).

It also helps if you can say whether this problem happens consistently or only some of the time. If the error appears only sporadically, try to identify any patterns that you've noticed when the error occurs:

- Does it always occur when you're trying to perform some specific operation?
- Does it happen only under certain conditions?
- Have you found a way to get around the problem, even if it's not ideal?

And whenever possible, identify anything that could have possibly contributed to the problem:

- Can you say when the problem first appeared?
- Did you upgrade any software or hardware just before the problem started?
- Did you change any settings or preferences before the problem started?
- Do you remember doing or seeing anything unusual before the problem started?

The more information you can provide, the easier it will be for the technical support person to help you solve the problem. You can't know for sure in advance whether something is relevant to your problem, but it never hurts to be forthcoming about anything that might be relevant. The better prepared you are for your conversation with the technical support person, the better the outcome is likely to be.

APPENDIX C

HTML Tags and Attributes

This appendix contains the tags and attributes described in Chapter 4. This summary is consistent with HTML 3.0 and 4.0, but it is not a comprehensive list of HTML tags and attributes. For a complete description of all HTML tags and attributes, please consult online HTML documentation or a published HTML manual.

HEAD, TITLE, AND BODY

```
<HTML>
<HEAD>     <!-- the HEAD must precede the  BODY -->
<TITLE> Web Page Title </TITLE>
           <!-- the TITLE must go inside the HEAD -->
</HEAD>
<BODY BGCOLOR=#F8F8FF
      BACKGROUND=wrinkles.gif>
           <!-- use either a background color OR a
           background pattern -->
</BODY>
</HTML>
```

HEADINGS

```
<H1 ALIGN=LEFT | RIGHT | CENTER > </H1>
                        <!-- The largest heading -->
<H2>
<H3>
<H4>
<H5>
<H6>                    <!-- the smallest heading -->
```

PRESENTATION TAGS

```
<B></B>                <!-- boldface -->
<I></I>                <!-- italics -->
<TT></TT>              <!-- teletype font -->
<U></U>                <!-- underlining -->
```

INFORMATIONAL TAGS

```
<STRONG></STRONG>      <!-- stands out -->
<EM></EM>              <!-- emphasize -->
<CODE></CODE>          <!-- monospaced font -->
<PRE></PRE>            <!-- preserves all white spacing -->
<CITE></CITE>          <!-- citation -->
```

TEXT FORMATTING

```
<PRE></PRE>            <!-- reproduce all text as is -->
<BR CLEAR=LEFT | RIGHT | ALL>
                        <!-- go to next clear line -->
<P ALIGN=LEFT | RIGHT | CENTER>
                        <!-- start new paragraph -->
```

LISTS

```
<!-- an unordered (bulleted) list of three items -->
<UL>
<LI> Item X
<LI> Item Y
<LI> Item Z
</UL>
```

```
<!-- an ordered (numbered) list starting at #5 -->
<OL START=5>
<LI> Item #5
<LI> Item #6
<LI> Item #7
</OL>


<!-- a list of definitions with a heading -->
<DL>
<LH> <H3> Two Important Definitions </H3> </LH>
<DT> Term X <DD> Definition of Term X
<DT> Term Y <DD> Definition of Term Y
</DL>
```

GRAPHICS

```
<IMG SRC=iggy.gif  WIDTH=30pt  HEIGHT=40pt
     ALIGN= LEFT | RIGHT | BOTTOM | TOP | MIDDLE
     ALT=[INLINE: A CARTOON IG]>
                  <!-- an inline graphic -->
                  <!-- with text alternate -->
<HR  SIZE=1,2,3,... WIDTH=25% ALIGN=LEFT | RIGHT | CENTER>
                  <!-- a horizontal rule -->
<CENTER></CENTER>
                  <!-- center justify a graphic element-->
```

HYPERTEXT LINKS

```
<A HREF=igtext.html>Basic Iguana Care for Beginners</A>
     <!-- a link to another page -->
<A HREF=http://www.repti.com/pub/info/igtext.html>
     Iguana Care </A>
     <!-- a link to another page on another Web page
     server-->
<A HREF="#food">Your Iguana Needs a Healthy Diet</A>
     <!-- a named link (to a place on the same page) -->
<A HREF="igtext.html#food">Your Iguana Needs a Healthy
     Diet</A>
     <!-- a named link (to a place on a different
     page) -->
<A NAME ="food"> Iguana Dietary Needs </A>
     <!-- an anchor for the named link #food -->
<A HREF=iggy.gif WIDTH=200pt HEIGHT=300pt >
     <IMG SRC=iggy.gif WIDTH=20pt HEIGHT=30pt> </A>
     <!-- a clickable thumbnail graphic -->
```

TABLES

```
<TABLE  BORDER=0,1,2,3,... ALIGN=LEFT | RIGHT WIDTH=
    HEIGHT= >
<CAPTION ALIGN=TOP | BOTTOM > </CAPTION> <!-- optional -->
<TR><TD WIDTH= HEIGHT= ALIGN=LEFT | RIGHT | CENTER>
</TABLE>
```

FRAMES

```
<FRAMESET ROWS="30%, 70%" COLS="50%, 50%">
    <!-- sets up a 4-frame layout split evenly down
    the middle -->
<FRAME SRC="igtext.html">
    <!-- defaults to a frame with a scroll bar -->
<FRAME SRC="igpics.html" SCROLLING="no">
</FRAMESET>
```

Index

Credits

Figures 1.17, 2.3, 2.7(a), 2.7(b), 3.3, 3.9, 3.14, 4.4, and 4.41	Netscape Communicator browser window ©1999 Netscape Communications Corporation. Used with permission. Netscape Communications has not authorized, sponsored, endorsed, or approved this publication and is not responsible for its content.

Chapter 1

Figure 1.4	PC Pitstop LLC. Reprinted with permission.
Figure 1.7	©2000 Matrix.Net, Inc.
Figures 1.9(a) and (b)	From www.gwbush.com. Reprinted with permission.
Figure 1.11	http://www.nua.ie.surveys/ Nua Internet Surveys, 2000. Reprinted with permission.
Figure 1.12	Copyright 2000 internet.com Corporation. All Rights Reserved. Reprinted with permission from www.thelist.com.
Figure 1.12 (bottom)	From www.isps.com.
Figure 1.13	Andover.Net, Inc. Reprinted with permission.

Chapter 2

Figures 2.2 and 2.4	Courtesy of McAfee.com.
Figure 2.6	Screen shots reprinted by permission from Microsoft Corporation.

Chapter 3

Figure 3.5	Courtesy of David Fisher.
Figures 3.6, 3.12, 3.15, 3.16, and 3.19	Reproduced with permission of Yahoo! Inc. ©2000 by Yahoo! Inc. YAHOO! and the YAHOO! logo are trademarks of Yahoo! Inc.
Figure 3.7	From Individual.com. Reprinted with permission.
Figure 3.10	From MP3.com. Reprinted with permission.

Chapter 4

Figure 4.15	Reprinted with permission of Eric Mumpower, MIT
Figure 4.27	Copyright ©1994-2000 Wired Digital, Inc. All Rights Reserved.
Figure 4.27	Reprinted with permission from NewsScan Daily, www.news-scan.com.
Figure 4.31	From www.b-zone.de. Reprinted with permission.

Chapter 5

Figure 5.1	Copyright 2000 internet.com Corporation. All Rights Reserved.
Figures 5.2–5.7	Reproduced with permission of Yahoo! Inc. ©2000 by Yahoo! Inc. YAHOO! and the YAHOO! logo are trademarks of Yahoo! Inc.
Figure 5.8	©2000, licensed to About, Inc. Used by permission of About, Inc. which can be found on the Web at www.About.com. All rights reserved.
Figure 5.9	Netscape Communicator browser window ©1999 Netscape Communications Corporation. Used with permission.

Figures 5.10 and 5.11	©1993-00 David S. Blackmar. All Rights Reserved Worldwide.
Figures 5.12 and 5.13	©The Argus Clearinghouse. Reprinted with permission.
Figure 5.14	All images from www.google.com provided courtesy of Google, Inc. All rights reserved.
Figures 5.15 and 5.16	From Ask Jeeves.
Figures 5.17, 5.18, 5.22	Courtesy of Infind.com, Inc.
Figure 5.19, 5.20, and 5.21	Copernic.com. Reprinted with permission.
Figure 5.25	©2000 by Digital Tools & Designs, Inc. Email: findspot@cmpo.com.
Figures 5.26, 5.28, 5.29, 5.30, and 5.31	From AltaVista.com. Reprinted with permission.
Figure 5.33	Reprinted with permission of IntelliSeek.
Figure 5.34	©K. Clough, Inc. Reprinted with permission.
Figure 5.36	Copyright 2000 internet.com Corporation. All Rights Reserved. Reprinted with permission from www.bots.internet.com.
Figures 5.37, 5.38, 5.39, and 5.43	Courtesy of EntryPoint Incorporated. All Rights Reserved.
Figure 5.40	From InfoPager Technologies.
Figure 5.41 and 5.42	©2000 The New York Times Company. Reprinted with permission.